Transport Layer for Computer Networks

Hui Li · Zheming Bao

Transport Layer for Computer Networks

The Paradigm Shift from IP to Future Architecture

Springer

Hui Li
Shenzhen Graduate School
Peking University
Shenzhen, Guangdong, China

Zheming Bao
Shenzhen Graduate School
Peking University
Shenzhen, Guangdong, China

ISBN 978-981-95-7373-8 ISBN 978-981-95-7374-5 (eBook)
https://doi.org/10.1007/978-981-95-7374-5

This Springer imprint is published by the registered company Springer Nature Singapore Pte Ltd.
The registered company address is: 152 Beach Road, #21-01/04 Gateway East, Singapore 189721, Singapore

For the eternal peace of cyberspace and the end of cyber war, CoG-MIN is dedicated to all organizations and individuals of humanity now and in the future

为了网络空间永久的和平及终止战争,
*CoG-MIN*献给现在及未来的人类所有组织及个人

To My Mother Ms. Meiyuan Chen

and

My Father Mr. Qixiong Li

献给: 我的母亲陈美媛女士和
我的父亲李启雄先生

Foreword

We are living in a deeply interconnected digital age where cyberspace has emerged as the fifth domain alongside land, sea, air, and space. However, fundamental flaws in Internet governance—such as disorder, insufficient security, and controllability—are becoming increasingly apparent. Building a "community with a shared future in cyberspace" has become a global consensus, requiring not only innovative top-level governance models but also robust technological architecture as its foundation.

Regarding the recognition and practice of cyber sovereignty, advancing the formulation of international codes of conduct for the network based on national sovereignty represents the optimal choice aligned with the interests of most nations. At the institutional level, legal countermeasures and recommendations must be developed to safeguard international cyberspace sovereignty. Technologically, only by proposing a novel network architecture can we achieve equitable multilateral collaborative governance among nations and sovereignty autonomy within cyberspace. Identifier domains, as the key elements for recognizing entities within the network, are evolving into a new territorial space following land, sea, and air.

In this critical domain, Prof. Hui Li and his team are undoubtedly global pioneers. They have long been dedicated to addressing the fundamental challenges of future networks, proposing the world's first systematic technical solution to cyberspace sovereignty and governance issues. This represents one of the earliest and most comprehensive technical explorations toward realizing the vision of a "cyberspace community with a shared future." In constructing a unified global network architecture for the post-IP era, Prof. Hui Li has articulated three core principles: replacing monopolistic control with national sovereignty in virtual cyberspace, implementing unified identifiers for all entities that include authentic identity information, and enabling traceability of the origin of every data packet. The *Co-Governed Multi-Identifier Network* (*CoG-MIN*) architecture embodies this philosophy as an engineering solution. It employs a decentralized collaborative governance model based on consortium blockchain technology, incorporates intrinsic network genetics and advanced security techniques to safeguard communication security and data privacy, and proposes network evolution strategies. Its mission is to transform cyberspace from a "lawless frontier" into a territory governed by the rule of law.

I am delighted to see Prof. Li's team document their profound research in published volumes, released sequentially by Springer. This constitutes a comprehensive theoretical and practical framework: Firstly, the 2021 publication *Co-governed Sovereignty Network: Legal Basis and Its Prototype and Applications with MIN Architecture* establishes a robust foundational framework for network sovereignty through legal theory and conceptualization; second, the 2025 publication *Principles of Architecture, Protocol, and Algorithms for CoG-MIN: A Sustainably Ecological and Evolutionary Solution for Packet Network System* constructs the grand top-level architecture and systemic principles of *CoG-MIN*.

Today, we are delighted to welcome the third pivotal work in this system—*Transport Layer for Computer Networks: The Paradigm Shift from IP to Future Architecture*. Transport layer protocols serve as the critical link connecting network theory to practical application.

The core value of this book lies in its profound revelation of the new mission borne by the transport layer during the paradigm shift from IP to future network architectures. It not only systematically explains the principles and core mechanisms of classic protocols like TCP and UDP but also focuses on emerging protocols represented by QUIC and their application optimization strategies in scenarios such as mobile networks, data centers, and high-performance computing. Simultaneously, the book showcases Prof. Li's team's pioneering research in future network architectures, including high-performance, high-security transmission solutions like *MIN-QUIC* designed for *MIN*, and the adaptive redundancy transport control protocol *MIN-SANC-TCP* that integrates network coding.

The book also integrates real-world application cases of transport layer protocols in large tech enterprises (such as leading companies' large-scale deployment practices of QUIC) and carefully designed hands-on experiments in each chapter (e.g., enabling HTTP/3 in browsers, packet capture analysis). This integration of theory with enterprise-level applications helps readers enhance their engineering practice capabilities.

I highly recommend this book. For networking students, frontline engineers, and even policymakers concerned with cyberspace governance, this work is an indispensable resource. I firmly believe that the pioneering contributions of Prof. Hui Li's team will profoundly impact the advancement of global networking technologies and the peaceful governance of cyberspace.

Jun Lu
Academician of Chinese Academy
of Engineering
Beijing, China

Preface

Undoubtedly, the computer network is the cornerstone of the information age, and the transport layer protocols are the key pillars that connect and sustain this magnificent architecture. The transport layer builds a crucial bridge between the complex network layer and the diverse application layer. Its protocols, such as TCP and UDP, provide reliability, efficiency, and fundamental guarantees for end-to-end communication. They have quietly supported information exchange, entertainment, work, and value creation for billions of users around the world. We must pay our highest respect to the inventors and contributors of these foundational protocols.

The Internet is the most important global infrastructure in the era of the digital economy. As the Internet has evolved from simple information exchange to personal consumption, e-commerce, live streaming, and now to high-performance computing networks and data center interconnections, its applications have grown in both breadth and complexity. Technological innovation has driven the continuous evolution of 5G, data centers, high-performance computing, and the Industrial Internet, imposing unprecedented demands for ultra-low latency, high reliability, and massive throughput on network transmission. At the same time, the limitations of traditional transport protocols in terms of performance, security, and evolution have become increasingly evident.

The Challenges and Opportunities of Transport Layer Protocols

With the deep development of the digital economy, the Internet has become the most important global infrastructure. However, driven by emerging scenarios such as 5G, computing networks, and data centers, traditional transport protocols are facing unprecedented challenges:

1. **The first challenge is the bottleneck of performance and efficiency.** The mechanisms designed by traditional TCP to ensure reliability—such as the three-way

handshake, head-of-line blocking, and fixed congestion control strategies—often perform poorly in high-latency and high-packet-loss environments such as 5G or satellite networks. These limitations make it difficult to meet the extreme experience requirements of real-time interactive applications.
2. **The second challenge is the rigidity and difficulty of network evolution.** Transport layer protocols are deeply embedded in the operating system kernel, which makes any improvement or evolution—such as the transition from TCP to QUIC—a long and costly process. The solidified architecture limits the ability of transport protocols to adapt quickly to new technologies and application demands.
3. **The third challenge is the lack of security gene.** Traditional protocols are based on the underlying logic of "IP address equals identity." However, the IP network lacks inherent security genes. Due to the uniqueness of IP addresses, this semantic overload causes vulnerabilities in security, mobility, and quality of service, making the IP-based transmission system unsuitable for modern technological and application development. In addition, IP networks lack mechanisms to protect data ownership, posing risks to data privacy and property rights. Attackers can exploit vulnerabilities in the IP network to gain unauthorized access to sensitive user information for profit.

The theme of this book is a comprehensive analysis and sustainable evolution of transport layer protocols.

How to systematically and deeply understand and address the challenges outlined above is the central theme of this book. Through this work, we aim to build for readers a complete transport layer knowledge system that spans classical theory and cutting-edge practice.

This book offers an in-depth analysis of the theoretical foundations and emerging application scenarios of transport layer protocols. It not only systematically presents the principles and core mechanisms of classical protocols such as TCP and UDP, but also focuses on emerging protocols represented by QUIC and their application-specific optimization strategies in scenarios including 5G, data centers, computing networks, and ICN.

Beyond current protocols, the book looks toward future network architectures. We recognize that evolution at the transport layer cannot be decoupled from innovations in the underlying network architecture. Therefore, the text specifically examines how transport layer protocols can be adapted and deeply optimized for novel architectures that represent future directions—such as Co-governed Multi-identifier Networks (CoG-MIN, shortly MIN)—by introducing designs like MIN-TCP and MIN-QUIC. This ensures readers gain forward-looking knowledge relevant to future deployments.

Key features of this book:

1. **Balancing Classical Foundations and Frontier Advances.**
   The book provides detailed analyses of TCP (Chap. 2) and UDP (Chap. 3)—including header formats and core mechanisms such as connection management, congestion control, and sliding windows—and presents an extended treatment

of QUIC (Chap. 4). Chapter 5 is devoted to transport layer security (TLS). Together, these chapters equip readers with up-to-date technical knowledge of the transport layer.

2. **Focusing on Emerging Scenarios and Future Architectures.**
   The book concentrates on the application and optimization of transport protocols in scenarios such as 5G, data centers, and computing networks (Chap. 6). Based on our understanding of future network architectures, we present the team's frontier explorations in transport optimization, including MIN-NC-TCP (TCP optimized with network coding), MIN-SANC-TCP (adaptive redundancy), and MIN-QUIC (QUIC enhancements for multi-identifier networks).
3. **Bridging Theory and Practice.**
   To overcome the limitations of purely theoretical texts, the book supplements theory with rich application examples and enterprise case studies (Chap. 7), offering in-depth analyses of production deployments and protocol optimizations by leading companies such as Meta, Tiktok Group, Tencent, and Alibaba. In addition, each chapter includes carefully designed practical exercises—packet capture analysis, code labs, and performance tests—providing readers with direct, hands-on insight.

Chapters Arrangement

This book comprises seven chapters. Chapter 1 provides an overview of computer networks and the transport layer, introducing key technologies and development trajectories. Chapters 2 and 3 offer detailed treatments of TCP and UDP, respectively, and introduce TCP optimization schemes designed for future network architectures. Chapter 4 focuses on the QUIC protocol and its MIN-QUIC enhancements tailored for novel architectures. Chapter 5 covers the transport layer security protocol TLS. Chapter 6 explores frontier topics in transport protocols—such as network coding, data center networking, and high-performance computing. Chapter 7 concentrates on concrete applications of transport protocols in web environments and enterprise deployments.

Intended Audience

This book is written as a systematic learning resource for graduate students and senior undergraduates, helping them understand the evolution of transport layer protocols and master technical concepts, details, and application scenarios. It can serve as a textbook or reference for students in computer science, network security, and communications; each chapter includes experiments to guide learners from basic concepts to hands-on practice.

At the same time, the book is an important guide for network engineers, system architects, and network-security practitioners. We hope it will serve as a bridge between academia and industry and provide actionable insights for real-world deployments.

Shenzhen, China

Dr. Hui Li
Director of Expert Committee
on Theoretical and Mathematical
Modeling of IEEE Blockchain Society,
Chair of IEEE Blockchain Shenzhen Branch

Chief Information Scientist
of the International Academician
Science and Technology Innovation Center,
IASTIC

Member of the National Academy
of Artificial Intelligence NAAI,
USA

Director of Asia Institute of NAAI
Director of Peking University-China
Mobile Group Joint Lab. of Sovereign
Trusted Network Technology
Foreign Academician of Russia
Academy of Natural Science
Technical Executive Director
of Sino-EU ICV and Autonomous
Driving Industry Innovation
Alliance (SASD), Germany

Member of Expert Committee of World
Digital Technology Academy,
UN, Geneva

Fellow of IET, British
Director of SZ-Branch Lab
of the China Major Science
and Technology Infrastructure
for Future Network
Vice Chairman of the World
Artificial Consciousness Association

Acknowledgements

This book originates from the research work of Prof. Hui Li's group at Peking University. We would like to express our sincere gratitude to all the students, engineers, and teachers who have contributed to the preparation of this textbook. Without their valuable efforts, this book could not have been completed.

Since 2010, Ph.D. students Kai Pan and He Bai and Master's students Sicong Song, Xudong Fan, Lihong Lin, Jianming Que, Mingrui Xiao, Zheming Bao, and others participated in different research works in this field at different times. Kai Pan, Sicong Song and Xudong Fan's research on the latest progress of network information theory, the integration of Network Coding theory and TCP transmission control, has provided corresponding NC-TCP materials and achievements for this book. Ph.D. candidate He Bai initiated the team of this laboratory, conducting research on machine learning, agents, and transmission congestion control algorithms that integrate AI theory under complex heterogeneous network conditions, providing corresponding background materials for MIN-TCP in this book. The research achievements of Lihong Lin and Jianming Que on the Transmission Control Protocol integrating the future network architecture MIN have provided corresponding materials and results for this book, namely MIN-NC-TCP and MIN-SAC-TCP. Mingrui Xiao and Zheming Bao conducted research on the integration of QUIC with the future network architecture MIN, providing corresponding materials and achievements for MIN-QUIC and TLS-MIN-QUIC for this book.

This book is divided into seven chapters. Professor Hui Li, the first author, is responsible for the overall planning and coordination to ensure that the structure and content of this book meet the expected goals. He is responsible for the writing of Chaps. 2, 4, 5, and 7. Graduate Student Zheming Bao is responsible for writing Chaps. 1, 3, and 6 and also completed the experimental part of the textbook.

We sincerely thank to Prof. Jun Lu, academician of the Chinese Academy of Engineering, for writing the recommendation foreword for this book.

We would like to sincerely appreciate the funding support for CoG-MIN research, including but not limited to: PKUSZ-China Mobile Internet Joint Lab. for Sovereign and Trustworthy Internet funded by The China Mobile Internet Co. Ltd. [No. CMIC-202400488]; Guangdong Provincial Key Laboratory of Ultra

High Definition Immersive Media Technology; Kunlun Talent Program—High-End Innovative and Entrepreneurial Talent No. 2024-25-27; Open Project of Key Laboratory of Yunnan University of Finance and Economics YNCJDX-2024-21; Key Laboratory Development Project of Huanghe Science and Technology College HHSCU-2023-021; Guangxi institute of artificial intelligence research and development plan GX—AIC No. 2026007; Open Fund Project KLF-2021-01 of Guangxi Key Laboratory of Multimedia Communication and Network Technology; China Environment for Network Innovations (Grant GJFGW[2016]No. 2533, [2018]No. 775, [2020]No. 386, SZFGW[2019]No. 261); National Key Research and Development Program of China (Grant No. 2020AAA0104203, Grant No. 2017YFB0803204, Grant No. 2016YFB0800101, Grant No. 2012CB315904); National Natural Science Foundation of China (Grant No. 61671001, Grant No. 61179028); Basic Research Enhancement Program of China (Grant No. 2021-JCJQ-JJ-0483); Key Research and Development Program of Guangdong Province, China (Grant No. 2019B010137001, Grant No. 2018B010124001); Natural Science Foundation of Shenzhen, China (Grant No. JCYJ20220531093206015, Grant No. JCYJ20210324122013036, Grant No. JCYJ20190808155607340, Grant No. GXWD20201231165807007-20200807164903001); Huawei Funding (Grant No. YBN2017125, Grant No. TC20201222002); ZTE Funding (Grant No. 2014ZTE03-01-01, Grant No. 2019ZTE03-01); PCL Future Regional Network Facilities for Large-scale Experiments and Applications (Grant No. LZC0019), Foshan Innovation Team (Grant No. 2018IT100082); and Shenzhen Smart City Tech. Group (Grant No. SZSCG-HT-2021-012).

Finally, we would like to express our sincere thanks to the dedicated staff at Springer Nature for their invaluable assistance and unwavering support throughout the publication process. Additionally, we extend our heartfelt thanks to each reader for engaging with this book and contributing to the ongoing discourse in this field.

Shenzhen, China
October 2025

Prof. Hui Li
Zheming Bao
R&D Engineer

Contents

About the Authors

Dr. Hui Li is Professor at Peking University. He was the First Scholar in the world who systematically points out the three gene defects of the current IP-based network: (A) IP-based cyberspace sovereignty is a unilateral monopoly. (B) There is a lack of security genes, resulting in frequent security incidents and difficulties in privacy protection. (C) The protocol is solidified, leading to long upgrade times and high costs.

Professor Hui Li proposed that corresponding to Principles of Classical Mechanics, there exist Newton's three laws in cybersecurity, briefly as NTLinCS. NTSinCS points out a truly feasible direction and path for the international community to fundamentally solve the problems of by the rule of law, security, peace, and the end of war in cyberspace.

Newton's First Law in the Cybersecurity: Insecurity is the inertia of the IP network. In other words, it is impossible to completely solve the security, peace, and end cyber wars in the current IP cyberspace. The international community must switch to a new track. It can be proved by using the method of contradiction followed by the method of enumeration.

Newton's Second Law on Cybersecurity states that the increase in the security coefficient of future networks is directly proportional to the investment in security resources, that is, the magnitude of the reaction force is equal to the action force. The security of IP network has a distinct barrel effect. There exist quantifiable deterministic technical solutions that can exponentially enhance security performance in the future networks.

Taking the IP network-security coefficient 1 as a reference, the improvement of the security coefficient in the future cyberspace is directly proportional to resources invested. The MIN architecture proposed by Prof. Hui Li is an example and has been verified in experiments, practices in offensive and defensive competitions.

Newton's Third Law of Cybersecurity: The Law of Acceleration: In the cyberspace of post IT future network, a multi-loop feedback system integrating technology, management, and the global court system can ensure that the cyberspace remains in a stable state by the rule of law, peace, and security forever. Because any unstable appearance will be rapidly brought back or transformed into a stable state by the acceleration of multi-dimensional powerful forces. And there will never be war in this cyberspace.

Major academic and social contributions of Prof. Hui Li include:

(1) He proposed the first Co-Governed Multi-Identifier Network (CoG-MIN, or MIN), or Co-governed sovereignty network with properties of multilateral governance, independent sovereignty, security, peace, and the rule of law. MIN is based on blockchain technology and the future network. He implemented its prototype on the Operator's Network in the world. MIN was obtained the award of the World Leading Internet Scientific and Technological Achievements at the 2019 World Internet Conference in Wuzhen, China. In 2021, the first English monograph on the theme of "Cyberspace UN" in the world, titled "Co-governed Sovereignty Network: Legal Basis and Its Prototype and Applications with MIN Architecture," was published by Springer Publisher. MIN was also awarded the unique Diamond Award among all Golden Awards at the 2022 British International Invention Exhibition.

(2) He put forward a complete set of patent solutions to solve the CAP trilemma of consortium blockchain. The monograph "Principle and Applications of Blockchain Systems: How to Overcome the CAP Trilemma in Consortium Blockchain" was jointly published by Wiley and IEEE Press, providing a solid technical foundation for the security of the community with a shared future in cyberspace and core systems of the digital economy.

(3) He was granted patents for maximum distance separable code for distributed storage systems in both China and the USA. He also proposed practical G(2) regeneration code patents, which have become the de facto global industry standard, saving at least 50% of storage equipment and space investment costs for global IDC centers and achieving significant economic and environmental benefits.

(4) He was the first to apply the theory of stochastic process martingale to the network anti-attack quantitative security analysis model, and the patent was granted in both China and the USA. This provides a mathematical model for endogenous security and AI-enabled network security.

(5) He has made extensive important social contributions, particularly in the proposal writing and project defense of two major scientific platforms, namely "Cyberspace Technology National Laboratory Construction Plan" and the "National Major Science and Technology Infrastructure Proposal for Future Network," commissioned by the Shenzhen Municipal Government. Prof. Hui Li's efforts have played a significant role in their successful implementation in Shenzhen.

Prof. Hui Li is Chief Information Scientist of the International Academician Science and Technology Innovation Center; Director of Expert Committee on Theoretical and Mathematical Modeling of IEEE Blockchain Society, Chair of IEEE Blockchain Shenzhen Branch, Foreign Academician of the Russia Academy of Natural Science, Member of the National Academy of Artificial Intelligence NAAI, USA, Member of the Expert Committee of the World Digital Technology Academy under the guidance of the UN Commission on Science and Technology for Developments, Fellow of IET, Director of PKU Lab of China Environment for Network Innovations, National Major Research Infrastructure, and the Technology Executive Director of the Sino-EU Intelligent Connected Vehicle and Autonomous Driving Industry Innovation Alliance (SASD). He received his B.Eng. and M.S. degrees from the School of Information Engineering, Tsinghua University, Beijing, China, in 1986 and 1989, respectively, and his Ph.D. degree from The Chinese University of Hong Kong in 2000.

In recent years, Prof. Hui Li has been invited to deliver keynote speeches on the topic of MIN/Cybersecurity/Blockchain/Web 3.0 over 200 conferences, including the 27th Annual Science and Technology Conference of the United Nations Science and Technology Commission at Geneva, the World Internet Conference in Wuzhen, China, Digital Economy Conference, and the Web 3.0 and AI Conference hosted by IEEE, etc.

Prof. Hui Li is First Inventor of 8 US granted patents and more than 50 Chinese granted patents. He is First Author of 9 monographs, with 9 in English (5 published) and 10 in Chinese (6 published). He has also published more than 300 papers in mainstream journals and conferences.

Zheming Bao is Research and Development Engineer at the Peking University Shenzhen Graduate School, China. His research interests focus on transport protocols and network architectures.

Chapter 1
Overview of Transport Layer Protocols

In our interconnected digital world, the need for seamless and reliable data exchange is paramount, and the transport layer is where this crucial work is done, acting as the logical communication bridge between application processes.

This chapter provides a fundamental overview of the transport layer. It begins by introducing computer networks, their history, and layered models (e.g., OSI). The focus is on defining the transport layer, its core protocols (TCP, UDP, and QUIC), key technologies (connection management, reliable transmission, flow and congestion control), and the protocol evolution path, including the paradigm shift toward future network architectures. Through packet capture experiments and exercises, students will deepen their understanding of these protocols.

1.1 Overview of Computer Networks

1.1.1 Definition of Computer Networks

Computer networks, as a vital component of modern information infrastructure, are systems formed by connecting multiple computers and their peripheral devices through communication links and network protocols. Their core objective is to achieve information sharing and resource sharing [1]. Within the network, various hardware devices (such as routers, switches, network cards, and servers) and software systems (including network operating systems, network management software, and diverse applications) collaborate through standardized communication protocols to ensure data transmission, exchange, and security [2].

Computer networks constitute complex and extensive systems that connect geographically dispersed computers with independent functions and their peripheral devices via communication lines. Under the management and coordination of network operating systems, network management software, and network

H. Li and Z. Bao, *Transport Layer for Computer Networks*,
https://doi.org/10.1007/978-981-95-7374-5_1

communication protocols, these networks enable resource sharing and information transmission.

Computer networks comprise hardware, software, and protocols. Hardware components primarily include computers, servers, routers, switches, network interface cards, and similar devices. Software components encompass operating systems, network management software, applications, and related programs. Protocols define the rules and standards for communication between different devices within a computer network.

The primary functions of computer networks can be summarized as follows:

Resource Sharing: Users within the network can share hardware resources such as printers and scanners; software resources like operating systems and applications; and data resources including files and databases.

Data Communication: Enables data exchange and information transfer between computers located in different places. Communication can occur via email, instant messaging, file transfers, and other methods.

Distributed Processing: Breaking large tasks into smaller components and assigning them to different computers within the network for processing, thereby enhancing efficiency. For instance, in scientific computing and big data processing, distributed processing fully leverages the computational resources available across the network.

Enhancing System Reliability: Through redundancy and backup mechanisms, ensuring that if one computer fails, others can continue operations, maintaining the system's normal functioning [3].

1.1.2 Evolution of Computer Networks

The development of computer networks has progressed through multiple stages, from standalone computing to global interconnection.

During the early standalone era, computers operated independently and lacked the ability to interact with external systems. With advances in hardware and communication technologies, people began utilizing simple communication lines and terminal devices to achieve point-to-point communication between computers, thereby gaining preliminary capabilities for information exchange [4].

In the 1960s, the US Department of Defense's Advanced Research Projects Agency (ARPA) developed ARPANET, the world's first packet-switched network, marking the birth of computer networking. ARPANET employed packet-switching technology, dividing data into small packets for transmission, thereby enhancing network efficiency and reliability.

From the 1970s to the 1980s, various network technologies and protocols emerged, such as Ethernet and the TCP/IP protocol. Ethernet is a local area network (LAN) technology that employs bus or star topologies to enable high-speed data transmission between computers. The TCP/IP protocol suite comprises a set of protocols for computer network communication, including the Transmission Control Protocol

(TCP) and the Internet Protocol (IP). TCP ensures reliable end-to-end data transmission, while IP enables addressing and routing across heterogeneous networks. Together, they form the foundation of the modern Internet [5].

With the rapid development and widespread adoption of the Internet, increasing emphasis has been placed on network openness and freedom. Growing demands for security, sharing, trustworthiness, and decentralization often exceed the capabilities of traditional network systems. Consequently, network researchers have begun exploring novel network architectures.

In August 2010, the National Science Foundation launched the Future Internet Architecture (FIA) initiative for US cybersecurity, funding four forward-looking network research projects: NDN, MobilityFirst, NEBULA, and XIA. The NDN project aimed to develop a novel network architecture, establishing a content-centric, expressive Internet framework. The MobilityFirst project treats node mobility as the norm, employing Generalized Delay Tolerant Networking (GDTN) to enhance network robustness and availability. With the participation of the NSF and 18 leading universities and research institutions, the FIA initiative progressed to the FIA-NP phase in 2015, planning to build a new global Internet based on these network architectures. However, a critical flaw in these approaches is that their novel identifiers remain anchored to IP addresses, adhering to DNS management and resolution mechanisms under the traditional IP system. This prevents them from escaping the political implications tied to IP identifiers.

In 2007, China's 973 Program launched the "Fundamental Research on Measurable, Controllable, and Manageable IP Networks" project, focusing on deepening research into the measurability, controllability, and manageability of existing IP networks.

In 2008, the National 973 Program funded the "Fundamental Research on Next-Generation Internet Architecture and Protocols" project, aiming to explore future-oriented next-generation Internet architectures and protocols.

Additionally, in 2011, the National 973 Program supported two projects: "Research on Service-Oriented Future Internet Architecture and Mechanisms" and "Research on Reconfigurable Information Communication Infrastructure Network Architecture."

In 2011, Peking University Shenzhen Graduate School collaborated with Academician Wu Jiangxing's team to pioneer the revolutionary coexistence system of multi-mode addressing at the network layer, breaking through the single IP identifier bottleneck. The 973 project "Addressing and Routing Switching for Reconfigurable Basic Networks" was successfully completed and rated excellent.

In 2019, Professor Li Hui's team proposed and implemented the prototype of Co-Governed Multi-Identifier Network (CoG-MIN or shortly MIN) system globally. MIN integrates future networks with IP through blockchain technology, establishing a multi-stakeholder governance framework. Addressing the international consensus on multilateral governance of cyberspace, the MIN system overcomes IP limitations by resolving issues such as single-entity control of the DNS root zone database, address semantic overload, and security deficiencies. It enables multilateral management of cyberspace—the top-level multilateral governance of humanity's fifth domain—ensuring global interconnectivity. While enabling domestic domain name sovereignty autonomy at all levels, this grants nations their first-ever autonomous cyberspace territories—a multilaterally governed sovereign Internet—effectively establishing a United Nations for cyberspace.

Meanwhile, with the emergence of new technologies such as cloud computing, big data, and the Internet of Things in recent years, computer networks face new challenges and opportunities. Cloud computing enables the sharing and allocation of computing resources over networks, enhancing resource utilization. Big data demands efficient network transmission and processing capabilities to meet data storage and analysis requirements. The Internet of Things connects various devices to networks, enabling intelligent interaction between them.

Amid the exponential growth of Internet applications, explosive expansion of user bases, rapid advancement of artificial intelligence, and surging demand for big data applications, computer networks once again stand at a crossroads of technological innovation, facing a new wave of transformation challenges and opportunities. Cloud computing technology has rapidly risen with its novel computing power supply model and resource allocation philosophy, reshaping the entire IT industry ecosystem. As the physical foundation of cloud computing, data centers continue to expand in scale and undergo continuous architectural optimization. They routinely house tens of thousands of servers, with some hyperscale facilities reaching millions. These facilities must not only accommodate massive data storage but also handle high-concurrency, low-latency data read/write, and computational tasks, imposing near-demanding requirements on network bandwidth, transmission stability, and reliability [6].

Simultaneously, the rapid rise of large-scale artificial intelligence models has injected powerful momentum into computer network development while presenting unprecedented challenges. Massively pre-trained language models like the GPT series, with parameters often reaching tens or hundreds of billions, require coordinating computational resources from data centers worldwide during training.

The resulting data transmission volumes are immense, demanding extremely high network speeds, low latency, and exceptional stability. This necessitates that computer networks accelerate their evolution toward ultra-high speeds, ultra-low latency, intelligent dynamic scheduling, and high reliability. It drives the accelerated research, development, and commercialization of technologies like 5G, 6G, and even more advanced future wireless communications. It also demands optimization of internal data center network architectures to better accommodate the stringent network requirements emerging from the iterative development of new technology industries. Ultimately, this empowers the digital economy to advance toward higher-quality development stages.

1.1.3 Network-Layered Model

To enable communication between different computers, computer networks employ a layered model. This model divides network communication functions into multiple layers, with each layer responsible for specific functions and interacting with adjacent layers through interfaces.

Common network-layered models include the OSI reference model and the TCP/IP model.

Figure 1.1 shows the architecture of the network-layered model. The OSI reference model divides network communication into seven layers: physical layer, data link layer, network layer, transport layer, session layer, presentation layer, and application layer. The physical layer transmits bit streams over physical media; the data link layer assembles bit streams into frames and performs error detection and correction; the network layer handles routing decisions and packet forwarding between different networks; the transport layer provides reliable end-to-end data transmission; the session layer establishes, maintains, and manages sessions; the presentation layer handles data formatting and encryption/decryption; the application layer delivers various network application services to users.

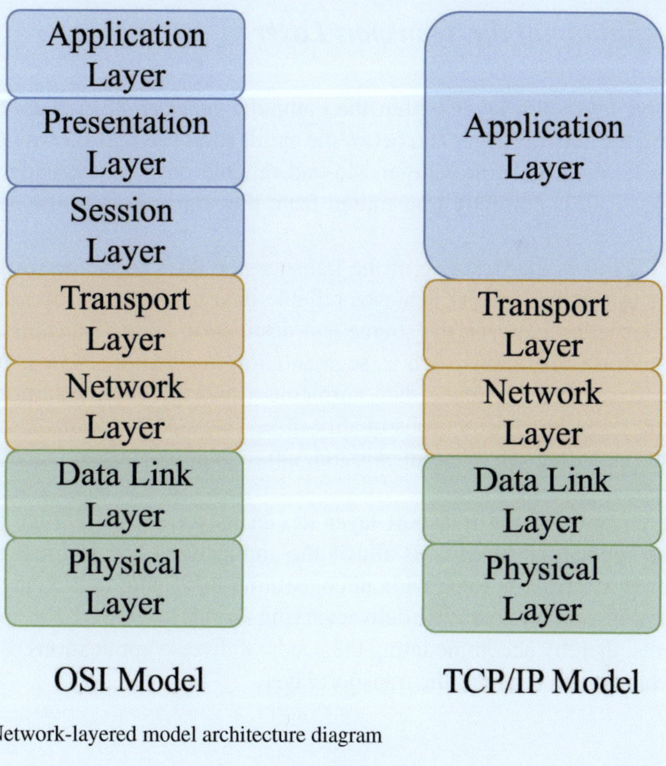

Fig. 1.1 Network-layered model architecture diagram

The TCP/IP model divides network communication into five layers: physical layer, data link layer, Internet layer, transport layer, and application layer. The physical layer and data link layer correspond to the physical layer and data link layer of the OSI reference model and are responsible for transmitting data packets over physical media; the Internet layer corresponds to the network layer of the OSI reference model, responsible for routing and packet forwarding between different networks; the transport layer provides reliable end-to-end data transmission; the application layer corresponds to the session layer, presentation layer, and application layer of the OSI reference model, responsible for providing various network application services to users.

The advantage of the network-layered model is its ability to decompose complex network communication problems into multiple relatively simple subproblems, facilitating design, implementation, and maintenance. Simultaneously, the layered model enables interconnection between devices from different manufacturers through standardized interfaces, thereby promoting the advancement of network technology.

1.2 Overview of the Transport Layer

1.2.1 Definition of the Transport Layer

The transport layer is a layer within the computer network-layered model, positioned above the network layer and below the application layer, as shown in Fig. 1.2. Its primary function is to provide end-to-end reliable data transmission services, ensuring that data is correctly transmitted from the source host to the destination host [7].

Figure 1.2 shows the structure of the transmission layer in the network-layered model. The transmission layer achieves reliable data transmission by establishing a logical connection between the source and destination hosts. Transmission layer protocols perform operations such as segmentation, reassembly, flow control, and congestion control to guarantee data correctness and integrity. Additionally, the transmission layer provides various quality-of-service (QoS) options to the application layer, including reliable transmission, unreliable transmission, and real-time transmission.

The significance of the transport layer lies in its provision of a unified interface for the application layer. This allows the application layer to focus solely on implementing its business logic without concerning itself with underlying network details. The transport layer can also deliver varying service levels based on application requirements, thereby accommodating the needs of diverse applications. Figure 1.3 shows a schematic diagram of the transport layer.

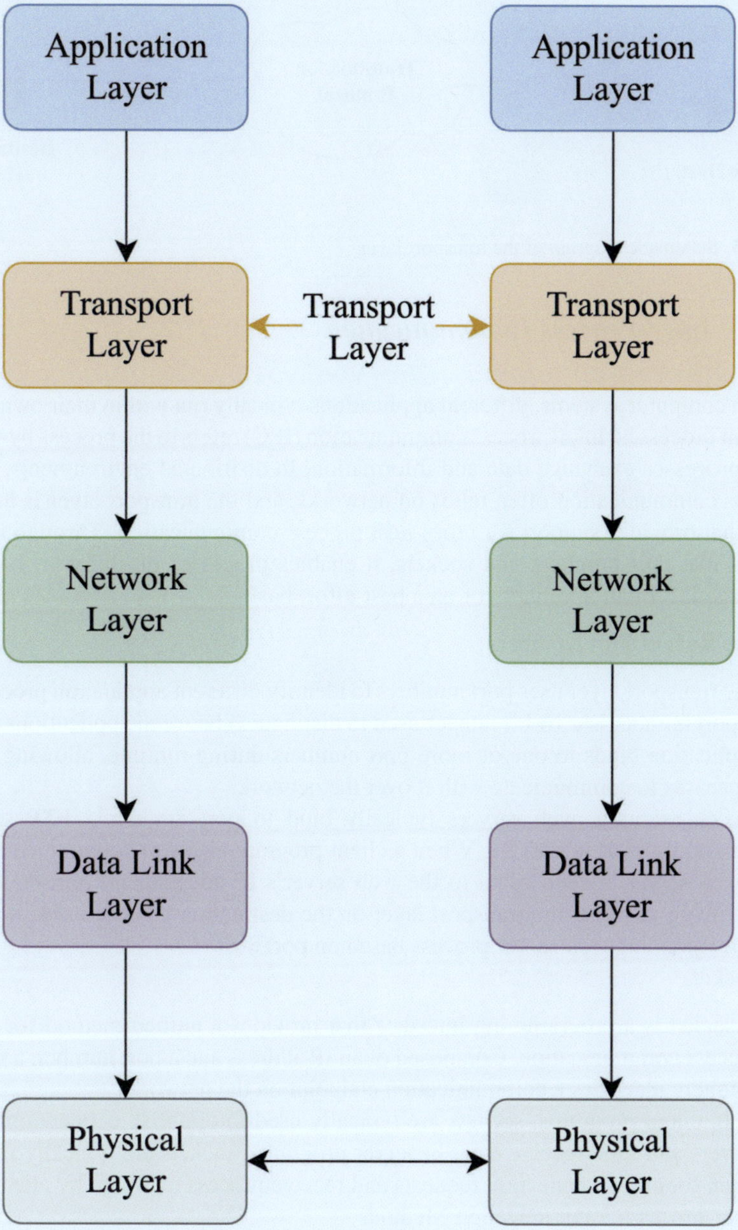

Fig. 1.2 Transmission layer structure in the network-layered model

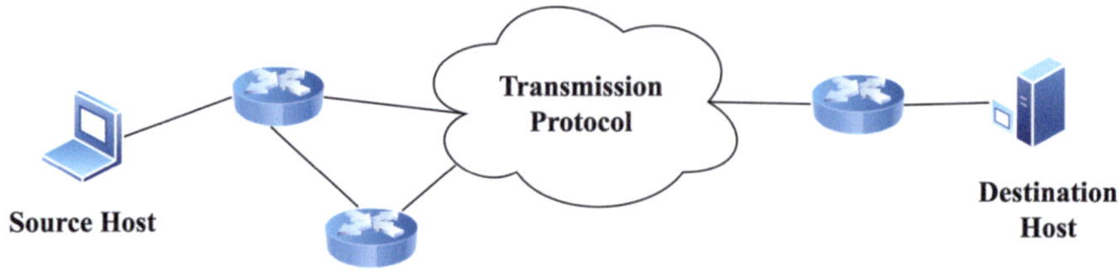

Fig. 1.3 Schematic diagram of the transport layer

1.2.2 Inter-Process Communication

Within computer systems, different applications typically run within their own independent processes. Inter-process communication (IPC) refers to the process by which these processes exchange data and information. In distributed environments, inter-process communication often relies on networks, and the transport layer is the key layer that provides support for cross-host process communication. Through mechanisms like port numbers and sockets, it enables processes on different hosts to exchange information reliably or on a best-effort basis.

1. The Role of Port Numbers

   The transport layer uses port numbers to identify different application processes. A port number is a 16-bit integer used to distinguish between applications. Each application binds to one or more port numbers during runtime, allowing other processes to communicate with it over the network.

   For example, web servers typically bind to port 80, while FTP servers commonly bind to port 21. When a client program needs to communicate with a web server, it sends data to the web server's IP address and port 80. Upon receiving the data, the transport layer on the destination host forwards it to the corresponding web server process based on port 80.
2. Socket

   A socket is a programming interface that provides a unified method for inter-process communication. Composed of an IP address and a port number, a socket uniquely identifies a communication endpoint on the network.

   In client programs, sockets are typically used to establish connections with servers and send/receive data. In server programs, sockets are typically used to listen for client connection requests and receive/process data sent by clients.
3. Inter-process Communication Methods

   The transport layer supports multiple inter-process communication methods, including connection-oriented and connectionless communication.

   Connection-Oriented Communication: In connection-oriented communication, a logical connection is first established between the source and destination hosts before data transmission occurs over that connection. Connection-oriented communication typically uses the Transmission Control Protocol (TCP), which provides reliable data transmission services, ensuring data correctness and integrity.

Connectionless Communication: In connectionless communication, the source host directly sends data to the destination host without establishing a logical connection. Connectionless communication is typically implemented using the User Datagram Protocol (UDP), which provides unreliable data transmission services and does not guarantee data correctness or integrity.

1.2.3 Primary Protocols

The primary protocols at the transport layer include the Transmission Control Protocol (TCP), the User Datagram Protocol (UDP), and emerging protocols designed for new application scenarios.

1. **Transmission Control Protocol (TCP)**

TCP is a connection-oriented, reliable transport layer protocol. It ensures reliable data transmission by establishing a connection between the source host and the destination host. TCP features the following characteristics:

1. Connection-Oriented: A logical connection is established between the source and destination hosts prior to data transmission, ensuring reliability and ordered delivery.
2. Reliable Transmission: Data correctness and integrity are guaranteed through acknowledgment and retransmission mechanisms. If the sender does not receive an acknowledgment from the receiver within a specified timeframe, the data is retransmitted.
3. Flow Control: The sender's data transmission rate is regulated via a window mechanism to prevent receiver overload. The receiver notifies the sender of a window size based on its processing capacity, and the sender adjusts its transmission rate accordingly.

Congestion Control: Monitors network congestion and adjusts the sender's transmission rate to prevent network congestion. TCP employs multiple congestion control algorithms, such as slow start, congestion avoidance, fast retransmission, and fast recovery.

Therefore, TCP finds extensive application in scenarios requiring highly reliable data transmission, such as:

1. File Transfer: Requires guaranteed data correctness and integrity. TCP's reliable transmission characteristics make it highly suitable for file transfer scenarios.
2. Email: Email transmission also demands reliable data delivery. TCP ensures that email content arrives at its destination accurately and without error.
3. Remote Login: Remote login requires reliable data transmission and interactivity. TCP meets these requirements.

2. **User Datagram Protocol (UDP)**

   UDP is a connectionless, unreliable transport layer protocol. It does not establish a connection between the source and destination hosts, instead sending data directly. UDP features the following characteristics:

   1. Connectionless: Data is sent directly to the destination host without establishing a logical connection, reducing the overhead of connection setup and teardown while improving transmission efficiency.
   2. Unreliable Transmission: Does not guarantee data correctness or integrity, potentially resulting in data loss, duplication, or out-of-order delivery.
   3. Efficient Transmission: Lacks acknowledgment and retransmission mechanisms, enabling high data transmission efficiency. Suitable for scenarios demanding high real-time performance with relatively lower reliability requirements.

   Consequently, UDP is better suited for applications requiring high real-time performance with relatively lower reliability demands, such as:

   1. Video Conferencing: Demands high real-time performance while tolerating some data loss. UDP rapidly transmits video data, and minor data loss rarely impacts video quality.
   2. Real-Time Gaming: Requires instantaneous responses to player actions with extreme real-time demands. UDP's high-efficiency transmission makes it the preferred protocol for real-time gaming.
   3. Domain Name System (DNS): DNS queries involve small data volumes with low reliability requirements. UDP enables rapid responses to DNS lookup requests.

3. **Emerging Protocols**

   Despite remaining suitable for most scenarios, traditional TCP and UDP protocols face limitations in connection establishment speed, real-time guarantees, and multipath support as computer networks continue to evolve. Consequently, researchers have proposed a series of novel transport layer protocols to better address diverse application demands.

   Common emerging transport layer protocols include:

   Quick UDP Internet Connections (QUIC) Protocol: QUIC is a transport layer protocol based on UDP, initially proposed by Google and later standardized by the IETF. It introduces mechanisms such as fast handshake, multiplexing, forward error correction, and mandatory encryption on top of UDP, significantly reducing connection establishment latency while enhancing transmission efficiency and security. Currently, QUIC is widely adopted in mobile Internet and cloud computing environments and serves as the underlying transport protocol for HTTP/3 [8].

   Real-Time Transport Protocol (RTP): RTP is specifically designed for real-time audio and video data transmission. It ensures data timeliness and ordering by adding timestamps, sequence numbers, and payload type information to packets. RTP is typically used in conjunction with Real-time Transport Control Protocol (RTCP), which provides statistical and feedback functions to support jitter compensation, bandwidth adaptation, and quality-of-service control. This protocol plays a vital role in video conferencing, Internet telephony, and real-time streaming media transmission [9].

Stream Control Transmission Protocol (SCTP): SCTP is a connection-oriented, reliable transport layer protocol originally designed by the IETF for telecommunications signaling transmission. Compared to TCP, SCTP supports multi-stream transmission, thereby reducing head-of-line blocking issues; it also supports multi-host connections, enhancing link fault tolerance. Furthermore, SCTP permits partially reliable transmission to accommodate applications requiring low latency over less reliable networks. This protocol remains widely deployed in telecommunications networks and certain industrial control systems [10].

These emerging protocols play vital roles in their respective domains: QUIC excels in high-latency networks and mobile scenarios; RTP resolves timing and synchronization challenges in multimedia transmission; and SCTP delivers enhanced reliability and flexibility for telecommunications and critical infrastructure. As network demands continue to evolve, transmission layer protocols will likely pursue increasingly diverse and specialized development paths.

1.2.4 Port Numbers

Port numbers serve as a mechanism within transport layer protocols to identify different application processes. A port number is a 16-bit integer ranging from 0 to 65,535.

1. Classification of Port Numbers

   Well-Known Ports: Range from 0 to 1023. These ports are uniformly allocated and managed by Internet Assigned Numbers Authority (IANA) for common or critical network services. For example: HTTP uses port 80, and FTP control connections use port 21.

   Registered Ports: Range 1024–49,151. These ports can be registered with IANA by organizations or application developers for specific applications.

   Dynamic/Private Ports: Range 49,152–65,535. These ports do not require registration and are typically assigned temporarily by client programs during runtime for short-term communication.
2. Port Number Allocation and Management

   Port number allocation and management are handled by IANA. IANA regularly publishes port number allocation lists for reference by users and application developers. When assigning port numbers, the following principles should be followed:

Avoid using well-known port numbers unless necessary for compatibility with standard applications.

Select an unused registered port number to prevent conflicts with other applications.

Within applications, dynamically assigned port numbers can be used to improve port number utilization.

1.3 Key Technologies of the Transport Layer

The transport layer plays a crucial role in computer networks, not only ensuring reliable data transmission but also encompassing multiple key technologies. Figure 1.4 shows a schematic of the transmission layer.

Below is a detailed description of some core technologies within the transmission layer.

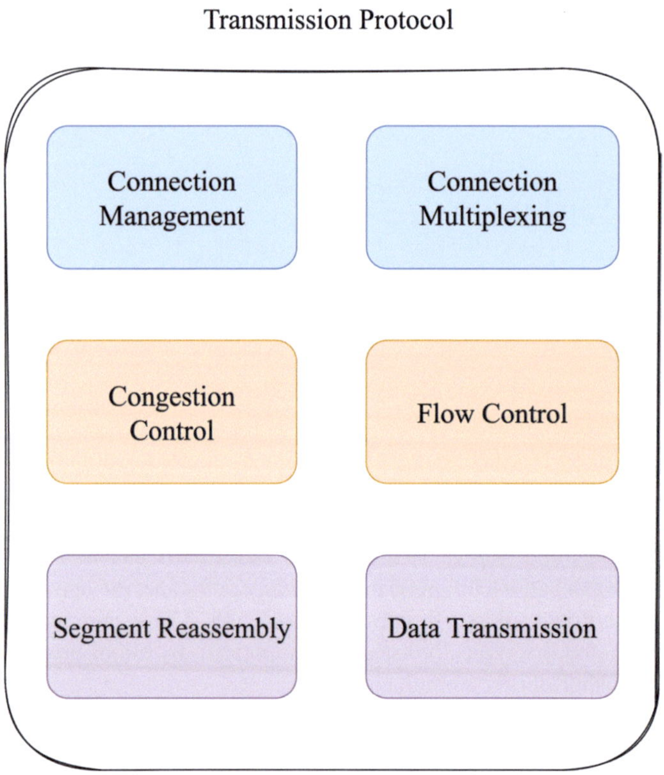

Fig. 1.4 Transmission layer schematic

1.3.1 Connection Management

Connection management is one of the fundamental functions of the transmission layer, ensuring reliable data transmission. It extends beyond traditional connection-oriented protocols to encompass broader protocol frameworks, enabling the establishment, maintenance, and termination of communication across various scenarios. Generally, connection management functions include:

1. Connection Establishment

   Within the transport layer, connection establishment typically involves a series of handshake processes. Taking connection-oriented protocols as an example, the sender and receiver exchange specific control information to confirm each other's identity and communication intent and negotiate key parameters such as the initial sequence number. This process ensures that both parties are prepared and capable of correctly identifying and processing each other's data before data transmission begins.

   For instance, in the TCP protocol, connection establishment is achieved through a three-way handshake. First, the client sends a packet with the SYN flag set to the server, requesting a connection. Upon receiving this packet, the server responds with a packet containing both SYN and ACK flags, acknowledging the client's request while simultaneously initiating its own connection request. Finally, the client replies with an ACK packet, confirming the server's connection request, thereby completing the connection establishment.
2. Connection Maintenance

   Once a connection is established, the transport layer continuously monitors its state to ensure reliable data transmission. This involves detecting and handling various potential error conditions, such as packet loss, duplication, or out-of-order delivery. Simultaneously, the transport layer dynamically adjusts connection parameters—like send window size and congestion control strategies—based on network conditions and the needs of both communicating parties.

   For example, the TCP protocol maintains connection reliability through acknowledgment mechanisms, retransmission mechanisms, flow control, and congestion control. Upon receiving data, the receiver sends an acknowledgment packet to the sender, indicating that the data was correctly received. If the sender does not receive an acknowledgment within a certain timeframe, it assumes data loss and initiates retransmission. The flow control mechanism prevents data overflow at the receiver by adjusting the send window size when the receiver's processing capacity is insufficient. The congestion control mechanism adjusts the sender's data transmission rate based on network congestion to prevent network congestion.
3. Connection Termination

   After completing data transmission, both parties must properly terminate the connection to release occupied resources. Connection termination typically involves a series of interactions to ensure both sides acknowledge the connection's end and no further data transfer occurs.

For example, in the TCP protocol, connection termination is achieved through a four-way handshake. First, one party (usually the client) sends a segment with the FIN flag set, indicating it has no more data to transmit. Upon receiving this packet, the other party responds with an ACK packet, acknowledging receipt of the FIN packet. Then, the other party also sends a packet with the FIN flag set, indicating it too has no more data to send. Finally, the party that originally sent the FIN packet responds with an ACK packet, acknowledging receipt of the other party's FIN packet, thereby completing the connection termination.

1.3.2 Reliable Data Transmission

In general network architectures, reliable data transmission is accomplished at the transport layer. Ensuring reliable data transmission is one of the core tasks of the transport layer, guaranteeing that data is accurately delivered from sender to receiver.

1. Acknowledgment Mechanism

   The acknowledgment mechanism is key to achieving reliable data transmission. Upon receiving data, the receiver sends an acknowledgment message to the sender, indicating that the data has been correctly received. The sender uses these acknowledgments to determine which data segments have been successfully received and which require retransmission.

   For example, in the TCP protocol, the receiver immediately sends an acknowledgment packet upon receiving data. This packet contains an acknowledgment number indicating the sequence number of the next data segment expected to be received. The sender uses this acknowledgment number to determine which data segments have been confirmed and which require retransmission. If the sender does not receive an acknowledgment within a specified timeout period, it assumes data loss and initiates retransmission.
2. Sequence Numbers and Acknowledgment Numbers

   Sequence numbers and acknowledgment numbers are crucial mechanisms for ensuring ordered data transmission. The sender assigns a sequence number to each transmitted data segment. The receiver sorts the data based on these sequence numbers and uses acknowledgment numbers to inform the sender of the next expected sequence number.

   For example, in the TCP protocol, when sending data, the sender places the sequence number of each segment in the TCP header. Upon receiving data, the receiver sorts it based on sequence numbers and includes an acknowledgment number in the acknowledgment packet, indicating the next sequence number of data expected to be received. This allows the sender to determine which data segments have been successfully received and which require retransmission.
3. Checksum Mechanism

   The checksum mechanism detects errors that may occur during data transmission. When sending data, the sender calculates a checksum for the data and includes it in the datagram. Upon receiving the data, the receiver recalculates the checksum and compares it with the received checksum. If the two checksums do not match, it indicates an error occurred during transmission.

For example, both the TCP and UDP protocols utilize the checksum mechanism to detect data errors. When calculating the checksum, the sender includes both the header and the data portion of the datagram. Upon receiving the data, the receiver recalculates the checksum and compares it with the received checksum. If the two checksums do not match, the receiver discards the datagram and sends an error report to the sender.

4. Retransmission Mechanism

   When the sender detects data loss or corruption, retransmission is required. The retransmission mechanism ensures that data is ultimately received correctly by the receiver.

   For example, in the TCP protocol, the sender starts a timer after sending data. If no acknowledgment is received before the timer expires, the sender assumes data loss and initiates retransmission. The number of retransmissions and time intervals can be adjusted based on the specific protocol and network conditions.

1.3.3 Flow Control

The purpose of flow control is to ensure that the sender's data transmission rate does not exceed the receiver's processing capacity, thereby preventing data loss or delays.

Most transport layers typically implement dynamic flow control through a window mechanism. This dynamic adjustment allows the sender to optimize the window size for data transmission based on network conditions and receiver capacity. The window mechanism is the primary means of achieving flow control. The receiver notifies the sender of a window size based on its processing capability, indicating the amount of data the sender can transmit. The sender then adjusts its transmission rate according to the window size communicated by the receiver.

Flow control is crucial for ensuring the reliability and stability of data transmission. If the sender transmits data too rapidly, the receiver may be unable to process it in time, leading to data loss or overflow. Through flow control, the sender can adjust its transmission rate based on the receiver's processing capacity, ensuring that data is correctly received and processed.

1.3.4 Congestion Control

Congestion control refers to a series of measures implemented to prevent network congestion. When data traffic in a network becomes excessive, it may cause congestion, thereby reducing the efficiency and reliability of data transmission. Compared to flow control, congestion control is more comprehensive. Flow control applies to a single connection, while congestion control governs the entire network.

Congestion control is a critical transmission layer technology for ensuring stable and efficient network operation. Strategies and methods vary across different network architectures.

1. **Congestion Control in TCP/IP Networks**

   In traditional TCP/IP networks, congestion control [11] is primarily implemented through the following approaches:

   1. Slow Start and Congestion Avoidance:

      During the slow-start phase, the sender begins transmitting data with a small send window, gradually increasing it as acknowledgments are received. This process prevents initial network congestion caused by sending large volumes of data too quickly.

      Once the send window reaches a certain threshold, the congestion avoidance phase begins. Here, the send window increases slowly in a linear manner to prevent the network from entering a congested state too rapidly.

      For example, in file transfer scenarios, the sender may initially transmit only a small number of data segments. As acknowledgments continuously arrive from the receiver, the send window gradually increases, accelerating data transmission.
   2. Fast Retransmission and Fast Recovery:

      When the receiver receives three duplicate acknowledgment messages, it assumes data segments may be lost and immediately retransmits the missing segments without waiting for a timer to expire.

      Entering the fast recovery phase, the send window size is reduced to half its current value and begins linear growth to restore data transmission as quickly as possible.

      For instance, during brief network congestion causing data loss, the fast retransmission and fast recovery mechanism can rapidly resume data transmission, minimizing transmission delays.
   3. Congestion Window Adjustment:

      Dynamically adjusts the send window size based on network congestion. When congestion occurs, the send window shrinks. When network conditions improve, increase the transmission window.

      For instance, network congestion levels are assessed by monitoring metrics such as packet loss rate and round-trip time, subsequently adjusting the transmission window size.

2. **Congestion Control in Information-Centric Networking (ICN)**

   Information-Centric Networking (ICN) is a novel content-centric network architecture that differs significantly from traditional end-to-end communication-based TCP/IP systems. In ICN, users request specific content by sending interest packets. Upon receiving these packets, network nodes forward them based on name matching and return corresponding data packets. Under this architecture, congestion control exhibits distinct characteristics from traditional networks:

First, congestion control based on interest packets and data packets is a core mechanism of ICN. Since content retrieval is driven by interest packets, congestion control can be achieved by regulating the transmission rate of these packets. When a node detects excessive link load or cache queue backlog, it can proactively reduce the forwarding rate of interest packets, thereby decreasing the generation of new data packets. This approach resembles the congestion avoidance mechanism in traditional TCP, but it adjusts the frequency of content requests rather than the transmission window size.

Second, caching mechanisms play a crucial role in congestion control. ICN nodes can cache passing data, enabling subsequent user requests to directly hit caches at nearby nodes and return results, thereby reducing traffic load on core links. During network congestion, caching strategies can coordinate with congestion control—for example, prioritizing caching of popular content to avoid redundant requests for the same data that waste link resources. In typical video-on-demand scenarios, widespread storage of popular video segments across distributed caching nodes allows user requests to be fulfilled directly at access or edge nodes. This not only reduces transmission latency but also significantly alleviates network congestion.

Therefore, congestion control in ICN relies not only on adjusting the rate of interest packets but also integrates the network's built-in caching mechanisms. This makes congestion control strategies more flexible and efficient in content distribution scenarios. This content-driven congestion management model represents a key future development direction for network architectures in data acquisition and resource optimization.

1.3.5 Segmentation and Reassembly

1. Purpose and Principles of Segmentation

   At the transport layer, segmentation refers to the process of dividing larger application layer messages into multiple smaller data segments. Its primary purpose is to accommodate network layer transmission constraints and enhance overall transmission efficiency. Network layers typically impose constraints on datagram length, known as the Maximum Transmission Unit (MTU). If application layer packets are too large and not segmented, they may exceed the network layer's capacity, preventing successful transmission. By segmenting packets, each data segment remains within the MTU limit, ensuring smooth traversal across various network links and routing devices.

   Beyond adapting to network constraints, segmentation enhances transmission efficiency. Smaller segments are easier to schedule and transmit across networks, reducing congestion and packet loss risks under varying link conditions. Additionally, segmentation makes error recovery more efficient: if a segment is lost or corrupted, only that segment needs retransmission, not the entire datagram.

2. The Process and Methods of Fragmentation
   Determining Fragment Size: The transport layer protocol determines the fragment size based on the network layer MTU, the receiver's receive window, and the characteristics of the application layer. For example, in TCP, the sender dynamically adjusts the fragment size based on the receiver's advertised window size and network conditions to achieve optimal throughput and fairness.
   Adding Header Information: Each data segment is generated with a transport layer header, containing common fields such as sequence numbers, acknowledgment numbers, control bits, and checksums. This information facilitates data reassembly at the receiver and supports reliability mechanisms like error detection and flow control.
3. Reassembly Process and Challenges
   At the receiver, the transport layer must reassemble fragmented data. Specifically, the receiver sorts fragments based on sequence numbers and stitches them into application layer packets. When fragments are missing, the receiver requests retransmission via acknowledgment and retransmission mechanisms. Due to complex network conditions, reassembly often faces these challenges:
4. Fragments may arrive lost, duplicated, or out of order, necessitating acknowledgment and retransmission mechanisms for correction.
5. Fragment reordering and loss detection incur computational and memory overhead, particularly pronounced in high-bandwidth, high-concurrency scenarios;
6. To ensure performance for real-time applications, the transport layer must balance error recovery with latency.

In summary, segmentation and reassembly mechanisms form the critical foundation for reliable communication at the transport layer. By adapting to network constraints, enhancing error recovery efficiency, and ensuring ordered data transmission, they enable stable and efficient information exchange between application processes.

1.3.6 Multiplexing and Demultiplexing

Multiplexing and demultiplexing are key mechanisms enabling the transport layer to support multiple application processes sharing network communication capabilities. They enable multiple communication streams from different applications to coexist over a single logical host-to-host connection. For example, in the QUIC protocol, multiplexing is achieved through the abstraction of "streams," allowing multiple requests and responses to be multiplexed over a single QUIC connection. This avoids the head-of-line blocking issue common in traditional TCP during multi-request scenarios.

1. Multiplexing
   Multiplexing refers to the capability of multiple application processes to transmit data using the same transport layer protocol. At the sender, the transport

layer appends header information to data from different application processes and transmits it over a single network connection.

2. Demultiplexing

   Demultiplexing involves the transport layer correctly delivering received data to the appropriate application process based on specific identifiers (such as port numbers). At the receiver, the transport layer uses information like port numbers within datagrams to deliver data to the correct application process.

3. Importance of Multiplexing and Demultiplexing

   Multiplexing and demultiplexing enhance network resource utilization and reduce the number of network connections. Through multiplexing, multiple application processes can share a single network connection, thereby minimizing network resource consumption. Simultaneously, demultiplexing ensures that data is correctly delivered to the intended application process, guaranteeing the accuracy and reliability of data transmission.

1.4 Evolution Path of Transport Layer Protocol

1.4.1 Overview of TCP and UDP

As a critical layer in the computer network-layered model, the evolution and development of transmission layer protocols have always been closely tied to the demands of network applications. With the continuous advancement of network technology and the increasing diversity of application scenarios, transmission layer protocols are undergoing ongoing optimization and innovation to better meet data transmission requirements across different contexts. Within this developmental trajectory, Transmission Control Protocol (TCP) and User Datagram Protocol (UDP) stand as two foundational pillars of the transport layer. They play pivotal roles in diverse application scenarios and form the basis for numerous application layer protocols.

Transmission Control Protocol (TCP) and User Datagram Protocol (UDP) are the two primary transport layer protocols. They serve critical functions across various application scenarios and constitute the foundation for many application layer protocols.

1. Characteristics and Application Scenarios of TCP

   TCP is a connection-oriented, reliable transport layer protocol. It ensures reliable data transmission by establishing a logical connection between sender and receiver. TCP features the following characteristics:

   Connection-Oriented: A connection must be established before data transmission to ensure reliability and order.

   Reliable Transmission: Ensures data correctness and integrity through acknowledgment and retransmission mechanisms.

   Flow Control: Regulates sender data transmission rates via window mechanisms to prevent receiver overload.

Congestion Control: Monitors network congestion and adjusts sender rates to avoid network bottlenecks.

TCP is suitable for applications demanding high data reliability, such as file transfers, email, and remote logins. In these scenarios, data accuracy and integrity are critical, necessitating a reliable transport layer protocol to guarantee transmission quality.

2. Characteristics and Use Cases of UDP

   UDP is a connectionless, unreliable transport layer protocol. It transmits data directly without establishing a connection between sender and receiver. UDP features:

   - Connectionless: Sends data directly to the destination host without establishing a connection, reducing overhead from connection setup/teardown and improving transmission efficiency.
   - Unreliable Transmission: Does not guarantee data correctness or integrity, potentially resulting in data loss, duplication, or out-of-order delivery.

   High-Efficiency Transmission: Lacks acknowledgment and retransmission mechanisms, enabling high data transmission efficiency. Suitable for scenarios demanding high real-time performance with relatively lower reliability requirements.

   UDP is suitable for applications demanding high real-time performance but relatively low data reliability, such as video conferencing, real-time gaming, and the Domain Name System (DNS). In these scenarios, data timeliness is critical, necessitating efficient transport layer protocols to ensure transmission speed.

1.4.2 Communication Requirements for Future Networks

The current Internet architecture was originated in the 1960s and 1970s. Constrained by hardware performance and resources, computer networks at that time primarily addressed the challenge of sharing scarce resources between hosts. Consequently, the end-to-end push-based interaction design effectively met the demands of the era [12]. Over the subsequent decades, rapid advancements in integrated circuits led to increasingly sophisticated network devices with enhanced computational power and reduced costs. This hardware evolution fueled the rapid expansion of computer networks. In the past decade, the explosive growth of network scale has accelerated the development of emerging applications like digital media, short videos, and social networks, making content distribution the primary function of the Internet. Users now prioritize content itself over how or where to access it. The current Internet architecture design is inconsistent with existing user demands, prompting researchers to continuously explore new architectural designs for future networks.

Academic circles have proposed two technical approaches to address the issues in the current Internet architecture: The first adopts an "incremental improvement" philosophy, revising and expanding existing network models to adapt to new network demands. A typical example is using IPv6 to solve the IPv4 address exhaustion problem. The second approach adopts a "revolutionary disruption" philosophy, reconstructing existing network architectures and redesigning future network frameworks. Representative architectures include Information-Centric Networking (ICN), Named Data Networking (NDN), and Co-Governed Multi-Identifier Networks (CoG-MINs) [13, 14].

The traditional IP address system can no longer meet future networks' demand for multiple identifiers, such as user identification and content identification. Future networks require support for multi-identifier systems to enhance reliability and efficiency.

Within these emerging network architectures, content identification and retrieval become central concerns. For instance, ICN adopts a content-centric approach where users request content by sending interest packets. Nodes in the network forward data packets based on these interest packets. This necessitates transport layer protocols capable of efficiently handling content-based requests and transmissions to ensure rapid and accurate content distribution. These network architectures employ disruptive design approaches, reconstructing a network layer that is difficult to scale. Consequently, they struggle to achieve seamless compatibility with existing IP networks and may fail to address emerging communication demands in the future.

Named Data Networks (NDNs), proposed in 2010, evolved from Content-Centric Networking (CCN). It replaces the sender-driven push communication semantics of IP networks with receiver-driven pull communication semantics. However, due to NDN's disruptive architectural design and reliance on a single communication semantics, it reconstructs a network layer that is difficult to scale. Consequently, it fails to achieve good compatibility with existing IP networks and cannot address new communication demands that may emerge in the future. When new communication requirements arise, it may necessitate a radical restructuring of the network architecture or even the introduction of an entirely new network architecture as a replacement.

To address the aforementioned issues with NDN, Professor Li Hui's team proposed MIN [15, 16], a Co-Governed Multi-Identifier Network architecture that integrates future networks with IP through blockchain technology. Figure 1.5 shows the architecture of the MIN network. Addressing the shortcomings of the IP Internet architecture in service quality, security, and mobility, as well as the US control over top-level domain root servers, the MIN network integrates blockchain technology to achieve decentralized identifier management and resolution. This enables multilateral, equal governance of global non-IP top-level identifiers, meeting the urgent needs of nations for independent cyberspace sovereignty, secure and orderly development, and future sustainability.

The MIN network possesses numerous innovative features. In terms of communication semantics, it inherits the superior designs from both IP networks and NDN networks while supporting both push and pull communication semantics. This design not only enhances compatibility with existing IP networks but also introduces greater operational flexibility. Users can flexibly select appropriate communication semantics based on different service scenarios, or even employ both push and pull methods

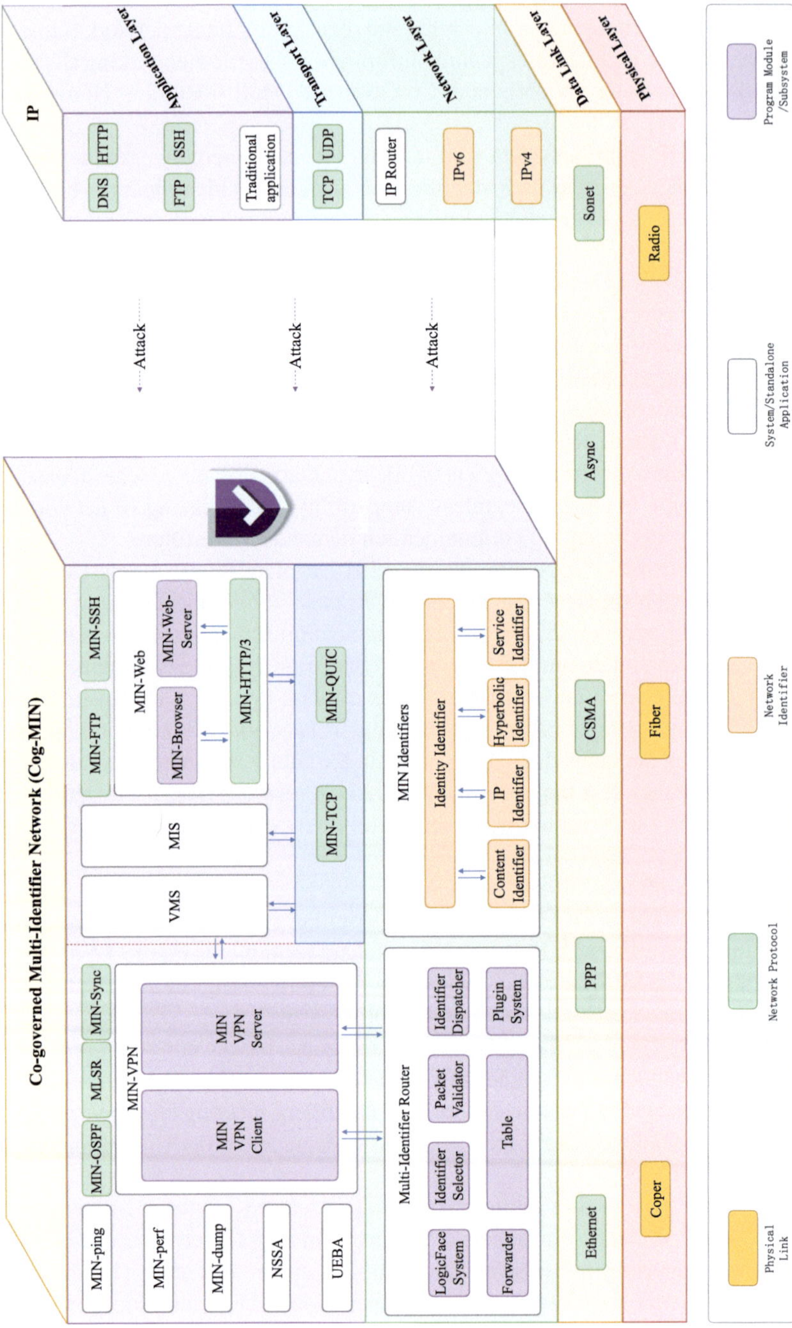

Fig. 1.5 MIN network architecture diagram

simultaneously within the same scenario. For instance, push semantics ensure timely information delivery in real-time interactive services, while pull semantics enable more efficient content retrieval in content-access services.

MIN network excels in security. It supports adding digital signatures to all types of network packets. Routers or edge nodes can verify these signatures to ensure data integrity and traceability. For identity management, MIN network supports multiple network identifiers, including identity identifiers, content identifiers, IP identifiers, hyperbolic identifiers, and service identifiers. This capability enables the network to adapt to more complex and diverse application scenarios.

In practical applications, the MIN network has demonstrated broad potential. It has undergone pilot testing and implementation across multiple domains, including supply chain financial management systems, industrial digital management systems, asset digital management and trading systems, industrial Internet, intelligent vehicle networking, and integrated space-ground satellite networks. In supply chain financial management systems, MIN network's multi-identifier capability and security mechanisms enable identity authentication and secure information sharing among supply chain participants, enhancing the trustworthiness and efficiency of financial transactions while mitigating risks. In intelligent connected vehicle networks, MIN network's high security and real-time communication capabilities provide reliable network support for autonomous driving and intelligent traffic management, ensuring driving safety and traffic flow.

As the technology continues to evolve and mature, the MIN network is poised to become a key development direction for future networks. Its design philosophy and characteristics offer practical solutions to challenges arising from the transition between traditional and future network requirements, laying a solid foundation for future network development. By balancing compatibility and utilization of existing networks with foresight into future demands, the MIN network achieves security and scalability through innovative technical approaches, positioning it as a significant developmental path for future network architectures.

1.4.3 Protocol Development for Emerging Scenarios

Having identified the communication demands of future networks and the challenges and opportunities facing current network architectures, we now focus on the specific development directions for transport layer protocols in emerging scenarios. With continuous technological advancement, new scenarios such as data centers and computing networks, mobile networks, real-time multimedia transmission, and blockchain applications are emerging rapidly. Each presents unique performance requirements and functional expectations for transport layer protocols. Against this backdrop, innovation and optimization of transport layer protocols are imperative to better accommodate these emerging scenarios. This will deliver superior, efficient, and reliable network service experiences to users, thereby propelling the entire field of computer networking technology toward greater intelligence, diversity, and security.

In data center scenarios, as the core hubs for processing and storing massive amounts of data, their internal networks impose stringent performance requirements on transport protocols. Data centers handle substantial real-time data processing and large-scale data transmission tasks, such as video streaming and big data analytics. This necessitates transmission protocols with high bandwidth and low latency to ensure rapid, stable data transfer between servers.

Additionally, data center networks feature a single control domain and homogeneous network architecture, enabling unified management policies for network device and protocol configuration, resulting in greater consistency and controllability. However, diverse application demands, complex traffic patterns, congestion control challenges, and issues like TCP Incast pose significant challenges to data center transport layer protocols. To address these challenges, host-based congestion control algorithms like DCTCP [17] emerged. Leveraging switches' explicit congestion notification capabilities, DCTCP enables fine-grained congestion control but suffers from limitations such as failing to distinguish between small and large flows. Switch priority scheduling ensures rapid forwarding of high-priority traffic, but hardware limitations restrict the number of priority queues.

Traditional TCP protocols have also shown limitations in data center networks, leading to the adoption of RDMA technology. RDMA enables direct access to remote host memory, reducing latency and CPU overhead, primarily implemented through InfiniBand, RoCE, and iWARP. However, it faces challenges such as congestion management in practical applications.

In computing network scenarios, generative large language models like ChatGPT and Sora are experiencing explosive growth, posing unprecedented challenges to network infrastructure. During training, these models involve diverse parallel approaches—data parallelism, pipeline parallelism, and tensor parallelism—making cross-server communication essential. Moreover, training scales are immense, potentially involving hundreds of thousands or even millions of GPUs.

Coordinating such vast computational resources imposes stringent demands on the network's hyperscale capabilities, requiring it to reliably and efficiently handle communication between an enormous number of compute nodes. Against this backdrop, Remote Direct Memory Access (RDMA) technology stands out due to its unique advantages. This technology enables applications to directly access remote node memory without operating system kernel intervention, delivering significant advantages such as high throughput, low latency, and zero CPU overhead. In large-model training scenarios, RDMA substantially enhances data transfer efficiency, effectively reducing time losses caused by data transmission and significantly boosting training efficiency, making it an ideal choice for such environments.

In mobile networking scenarios, the powerful impetus from 5G and future 6G technologies has directed transmission protocol optimization toward addressing challenges posed by frequent node mobility and unstable wireless links. The QUIC protocol enhances connection stability and data transmission performance in mobile environments by introducing connection migration and rapid recovery mechanisms.

For instance, when devices switch between Wi-Fi hotspots or transition from Wi-Fi to mobile data networks, QUIC rapidly detects network changes and restores transmission without requiring connection reestablishment—unlike traditional TCP. This minimizes transmission interruptions and improves user experience.

In practical scenarios like mobile video conferencing and live streaming, QUIC significantly outperforms traditional protocols by effectively preventing lag and interruptions. Furthermore, the application of network coding theory has become a crucial method for enhancing mobile network transmission reliability. Strategically introducing redundant information encoding during transmission significantly improves data resilience against packet loss and transmission success rates over unstable wireless links.

The rapid growth of real-time multimedia applications—such as high-definition video conferencing, large-scale interactive live streaming, and immersive online gaming—imposes extremely stringent demands on the real-time performance and efficiency of transmission protocols.

The RTP/RTCP protocol ensures the temporal accuracy and synchronization of multimedia data transmission through its precise timestamp and sequence number mechanisms, effectively safeguarding user viewing and interactive experiences. Real-time multimedia transmission solutions based on the QUIC protocol further leverage QUIC's low-latency advantages. Combined with its built-in high-strength encryption mechanisms, these solutions provide comprehensive security and efficiency guarantees for real-time multimedia data transmission.

1.5 Chapter Summary

This chapter introduces transmission layer protocols in computer networks, covering the following key topics:

1. Overview of computer networks.
2. Overview of the transmission layer.
3. Key technologies of the transmission layer.
4. Evolutionary path of transmission layer protocols.

1.6 Experiment—Introduction to Computer Network Transmission and Packet Capture Analysis

1.6.1 Experiment Objectives

1. Master the download, installation, and basic configuration of Wireshark.
2. Familiarize yourself with Wireshark's interface layout and core functional modules.

3. Learn to capture local network traffic and perform basic filtering and analysis.

1.6.2 Tools and Environment

1. Operating System: Windows 10/11, macOS, or Linux (Ubuntu 20.04 or later recommended).
2. Software: Wireshark (latest stable version).
3. Reference Resources: Wireshark official documentation (https://www.wireshark.org/docs/).

1.6.3 Experiment Steps

1. Download and Install Wireshark
   (1) Visit the Wireshark official website (https://www.wireshark.org/), click "Download" to access the download page.
   (2) Select the appropriate version based on your operating system (Windows users choose the 64-bit installer, macOS users select the.dmg file, Linux users can install via package managers—e.g., Ubuntu users run "sudo apt install wireshark").
   (3) During installation, macOS users must authorize system extensions; Linux users may need to configure permissions.
2. Wireshark Interface Overview
   (1) Launch Wireshark. The main interface consists of three sections:
      (a) Top: Menu bar and toolbar, containing capture controls, filters, and other functions.
      (b) Middle: List of network interfaces for capture, displaying currently available network adapters (e.g., Wi-Fi, Ethernet).
      (c) Bottom: Status bar, showing capture status, packet statistics, and other information (Fig. 1.6).
   (2) Capturing Local Network Traffic
      (a) In the interface list, select the currently active network adapter (e.g., "Wi-Fi" or "Ethernet"; identify active adapters by traffic fluctuations next to their names). Click the "Start Capture" button (shark fin icon) in the toolbar.
      (b) Open a browser and visit any website (e.g., https://www.baidu.com). After 30 s, click the "Stop Capture" button.
      (c) Observe the captured packet list, which includes fields such as timestamp, source address, destination address, protocol type, and message content (Fig. 1.7).

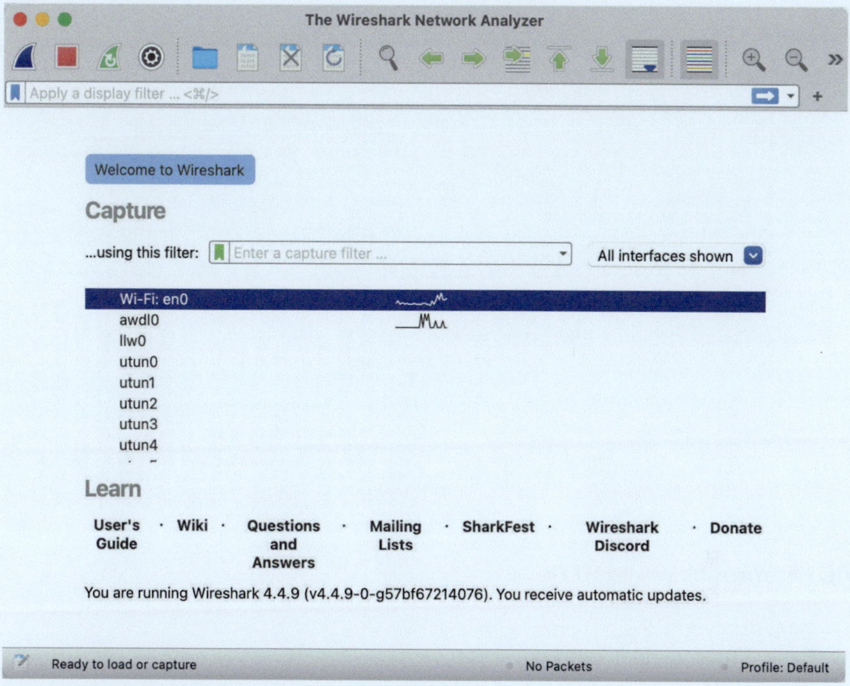

Fig. 1.6 Wireshark main interface

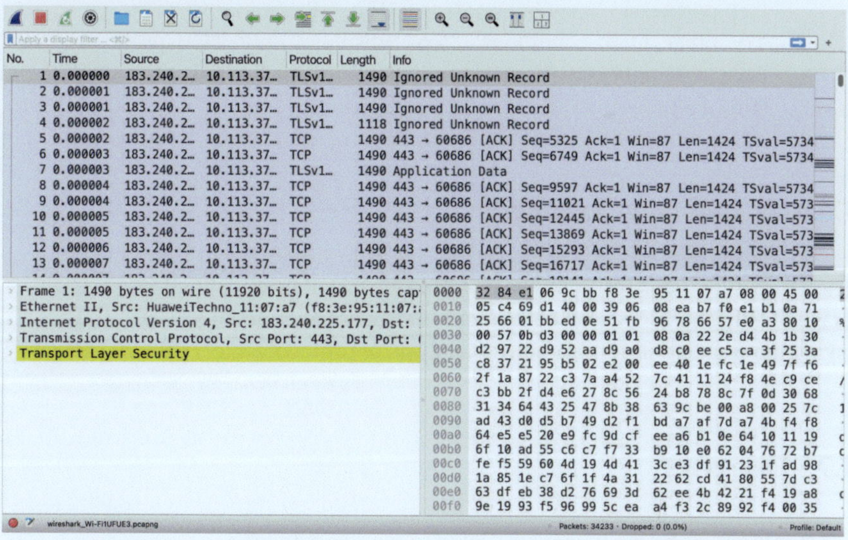

Fig. 1.7 Wireshark packet capture interface

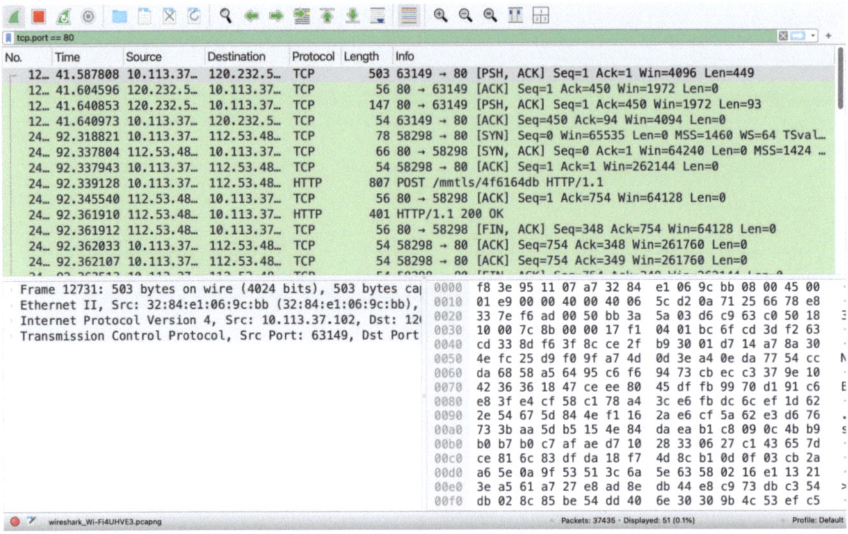

Fig. 1.8 Wireshark viewing HTTP

3. Basic Filtering and Analysis
   (1) Enter "http" or "tcp.port ==80" in the top filter bar to display only HTTP protocol packets (Note: Most modern websites use HTTPS; filtering by "tcp.port== 43" may be necessary) (Fig. 1.8).
   (2) Try other filter conditions: "tcp" (displays only TCP packets), "udp" (displays only UDP packets), "quic" (displays only QUIC packets) (Fig. 1.9).

1.6.4 Experiment Summary

Through this experiment, you have mastered the installation, configuration, and basic usage of Wireshark. You can now quickly locate target protocol packets using filters, laying the foundation for subsequent analysis of protocols like TCP and TLS.

1.7 Exercises

1. Briefly describe the layered model of computer networks.
2. Briefly describe the definition of the transport layer.
3. List at least three key technologies of the transport layer.
4. Briefly describe the core features of multi-identifier networks.

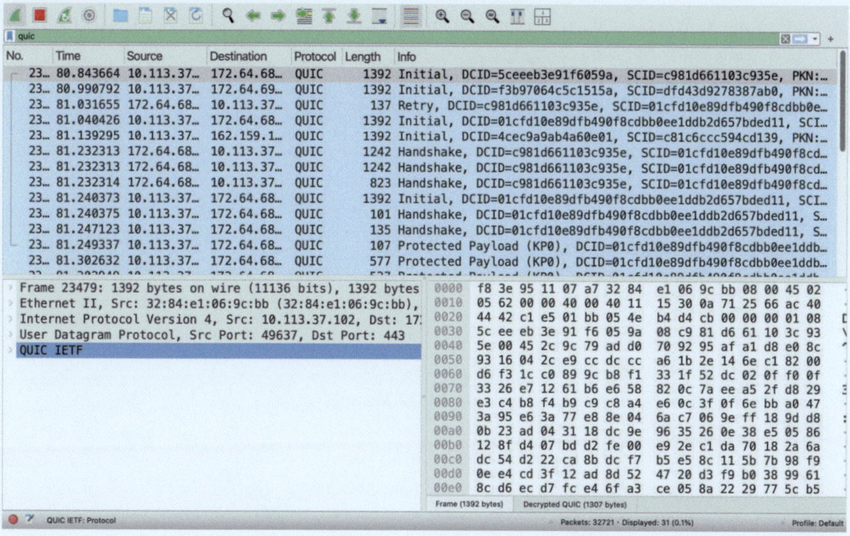

Fig. 1.9 Wireshark viewing QUIC protocol

References

1. Tanenbaum AS, Wetherall DJ. Computer networks. 5th ed. London: Pearson; 2010.
2. Kurose JF, Ross KW. Computer networking: a top-down approach. 8th ed. London: Pearson; 2021.
3. Stallings W. Data and computer communications. 10th ed. London: Pearson; 2015.
4. Halsall F. Computer networking and the internet. London: Pearson Education; 2005.
5. Leiner BM, Cerf VG, Clark DD, et al. A brief history of the internet. ACM SIGCOMM Comput Commun Rev. 2009;39(5):22–31.
6. Barroso LA, Hölzle U, Ranganathan P. The datacenter as a computer: designing warehouse-scale machines. Berlin: Springer; 2019.
7. Comer DE. Internetworking with TCP/IP. Boston: Addison-Wesley Professional; 2013.
8. Iyengar J, Thomson M. QUIC: a UDP-based multiplexed and secure transport. RFC 9000, IETF; 2021.
9. Schulzrinne H, Casner S, Frederick R, et al. RTP: a transport protocol for real-time applications. RFC 3550, IETF; 2003.
10. Stewart R. Stream control transmission protocol. RFC 4960, IETF; 2007.
11. Floyd S, Fall K. Promoting the use of end-to-end congestion control in the Internet. IEEE/ACM Trans Netw. 2002;7(4):458–72.
12. Forouzan BA. TCP/IP protocol suite. Columbus, OH: McGraw-Hill Higher Education; 2002.
13. Li H, Bai H. Principle of architecture, protocol, and algorithms for CoG-MIN: a sustainably ecological and evolutionary solution for packet network system. Berlin: Springer; 2025. https://doi.org/10.1007/978-981-96-3596-2
14. Li H, Yang X, Qi J. Multilateral co-governance of the sovereign internet: legal foundations, architectural framework, and prototype introduction. Tsinghua University Press; 2020. https://www.tup.tsinghua.edu.cn/upload/books/yz/086003-01. Accessed 14 Sept 2025.
15. Li H, Yang X. Co-governed sovereignty network: legal basis and its prototype and applications with MIN architecture. Berlin: Springer; 2021. https://doi.org/10.1007/978-981-16-2670-8.

16. Li H, Yang X, Wei G, et al. An evolutionary network layer for future network MIN architecture. IEEE Trans Netw Sci Eng. 2025.
17. Alizadeh M, Greenberg A, Maltz DA, et al. Data center TCP (DCTCP). In: Proceedings of the ACM SIGCOMM 2010 Conference. 2010. p. 63–74.

Chapter 2
Transmission Control Protocol

After systematically reviewing the evolution of transport layer protocols and their key enabling technologies in the previous chapter, this chapter turns to the core of the Internet's transport architecture—the Transmission Control Protocol (TCP). As a foundational protocol that has supported global networks for decades, TCP enables robust data exchange in complex network environments through its connection-oriented design and reliable transmission mechanisms.

This chapter details TCP's fundamental characteristics (connection-oriented, reliable transmission) and primary functions (reliable data delivery, flow control, and congestion control). This chapter analyzes TCP header structure, core mechanisms (connection management via three-way handshake/four-way teardown, data segmentation, sliding window, etc.), advantages and disadvantages, and optimization schemes (TCP Fast Open, selective acknowledgment, BBR congestion control). Finally, it introduces advanced TCP optimizations incorporating network coding within the MIN architecture for future networks. The chapter concludes with a TCP connection management experiment to help students grasp the protocol's practical operation.

2.1 Introduction to TCP

The Transmission Control Protocol (TCP) is one of the most fundamental transport layer protocols within the Internet Protocol Suite. TCP was initially formally defined by the IETF in RFC 793 [1] and underwent a comprehensive revision and updating in RFC 9293 in 2023 [2]. As a transport layer protocol operating atop the unreliable IP layer, TCP provides a reliable, connection-oriented byte-stream service. It ensures data is delivered in the correct order and error-free across complex network environments, making it the cornerstone of modern Internet data transmission [3].

H. Li and Z. Bao, *Transport Layer for Computer Networks*,
https://doi.org/10.1007/978-981-95-7374-5_2

TCP is designed to adapt to heterogeneous network environments, functioning effectively across varying bandwidths, delays, and topologies while maintaining robustness against link packet loss, node failures, and routing changes. Compared to the User Datagram Protocol (UDP), TCP incorporates mechanisms such as connection establishment (three-way handshake), sequence and acknowledgment numbering, retransmission policies, flow control, and congestion control to ensure reliable data transmission. This characteristic makes TCP the preferred transport layer protocol for core application protocols like HTTP, FTP, and SMTP.

TCP's development history is closely intertwined with the evolution of the Internet. Since its initial specification in 1981, TCP has undergone multiple critical expansions and optimizations. For instance, RFC 1323 [4] introduced window scaling and timestamp options to support high-bandwidth-delay-product networks; RFC 2018 [5] introduced selective acknowledgment (SACK) to enhance performance in high-packet-loss environments; and RFC 2581 [6] established the standard congestion control framework, laying the foundation for subsequent algorithms like TCP-Reno, NewReno, and CUBIC. These enhancements continuously strengthened TCP's scalability and adaptability, enabling it to sustain evolving application demands and Internet scale while solidifying its position as the core transport protocol of the Internet.

2.1.1 Fundamental Characteristics of TCP

The TCP protocol possesses five fundamental characteristics that collectively form its core distinguishing features from other transport protocols:

1. **Connection-Oriented Service**: TCP must establish a connection via a "three-way handshake" before data transmission and release the connection through a "four-way handshake" upon completion. This connection is logical rather than physical, termed a "virtual connection." The connection establishment process allows both communicating parties to negotiate key parameters, such as the initial sequence number and window size, laying the foundation for subsequent reliable transmission. The connection-oriented nature enables TCP to maintain connection state information, including sequence numbers and window sizes, which is essential for achieving reliable transmission.
2. **Reliable Delivery Service**: TCP ensures error-free, loss-free, non-duplicated, and in-order data arrival through mechanisms like sequence numbers, acknowledgments, timeout retransmissions, and data checksum [7]. Each transmitted byte receives a unique sequence number, while the receiver informs the sender of successfully received data ranges via acknowledgment numbers. Checksum mechanisms detect transmission errors, and timeout retransmissions handle lost packets. This reliability allows applications to focus on business logic without concerning themselves with how data traverses the network.

3. **Full-Duplex Communication**: TCP connections enable simultaneous, independent data transmission in both directions, with each end maintaining separate send and receive buffers. This bidirectional capability is achieved through distinct sequence number spaces—each data stream has its own sequence numbering. Full-duplex operation enhances bandwidth utilization and enables application layer protocols to design more flexible interaction models.
4. **Byte-Oriented**: TCP treats application layer data as unstructured byte sequences without preserving message boundaries. This contrasts with UDP's message-oriented nature. Data written in multiple segments may be combined for transmission, while a single large write may be fragmented. This design improves network utilization but requires applications to manage message boundaries themselves (addressing the "packet sticking" issue).
5. **Flow Control and Congestion Control**: TCP implements flow control based on the receiver's processing capacity through a sliding window mechanism, preventing sender buffers from overflowing due to excessive transmission rates. Concurrently, TCP's congestion control algorithms (such as slow start, congestion avoidance, fast retransmission, and fast recovery) dynamically adjust transmission rates according to real-time network conditions, preventing severe congestion caused by excessive data injection. These mechanisms collectively ensure TCP maintains robust performance and fairness across varying network conditions [8].

These fundamental characteristics establish TCP as the preferred transport protocol for most Internet applications, particularly those requiring reliable transmission. From web browsing to file transfers, from email to remote logins, TCP underpins the vast majority of critical services on the Internet.

2.1.2 Primary Functions of TCP

The Transmission Control Protocol (TCP) is one of the most critical core protocols within the Internet Protocol Suite, operating at the transport layer. Its primary function is to provide end-to-end reliable data transmission services for the application layer. Its design objectives ensure the reliable, ordered, and complete transmission of data across networks while balancing network congestion control and resource utilization efficiency. Figure 2.1 shows the TCP transmission protocol.

1. **Reliable Data Transmission**: TCP's most critical function is reliable data transmission. It employs a multi-stage mechanism to ensure dependable delivery from sender to receiver. Data is fragmented before transmission, with each segment assigned a unique sequence number. The receiver uses these sequence numbers to reorder and deduplicate out-of-sequence or duplicate segments. The sender initiates a timeout retransmission timer for each segment; if no acknowledgment (ACK) is received within the specified time, the data is automatically retransmitted. The receiver uses a cumulative acknowledgment mechanism to inform

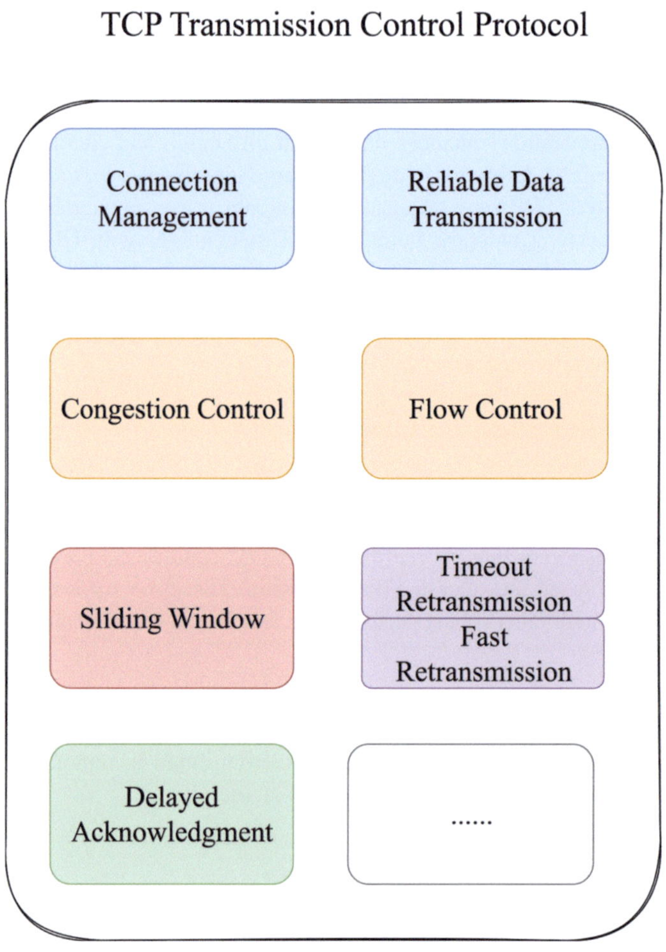

Fig. 2.1 Functional modules of the TCP transmission protocol

the sender of the range of successfully received data, enabling rapid detection and recovery of lost or corrupted segments. TCP achieves reliable data transmission through its acknowledgment (ACK) mechanism and retransmission techniques.

2. **Flow Control**: The receiver dynamically adjusts the sender's data transmission rate using a sliding window mechanism. The receiver's buffer capacity is finite. If the sender continuously transmits data at high speed while the receiver cannot read data promptly due to slow application processing or insufficient resources, unprocessed data accumulates in the buffer, eventually overflowing and being lost. To prevent the sender's rate from exceeding the receiver's processing capacity, TCP implements flow control. TCP achieves dynamic flow control through the sliding window mechanism. The receiver announces its current receive window size (RWND) in ACK packets, indicating the remaining buffer

capacity. The sender limits the transmission of unacknowledged data based on this value. If the receiver's buffer is exhausted, the window size is set to zero. The sender then pauses transmission and initiates a "Zero Window Probe," periodically sending single-byte data to trigger the receiver to update its window state. This mechanism effectively balances transmission rates with receiver processing capacity, preventing data overflow or resource contention.

3. **Congestion Control**: Congestion control functions prevent overall network overload, avoiding global performance degradation or even paralysis caused by router buffer overflows or link bandwidth saturation. It focuses on the global balance of network resources rather than the reception capacity of individual connections. If numerous TCP connections indiscriminately inject data into the network, it may cause router buffer overflows, triggering packet loss and retransmissions, forming a vicious cycle of "congestion collapse." Core congestion control algorithms include: Slow Start: During connection establishment, the congestion window begins at one Maximum Segment Size (MSS). Upon receiving each ACK, the window grows exponentially to rapidly probe network bandwidth capacity. Congestion Avoidance: Once the congestion window reaches the slow-start threshold (ssthresh), window growth switches to linear expansion to prevent aggressive scaling from inducing congestion. Fast Retransmit and Recovery: If the sender receives three consecutive duplicate ACKs, it immediately retransmits the suspected lost segment instead of waiting for a timeout. Simultaneously, ssthresh is set to half the current window, reducing the congestion window to a new threshold and entering the recovery phase.

2.2 TCP Header Structure Analysis

A TCP segment consists of a header and a data portion, with the header containing all information required for connection control and data transmission. The standard TCP header length is 20 bytes, plus up to 40 bytes of optional fields, resulting in a TCP header size ranging from 20 to 60 bytes. Understanding the TCP header structure is critical for analyzing protocol behavior and performance tuning.

Figure 2.2 shows the structure of the TCP header. The TCP header contains several key fields, each serving a specific function:

1. Source Port and Destination Port (16 Bits Each): Identify the sending and receiving applications. Together with IP addresses, they form socket addresses that uniquely identify communication endpoints. Common services use fixed port numbers (e.g., HTTP = 80, FTP = 21), while clients typically use temporary ports.
2. Sequence Number (32 Bits): Identifies the sequence number of the first data byte in this segment. During connection establishment, both parties randomly select an initial sequence number (ISN) to prevent misinterpretation of data from old connections. The sequence number space is modulo 2^{32}, wrapping around after approximately 4.3 GB.

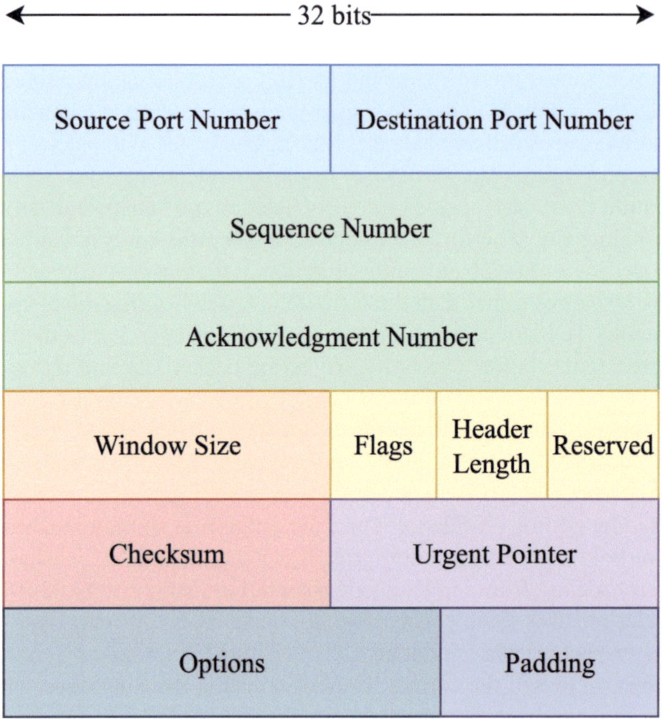

Fig. 2.2 TCP header

3. Acknowledgment Number (32 Bits): Valid when the ACK flag is set, indicating the sequence number of the next byte the receiver expects to receive. Using cumulative acknowledgment, an acknowledgment number N signifies that all bytes up to and including N-1 have been correctly received.
4. Reserved Field (6 Bits): Originally required to be set to 0 (RFC 793), though part of this field is repurposed by later extensions such as ECN.
5. Control Flags (6 Bits):
   (a) URG: Urgent pointer valid, indicating high-priority data.
   (b) ACK: Acknowledgment valid.
   (c) PSH: Push function, providing a hint for expedited data delivery (advisory, not guaranteed).
   (d) RST: Reset connection.
   (e) SYN: Synchronize sequence numbers for connection establishment.
   (f) FIN: Sender has completed data transmission.
6. Window Size (16 Bits): Available buffer space announced by the receiver for flow control. Window scaling options may extend this field.
7. Checksum (16 Bits): Checksum covering the header, data, and pseudo-header (source/destination IP, protocol number, TCP length) for error detection.

8. Urgent Pointer (16 Bits): Valid when URG = 1, indicating the end of urgent data.

Additionally, the TCP header supports protocol extensions and optimization via a variable-length options field (up to 40 bytes). Common options include:

Maximum Segment Size (MSS) negotiates the maximum acceptable data payload between peers (commonly 1460 bytes on Ethernet networks, based on a 1500-byte MTU) to avoid IP fragmentation. Timestamps precisely calculate round-trip time (RTT) and prevent ambiguity caused by sequence number wrap-around. Selective acknowledgment (SACK) allows receivers to report non-sequentially received data blocks, reducing redundant retransmissions; Window Scaling shifts the window value left by 0–14 bits, overcoming the 16-bit window size limitation. Finally, padding ensures that the header length is a multiple of 32 bits.

The overall design embodies TCP's layered extensibility: A fixed header fulfills core functions, while option fields support protocol evolution (e.g., SACK enhances retransmission efficiency, timestamps optimize congestion control). Through field coordination (e.g., sequence/acknowledgment numbers ensure ordered delivery, window/flag bits implement flow control), TCP constructs reliable byte-stream services over unreliable IP networks, forming the cornerstone of the Internet's core transport protocols.

2.3 Core Mechanisms of TCP

2.3.1 TCP Connection Management

Transmission Control Protocol (TCP) is a connection-oriented, reliable byte-stream protocol supporting full-duplex communication. It achieves stable data transmission between endpoints through three fundamental operations—connection establishment, data transfer, and connection release—with its core logic driven by a state machine.

Unlike UDP's connectionless, datagram-based transmission model, TCP requires establishing a logical connection through a "three-way handshake" before communication. This connection is not a physical link but a virtual session built upon sequence number synchronization, state management, and window control. During the connection establishment process, for example, the client and server exchange their initial sequence numbers (ISNs) in the three-way handshake to agree on the order of subsequent data byte streams.

As defined in RFC 793, the TCP state machine encompasses 11 connection states. This article will illustrate the transition of these states through the three-way handshake and four-way handshake processes. Figure 2.3 shows the TCP connection state diagram.

The 11 states of a TCP connection can be categorized into three major groups:

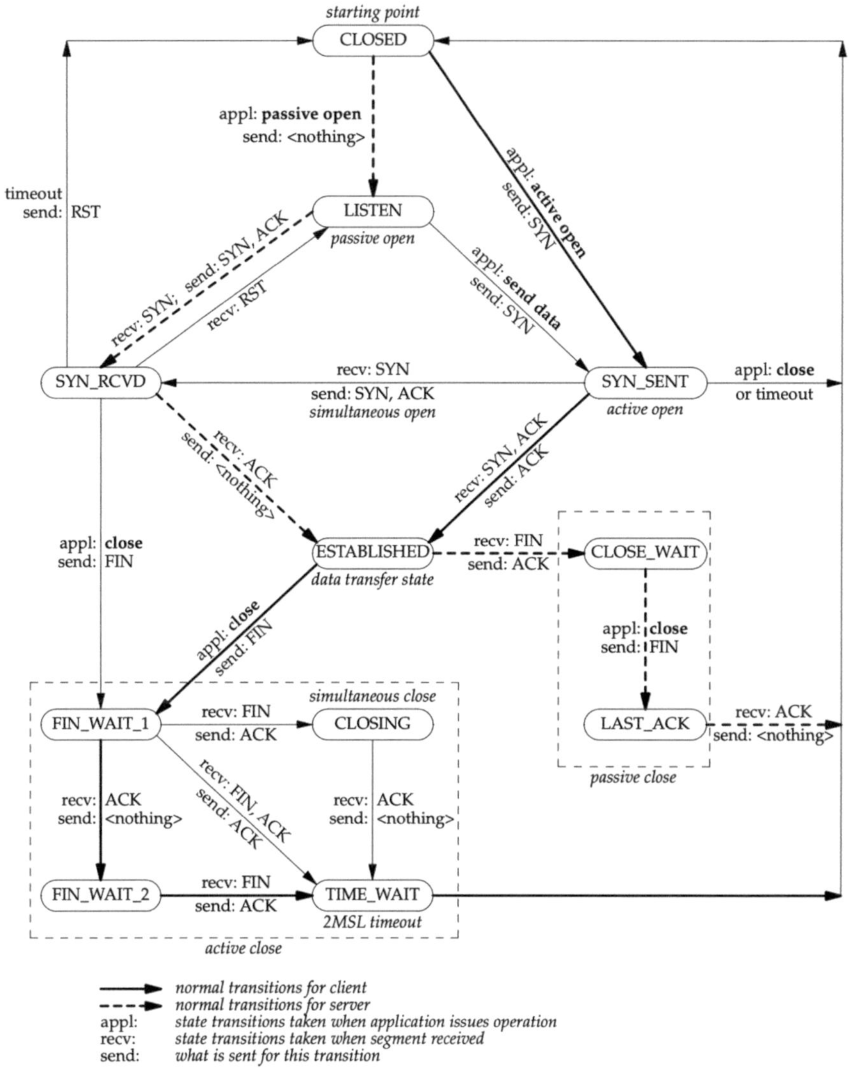

Fig. 2.3 TCP connection state diagram [3]

1. **Initial and Termination States**

   - CLOSED: The initial state, indicating the connection has not been established or has been fully closed.
   - TIME_WAIT: A waiting state entered by the initiator of closure, ensuring all residual segments in the connection have been cleared to avoid affecting subsequent connections.

2. **Connection Establishment Phase**
   - LISTEN: The server is in a listening state, awaiting a connection request from the client.
   - SYN_SENT: The client has sent a SYN segment and is waiting for the server's response.
   - SYN_RCVD: After receiving the SYN, the server sends a SYN-ACK segment and waits for the client's acknowledgment.
3. **Data Transfer and Connection Release Phase**
   - ESTABLISHED: The connection is established, and both parties can begin bidirectional data transfer.
   - FIN_WAIT_1: The initiator sends a FIN packet requesting to close the connection and waits for the other party's ACK.
   - FIN_WAIT_2: The ACK has been received, and the initiator continues waiting for the other party to send FIN.
   - CLOSE_WAIT: The recipient receives FIN and waits for the local application layer to close.
   - CLOSING: Both sides send FIN packets nearly simultaneously and await the other's ACK.
   - LAST_ACK: The passive closing party has sent FIN and awaits the final ACK from the other side. The essence of a TCP connection lies in establishing synchronized states between communicating parties through a three-way handshake and gracefully releasing resources via a four-way handshake. This mechanism ensures reliable and ordered data transmission while supporting full-duplex communication, enabling simultaneous sending and receiving of data.

Figure 2.4 shows the TCP connection establishment process. During TCP connection establishment, both client and server initially reside in the CLOSE state. To receive connection requests, the server first executes a listening operation on a designated port, transitioning to the LISTEN state. Subsequently, the connection is established through the "three-way handshake" process:

1. **First Handshake**: The client randomly generates an initial sequence number (client_isn), places it in the sequence number field of the TCP header, and sets the SYN flag to 1, forming a SYN packet. This packet is sent to the server requesting a connection, and the client enters the SYN-SENT state.
2. **Second Handshake**: Upon receiving the SYN packet, the server generates its own initial sequence number (server_isn), writes it into the sequence field, and sets the acknowledgment field to client_isn + 1. Simultaneously, it sets both the SYN and ACK flags to 1, forming a SYN-ACK packet which is returned to the client. The server then enters the SYN-RCVD state.
3. **Third Handshake**: Upon receiving the server's SYN-ACK packet, the client sends an ACK packet to the server. This packet sets the ACK field to server_isn + 1 and sets the ACK flag. It may also carry application layer data. The client

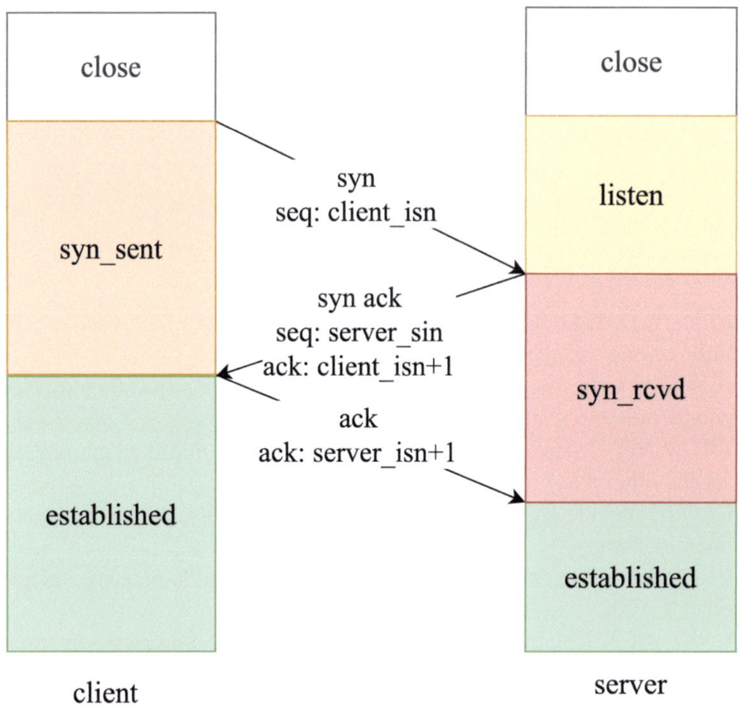

Fig. 2.4 TCP connection establishment process

then transitions to the ESTABLISHED state. After receiving this ACK, the server also enters the ESTABLISHED state, completing the connection establishment.

The three-way handshake mechanism not only ensures both parties correctly synchronize the initial sequence number (ISN) but also effectively prevents erroneous connections caused by historical residual packets. For instance, when delayed old SYN packets exist in the network, the TCP state machine can discard invalid requests through the check mechanism in the SYN_RCVD state. Furthermore, modern operating systems typically allocate full connection resources only after the third handshake completes, mitigating the risk of SYN flood attacks.

Figure 2.5 shows the TCP four-way handshake process. When a client intends to close a connection, the core of the four-way handshake involves bidirectional closure and resource reclamation. The process can be broken down as follows:

1. **First Handshake (FIN-Based Active Close Request)**
   The initiating party (typically the client) sends a segment with the FIN flag set, indicating it will no longer send data but remains ready to receive from the other party. The initiating party's state transitions from ESTABLISHED to FIN_WAIT_1. If no acknowledgment is received, TCP retransmits the FIN segment according to the tcp_orphan_retries parameter (Linux defaults to 5 retries).

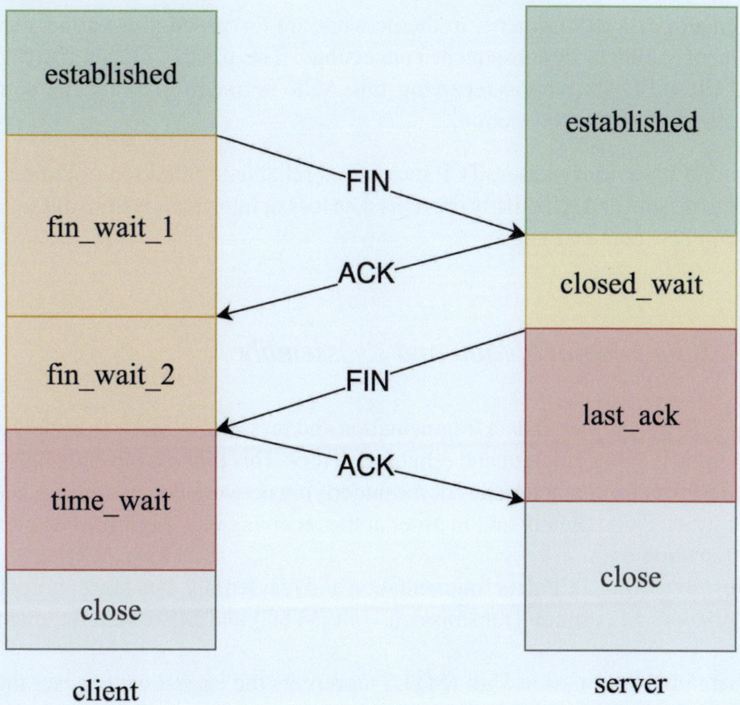

Fig. 2.5 TCP four-way handshake

2. **Second Handshake (Asynchronous ACK Response)**

   Upon receiving the FIN segment, the passive closing party immediately returns an ACK segment with an acknowledgment number equal to the FIN segment's sequence number plus one. The passive party's state then transitions to CLOSE_WAIT, while the active party enters FIN_WAIT_2 after receiving the ACK, continuing to await the passive party's closure operation. It is important to note that in the CLOSE_WAIT state, the server-side application must still complete sending any remaining data and call close(). Failure to do so may lead to a "CLOSE_WAIT pileup" issue.
3. **Third Handshake (Passive Party Sends FIN)**

   After the passive party completes data transmission and calls close() to close the socket, it sends a segment with the FIN flag set and enters the LAST_ACK state, awaiting the final acknowledgment from the other party. The acknowledgment number for this FIN segment is still the acknowledgment number from the previous phase, incremented by 1.
4. **Fourth Handshake (Active Closure Confirms and Enters TIME_WAIT)**

   Upon receiving the FIN segment, the active closure immediately sends an ACK confirmation and enters the TIME_WAIT state. The active closure must remain in this state for twice the Maximum Segment Lifetime (2MSL, typically 2 min) to ensure delayed segments in the network are discarded, preventing sequence number conflicts in subsequent connections. The passive closing party enters the CLOSED state upon receiving this ACK segment, marking the complete termination of the connection.

Through these four phases, TCP guarantees reliable termination of bidirectional data transmission and effectively prevents data loss or interference from old segments disrupting new connections.

2.3.2 *Data Fragmentation and Reassembly*

During TCP transmission, data fragmentation and reassembly serve as critical mechanisms for achieving efficient and reliable delivery. This process must not only adapt to the transmission characteristics of the underlying network but also ensure that data is reconstructed completely and in order at the receiving end. Figure 2.6 shows TCP data fragmentation.

Before exploring TCP data fragmentation and reassembly, two key concepts must be understood: Maximum Transmission Unit (MTU) and Maximum Segment Size (MSS).

Maximum Transmission Unit (MTU) represents the largest data packet that can be transmitted in a single hop at the data link layer, determined by the underlying network technology. For common Ethernet, the MTU is typically 1500 bytes. This value encompasses the data link layer header, IP layer header, TCP layer header, and the actual data payload. If the data exceeds the MTU size, it must be fragmented. However, fragmentation increases network transmission complexity and latency and may lead to issues like fragment loss. Therefore, fragmentation should be avoided whenever possible.

Maximum Segment Size (MSS) is the maximum length of the data portion within a TCP segment. It is calculated based on the MTU: MSS = MTU − IP header length − TCP header length.

In the absence of option fields, both the IP header and TCP header are 20 bytes each. Consequently, the default MSS in an Ethernet environment is 1460 bytes

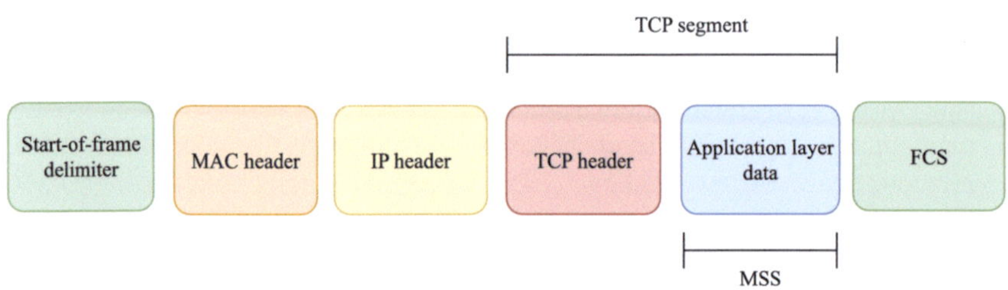

Fig. 2.6 TCP data fragmentation

(1500 – 20 – 20). Setting the MSS is critical, as it directly determines the size of TCP data segments, thereby impacting transmission efficiency and network resource utilization.

When application layer data requires TCP transmission, the TCP protocol segments the data into multiple packets based on the MSS. Suppose the application layer generates a 3000-byte data block, and the MSS is 1460 bytes. TCP will divide it into three packets: The first and second packets each contain 1460 bytes of data, while the third packet holds the remaining 80 bytes.

During segmentation, TCP appends a TCP header to each segment. This header contains key fields such as source port number, destination port number, sequence number, acknowledgment number, and flags. The sequence number field indicates the position of the segment's first byte within the entire data stream, providing a crucial reference for the receiver to reassemble the data.

Upon receiving TCP segments, the receiver must reassemble the fragmented data into a complete stream—a process known as data reassembly. The core reference for this reassembly is the sequence number field within the TCP header.

The receiver maintains a receive window to track the range of data already received and the expected range of data to be received. Upon receiving a TCP segment, the receiver checks whether its sequence number falls within the receive window. If within the window, the receiver stores the segment data in a buffer and determines its position within the entire data stream based on the sequence number.

If the received segments are consecutive, the receiver attempts to concatenate them with existing data. For example, if segments with sequence numbers 1–1460 arrive first, followed by segments 1461–2920, the receiver concatenates these two segments. Once the receiver confirms all intervening segments have arrived—meaning that the received data is contiguous and complete—it forwards this data to the application layer in sequence.

However, in real network environments, data segments may arrive out of order or even be lost. Upon receiving out-of-order segments, the receiver does not immediately submit them to the application layer. Instead, it temporarily stores them while waiting for missing segments to arrive. Concurrently, the receiver sends duplicate ACK messages to the sender, indicating which segments have been received and which are missing. Based on this information, the sender retransmits the missing segments to ensure that the receiver can fully reassemble the data.

2.3.3 Flow Control and Sliding Window Mechanism

In TCP transmission, flow control and the sliding window mechanism are crucial for ensuring stable data transfer, preventing network congestion, and avoiding receiver buffer overflows. During TCP data transmission, dynamic changes in network bandwidth and variations in receiver processing capacity can both lead to transmission issues. Flow control and the sliding window mechanism were designed to address these problems. By regulating the sender's transmission rate, they ensure the receiver can process data in a timely manner, preventing buffer overflows while enhancing network resource utilization efficiency.

The core objective of flow control is to coordinate the data transmission rates between sender and receiver, ensuring the sender's data transmission pace aligns with the receiver's processing capacity. If the sender transmits data too rapidly while the receiver has limited processing capability, the receiver's buffer may become full, causing subsequent data loss and triggering retransmissions that reduce transmission efficiency. Conversely, if the sender transmits data too slowly, network resources are wasted.

Consider web browsing: when a user requests webpage resources from a server via a browser, the server sends webpage data in TCP segments to the browser. If the server transmits large amounts of data within a short timeframe, and the browser cannot receive and process it promptly due to limitations like CPU processing power or memory, data loss occurs. The flow control mechanism dynamically adjusts the server's transmission rate based on the browser's reception capacity, ensuring stable and complete data transfer.

The sliding window protocol is the core mechanism for TCP flow control. In this mechanism, both sender and receiver maintain a window:

1. **Send Window**: The sender maintains a send window indicating the range of data that can be sent but has not yet been acknowledged. The size of the send window determines the amount of data the sender can transmit before receiving acknowledgment from the receiver. Figure 2.7 shows the TCP send window.
2. **Receive Window**: The receive window maintained by the receiver, indicating the amount of data the receiver can currently accept. The size of the receive window dynamically changes based on the remaining space in the receiver's buffer and is communicated to the sender via the window field in ACK packets. Figure 2.8 shows the TCP receive window.

The "sliding" aspect of the sliding window manifests in the dynamic changes to the window boundaries during data transmission:

During data transmission, the window continuously "slides": the sender continuously transmits data within the window range. After the receiver receives and acknowledges the data, the window advances forward, allowing new data to enter transmission. For example, after the sender transmits bytes 1–1000 and receives

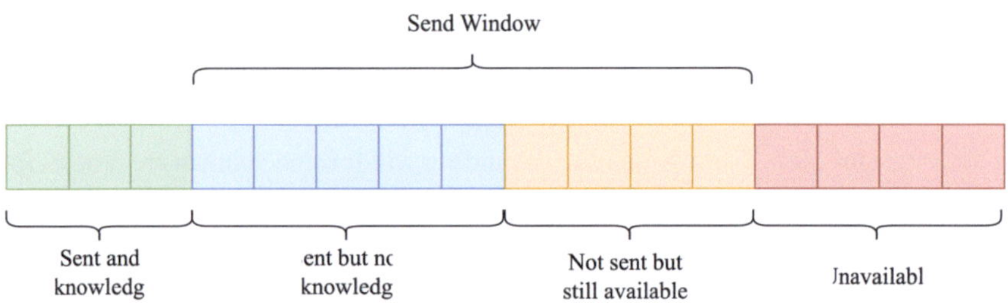

Fig. 2.7 TCP send window

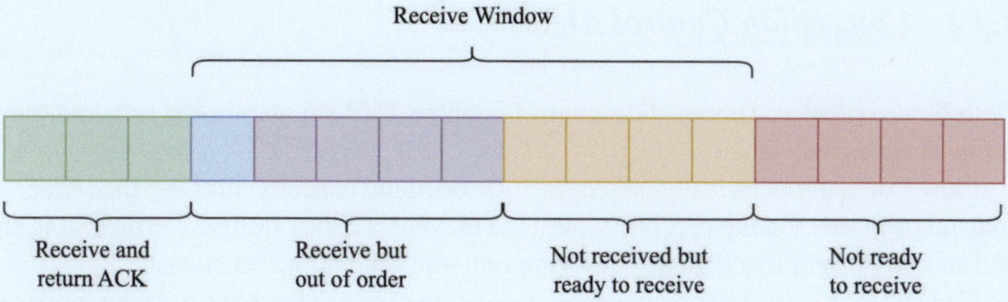

Fig. 2.8 TCP receive window

acknowledgment, the window start position slides to byte 1001 and subsequent sequences.

In the TCP protocol, window size information is conveyed via the 16-bit window field in the TCP header. This field indicates the current receive window size in bytes. However, in high-bandwidth, high-latency network environments, a 65,535-byte window size may prove insufficient. To address this, TCP introduces the Window Scaling Option, defined in RFC 1323. During the three-way handshake, the client and server negotiate a scaling factor (Shift Count) via the Window Scaling Option in the SYN packet. For example, if the negotiated scaling factor is 3, the actual window size is obtained by shifting the window field value left by 3 bits (i.e., multiplying by 8).

During flow control, Silly Window Syndrome (SWS) may also occur. When the receive window is extremely small (e.g., only 1 byte remains) yet the sender continues transmitting small segments, the network becomes flooded with numerous tiny packets. This leads to excessive header overhead and reduced bandwidth utilization. To prevent SWS, TCP employs several strategies:

Nagle Algorithm: Proposed by John Nagle, this algorithm caches subsequent small segments until the acknowledgment for the previous segment is received and then combines them into a larger segment for transmission. Data is sent immediately only when one of the following conditions is met:

1. The data length reaches the Maximum Segment Size (MSS).
2. An acknowledgment for the previously sent segment is received.

For example, if an application generates 100 bytes, 200 bytes, and 300 bytes of data consecutively, the Nagle algorithm buffers these segments until the previous ACKs are received. They are then combined into a single 600-byte segment for transmission.

Delayed Acknowledgment: Upon receiving data, the receiver does not immediately send an ACK confirmation packet. Instead, it waits for a period of time (typically not exceeding 500 ms). During this interval, if data needs to be sent to the sender, the ACK confirmation is sent along with the data (carry-along acknowledgment). If no data is sent, the ACK confirmation is still transmitted once the delay period expires. This approach reduces the number of ACK packets while giving the sender more time to accumulate data, thereby avoiding the transmission of small data segments.

2.3.4 Congestion Control Algorithms

Both flow control and congestion control regulate TCP's transmission rate, but they differ in focus and scope.

Flow Control: Focuses on the receiver's processing capacity, limiting the sender's transmission rate via the receive window to prevent receiver buffer overflow. It is an end-to-end control mechanism involving only the sender and receiver.

Congestion Control [9]: Focuses on the overall network load. It limits the sender's transmission rate through the congestion window to prevent network congestion. When congestion occurs, the congestion control mechanism reduces the transmission rate to alleviate network pressure. Congestion control is a global control mechanism involving all nodes and links in the network.

Within the TCP protocol framework, congestion control is a critical mechanism for ensuring network robustness. It dynamically adjusts the sender's transmission rate to prevent throughput degradation and latency spikes caused by network overload. Unlike flow control, which focuses on the receiver's processing capacity, congestion control addresses global network load. Through core parameters such as the congestion window (cwnd) and slow-start threshold (ssthresh), it achieves precise responses to network congestion states. Figure 2.9 shows a schematic of TCP congestion control.

The classic algorithms of TCP congestion control primarily include slow start, congestion avoidance, fast retransmit, and fast recovery. These algorithms work in tandem to form the foundational framework of TCP congestion control.

Slow start occurs during the initial phase of a TCP connection establishment or after a timeout retransmission. In this phase, the sender's congestion window (cwnd)

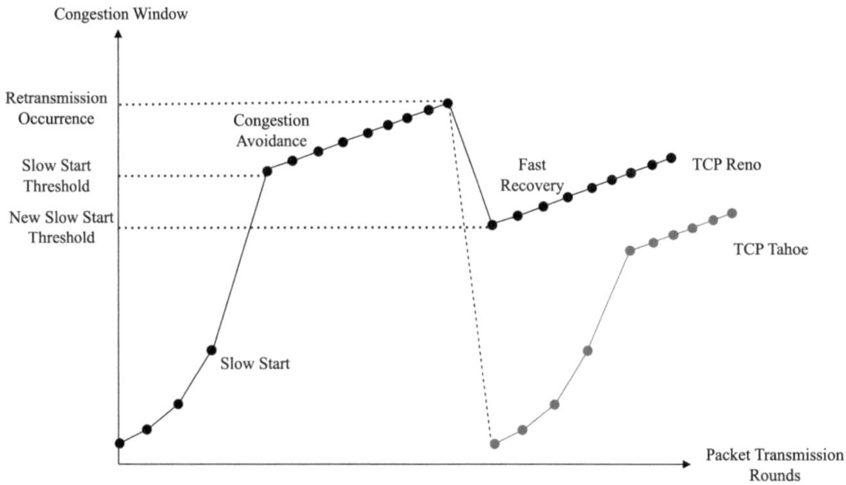

Fig. 2.9 TCP congestion control schematic

is initialized to one Maximum Segment Size (MSS), i.e., cwnd = 1 * MSS. Each received acknowledgment (ACK) increases cwnd by one MSS.

This exponential growth allows rapid sender rate scaling but carries risks, necessitating coordination with other mechanisms. Within each Round-Trip Time (RTT), cwnd doubles. For example: Initial cwnd = 1 * MSS. After 1 RTT: cwnd = 2 * MSS. After 2 RTTs: cwnd = 4 * MSS. When cwnd reaches the slow-start threshold (ssthresh), the congestion avoidance phase begins.

During congestion avoidance, cwnd no longer grows exponentially but follows a linear growth strategy. Each RTT increases cwnd by 1 MSS: cwnd = cwnd + 1 * MSS. This conservative growth approach helps prevent network congestion. When congestion occurs (e.g., upon detecting a timeout or receiving three duplicate ACKs), ssthresh is set to half the current cwnd, i.e., ssthresh = cwnd/2. Simultaneously, cwnd is reset to 1 * MSS, returning to the slow-start phase. This mechanism rapidly reduces the transmission rate to alleviate network congestion.

Traditional TCP requires waiting for the retransmission timer to expire before retransmitting upon packet loss detection, causing significant delays. The fast retransmission mechanism rapidly detects packet loss through duplicate ACKs. When the receiver detects out-of-order packets, it sends duplicate ACKs to the sender. Upon receiving three duplicate ACKs, the sender assumes intermediate packet loss and immediately retransmits the missing packet without waiting for the retransmission timer to expire. This mechanism significantly reduces retransmission time after packet loss, improving transmission efficiency.

Following fast retransmission, TCP enters the fast recovery phase. At this point, ssthresh is set to half of the current cwnd, i.e., ssthresh = cwnd/2, while cwnd is set to ssthresh + 3 * MSS. This is because receiving three duplicate ACKs indicates that at least three packets have successfully reached the receiver. Therefore, while lowering ssthresh, a portion of the packets already sent and acknowledged can be retained to prevent the transmission rate from dropping excessively. During the fast recovery phase, cwnd increases by one MSS for each new ACK received. Upon receiving a new non-repeated ACK, cwnd resets to ssthresh, transitioning back to the congestion avoidance phase. This fast recovery mechanism ensures a rapid response to packet loss while minimizing impact on transmission efficiency.

With advancements in network technology, TCP congestion control algorithms have continuously evolved, giving rise to various improved versions to adapt to different network environments and application requirements.

The Tahoe algorithm represents the original TCP congestion control mechanism, comprising three core components: slow start, congestion avoidance, and timeout retransmission. During the slow-start phase, the congestion window (cwnd) begins at one Maximum Segment Size (MSS) and grows exponentially after each acknowledgment received; upon reaching the slow-start threshold (ssthresh), the congestion avoidance phase begins, where the window increases linearly. When packet loss is detected (triggered by timeouts), Tahoe resets cwnd to 1 MSS and re-enters slow start. This conservative approach, while simple, recovers slowly after packet loss.

Reno Algorithm: Building upon Tahoe, Reno incorporates fast retransmission and fast recovery mechanisms. Upon receiving three duplicate ACKs, Reno triggers fast retransmission and fast recovery, enabling faster recovery from packet loss compared to Tahoe and improving transmission efficiency. The Reno algorithm is detailed in RFC 5681 [10]. Widely adopted in its early stages, it divides congestion control into three phases:

1. Slow-Start Phase: This phase continues until the congestion window reaches the slow-start threshold (ssthresh). The slow-start algorithm doubles the congestion window every RTT. Initially, ssthresh is set to infinity and subsequently depends on packet loss events. When the congestion window reaches ssthresh, the slow-start phase ends, transitioning to the Additive Increase Multiplicative Decrease (AIMD) phase.
2. Additive Increase Multiplicative Decrease (AIMD) Phase: Additive increase increases the window size by 1 each time, while multiplicative decrease halves ssthresh to half the current congestion window. Simultaneously, the congestion window is reset to its initial value, set to 10 in the Linux kernel.
3. Fast Recovery Phase: Triggered by receiving three redundant ACKs. Upon detection, ssthresh is set to the current congestion window size, and the congestion window is halved. The system then re-enters the AIMD phase. A limitation of this algorithm becomes apparent during packet loss: it remains in the AIMD phase indefinitely, bypassing the slow-start phase. Consequently, the window grows slowly even as network conditions improve.

NewReno Algorithm [11]: This algorithm addresses Reno's inefficiency in recovering from multiple packet loss scenarios. Upon receiving partial ACKs, NewReno more accurately determines which packets have been received and which require retransmission, avoiding unnecessary retransmissions and further enhancing recovery capabilities during multi-packet loss situations.

CUBIC Algorithm [12]: The default congestion control algorithm in Linux systems, CUBIC employs a cubic function model to dynamically adjust the congestion window (cwnd). It excels in high-bandwidth, high-latency networks by maximizing throughput while ensuring fairness through more precise congestion detection and adjustment strategies. Compared to traditional algorithms, CUBIC demonstrates superior adaptability and stability when handling burst traffic and complex network topologies. The implementation of the Cubic algorithm primarily references RFC 8312 [13]. As the default congestion control algorithm in the Linux kernel, it features a highly effective congestion control process, enhancing scalability and stability in high-speed, long-distance network environments.

The Cubic algorithm employs a cubic function to increase the window, with the specific formula as follows:

$$W_{\text{cubic}}(t) = C * (t - K)^3 + W_{\max}, \tag{2.1}$$

where C is a constant determining the aggressiveness of window increases in high BDP networks; t is the time elapsed since the onset of current congestion; K is the time required for the above function to increase the current window to $W_{\max}$.

Figure 2.10 shows the window function curve of the Cubic algorithm.

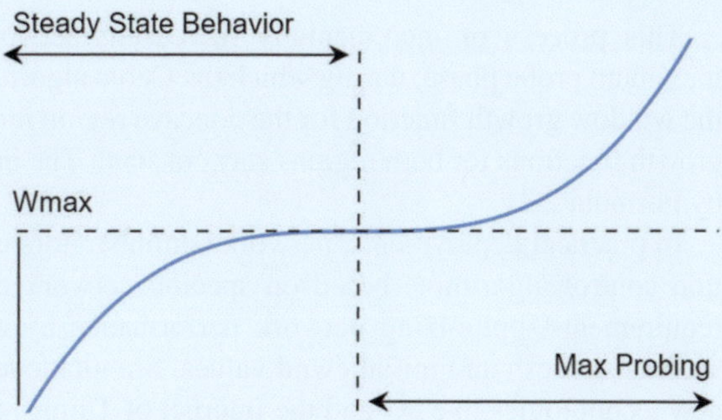

Fig. 2.10 Cubic algorithm window function curve

The calculation formula for K is as follows:

$$K = \sqrt[3]{\frac{W_{\max} * (1-\beta)}{C}}, \tag{2.2}$$

where β is the multiplicative decay factor for Cubic.

Based on the value of cwnd (congestion window), Cubic operates in one of three modes:

1. **TCP-Friendly Zone**: If cwnd is less than the window size reached by standard TCP at time t following the last packet loss event, Cubic enters TCP mode.

   Within the TCP-Friendly Zone, to achieve throughput equivalent to standard TCP, Cubic uses the following formula to estimate the window size:

$$W_{\text{est}} = W_{\max} * \beta + 3 * \frac{1-\beta}{1+\beta} * \frac{t}{\text{RTT}}. \tag{2.3}$$

2. **Convex Region**: When the congestion avoidance phase receives an ACK, if the protocol is not in TCP mode and cwnd is less than $W_{\max}$, the increment for cwnd in this region is:

$$\frac{W(t + \text{RTT}) - \text{cwnd}}{\text{cwnd}}. \tag{2.4}$$

3. **Concave Region**: When cwnd exceeds $W_{\max}$, it indicates that network conditions may have been disrupted since the last congestion event. This suggests potential fluctuations in network conditions, with some competing flows potentially leaving the network, thereby increasing available bandwidth.

Since networks are highly asynchronous, fluctuations in available bandwidth are always present. Consequently, the concave region grows relatively slowly at the outset. This is because it cannot yet determine whether the observed bandwidth increase stems from network fluctuations or genuine network capacity expansion. Thus, growth begins slowly before gradually accelerating.

This process of incrementally increasing network bandwidth is termed the maximum probe phase, during which the Cubic algorithm seeks a larger W_{max}. Since the window growth function for the concave region remains unchanged, the window growth functions for both regions stay constant. The increment of cwnd is expressed by Formula 2.4.

In practical deployments, network administrators can select appropriate congestion control algorithms based on specific network environments and application requirements, optimizing network performance by adjusting relevant parameters such as ssthresh and initial cwnd values. Simultaneously, with the advancement of new technologies like 5G and the Internet of Things, congestion control algorithms will face new challenges and opportunities, necessitating continuous innovation and refinement to meet the evolving demands of future networks.

As a core component of the TCP protocol, congestion control algorithms play a vital role in ensuring network stability and enhancing transmission efficiency through continuous evolution and innovation. From classical algorithms to modern optimization schemes, each approach embodies unique design philosophies and application scenarios. Together, they form the comprehensive framework of TCP congestion control, driving the ongoing advancement of network technology.

2.3.5 Acknowledgment and Retransmission Mechanism

In the TCP protocol, the acknowledgment and retransmission mechanism serves as the core pillar ensuring data reliability. Through the receiver's acknowledgment feedback and the sender's intelligent retransmission strategy, TCP achieves end-to-end reliable transmission even in unreliable network environments. This section will delve into the principles, implementation details, and optimization strategies of this mechanism.

TCP's acknowledgment mechanism uses sequence numbers and acknowledgment numbers to ensure data transmission order and completeness. Upon successfully receiving data, the receiver sends an acknowledgment packet (ACK) to the sender. This ACK contains the sequence number of the last byte received, incremented by one, i.e., Acknowledgment Number = Sequence Number of the Last Received Byte + 1. This design ensures that the sender precisely knows the range of data successfully received by the receiver.

Traditional TCP employs cumulative acknowledgment, where the receiver only confirms consecutively received data blocks. For example, if the receiver receives segments numbered 1–1000 and 1501–2000, it returns an acknowledgment number of 1001, indicating that data up to and including 1000 is confirmed, but segments 1001–1500 remain unacknowledged. The cumulative acknowledgment mechanism has limitations. If a data segment is lost in the middle, the receiver can only acknowledge the data received in sequence and cannot explicitly inform the sender which specific segment is missing. For example, if a segment with sequence number 2000 is lost, the receiver will still send an ACK packet with acknowledgment number 1000 upon receiving segment 3000, because it has not yet received all segments following 2000 in sequence. This may cause the sender to retransmit multiple segments starting from the lost segment without receiving confirmation, reducing transmission efficiency.

To address the limitations of cumulative acknowledgments, RFC 2018 introduced the SACK mechanism. The receiver reports non-sequentially received data blocks to the sender via the SACK option (Kind = 5). For example, if the receiver receives segments 1–1000 and 1501–2000, the SACK option will contain two blocks: [1, 1001) and [1501, 2001), informing the sender to retransmit only segments 1001–1500. SACK significantly improves retransmission efficiency in scenarios with multiple packet losses. To utilize the SACK mechanism, both communication parties must support this feature. In Linux systems, SACK functionality can be enabled by configuring the net.ipv4.tcp_sack parameter. Starting from Linux version 2.4, this feature is enabled by default.

When the sender fails to receive an acknowledgment in a timely manner, a retransmission mechanism is triggered. TCP implements efficient retransmission through multiple strategies:

1. **Timeout Retransmission**

   The sender sets a retransmission timer (RTO) for each segment. If the timer expires without acknowledgment, the sender retransmits the segment. Calculating RTO is critical; TCP dynamically adjusts it using the Jacobson algorithm [14]:

   Smooth Round-Trip Time (SRTT):

$$\mathrm{SRTT} = \alpha \times \mathrm{SRTT} + (1 - \alpha) \times \mathrm{RTT}. \tag{2.5}$$

   Round-Trip Time Variation (RTTVAR):

$$\mathrm{RTTVAR} = \beta \times \mathrm{RTTVAR} + (1 - \beta) \times |\mathrm{SRTT} - \mathrm{RTT}|, \tag{2.6}$$

$$\mathrm{RTO} : \mathrm{RTO} = \mathrm{SRTT} + 4 \times \mathrm{RTTVAR}. \tag{2.7}$$

   Timeout retransmission may occur in the following two scenarios:

   The Packet Fails to Reach the Receiver: Due to network congestion, link failures, or other reasons, the packet is lost during transmission. The receiver does not receive the packet and consequently cannot send an acknowledgment (ACK) message, causing the sender to retransmit due to a timeout.

   ACK Packet Loss: The receiver successfully receives the data packet and sends an ACK acknowledgment, but the ACK packet is lost en route back to the sender. The sender, not receiving the ACK, similarly triggers the timeout retransmission mechanism.

   If the retransmitted data time out again, TCP employs an exponential backoff strategy, doubling the next retransmission interval from the previous value. For example, if the initial timeout is 1 s, a retransmission timeout extends to 2 s, and so on. This strategy prevents excessive retransmissions during network instability, reducing congestion and bandwidth waste.

2. **Fast Retransmit**

   When the receiver detects out-of-order segments, it sends duplicate ACKs. If the sender receives three duplicate ACKs before the RTO expires, it assumes the segment is lost and immediately retransmits without waiting for the timeout. Fast retransmit significantly reduces recovery time after packet loss.

2.4 Analysis of TCP's Advantages and Disadvantages

2.4.1 Transmission Reliability

Transmission Control Protocol (TCP) excels in transmission reliability, which is one of the key factors driving its widespread adoption across numerous network scenarios. TCP employs a series of meticulously designed mechanisms to ensure data is transmitted accurately and completely from sender to receiver.

1. **Sequence Numbers and Acknowledgment Mechanism**

   TCP assigns a unique sequence number to each transmitted byte. The receiver uses these sequence numbers to confirm data reception. The receiver sends acknowledgment (ACK) packets to the sender, indicating the range of data successfully received. For example, if the sender transmits bytes with sequence numbers 1 through 1000, the receiver, upon successful receipt, sends an ACK with acknowledgment number 1001, indicating that it expects the next byte to have sequence number 1001. This mechanism allows the sender to clearly track which data has been received and which may be lost and requires retransmission.

2. **Retransmission Mechanism**

   If the sender does not receive an acknowledgment for a data segment within a specified timeframe, the retransmission mechanism is triggered. The retransmission mechanism primarily employs two methods: timeout retransmission and fast retransmission. Timeout retransmission involves the sender initiating a retransmission timer; if no acknowledgment is received by the timer's expiration, the segment is retransmitted. Fast retransmission occurs when the sender receives three consecutive duplicate ACK packets, indicating a lost segment between them, prompting immediate retransmission of that segment.

3. **Flow Control and Congestion Control**

   Flow control and congestion control are two core rate-limiting mechanisms in the TCP protocol. While neither directly implements reliable data transmission (such as sequence number acknowledgments or retransmission), they indirectly ensure transmission stability and reliability by regulating the sender's transmission rate, thereby establishing the foundational environment for dependable data transfer.

2.4.2 Adaptability

TCP provides flow control and congestion control mechanisms based on a sliding window. These two mechanisms work synergistically, enabling TCP to demonstrate strong adaptability in complex and dynamic network environments. By dynamically adjusting its transmission behavior, TCP can maximize the utilization of available network resources while ensuring reliability, thereby achieving efficient and stable data transmission.

It is important to emphasize that flow control and congestion control are not independent mechanisms; they jointly determine the sender's transmission rate. The actual send window size for a TCP sender is defined as:

$$\mathrm{swnd} = \min(\mathrm{rwnd}, \mathrm{cwnd}). \tag{2.8}$$

- rwnd (receiver window) is advertised by the receiver based on its buffer size and processing capacity, preventing sender overflow and receiver buffer overflow.
- cwnd (congestion window) is dynamically adjusted by the sender based on network congestion to prevent excessive traffic injection from causing network congestion.

This means that the sender must consider both the receiver's processing capacity (via rwnd) and the network's congestion state (via cwnd). When the receiver has a strong processing capacity but the network is congested, the congestion window (cwnd) limits the sender's transmission rate. When network conditions are favorable but the receiver's buffer space is limited, the receiver window (rwnd) takes precedence, restricting the sender's transmission rate.

This collaborative adaptive mechanism enables TCP to maintain efficient and stable data transmission across diverse network environments and application scenarios. Whether in high-speed, low-latency networks like LANs or in complex, dynamic environments such as WANs and mobile networks, TCP dynamically adjusts its transmission rate based on actual conditions. This ensures reliable data delivery while maximizing network resource utilization.

TCP's sliding window flow control and congestion control mechanisms endow it with powerful adaptability. This adaptability enables TCP to operate stably across diverse network conditions, providing reliable data transmission services to upper-layer applications. This is a key reason TCP has become one of the most widely used transport protocols on the Internet.

2.4.3 Head-of-Line Blocking

TCP is an ordered, byte-stream transport protocol. The receiver must deliver data to the application layer in sequence number order. When a byte segment is lost or delayed during transmission, even if subsequent segments have arrived at the receiver, the receiver must wait for the lost segment to be retransmitted and correctly received before delivering the subsequent data. This phenomenon, where subsequent packets cannot be processed due to blocking by preceding packets, is called head-of-line blocking (HOL Blocking).

The primary cause of head-of-line blocking stems from TCP's strict requirement for data delivery in sequence number order. Out-of-order data arriving in the receiver's buffer is temporarily stored (referred to as "out-of-order data") but not delivered prematurely to the application layer. Simultaneously, TCP's acknowledgment mechanism limits the receiver's ACK to confirming only the highest consecutive received byte sequence number. This prevents the sliding window from advancing rightward, causing subsequent data to be blocked.

2.4.4 Packet Coalescing and Fragmentation Issues

TCP is a byte-stream protocol that does not preserve "message boundaries." Data written by the sender may be fragmented into multiple segments (subject to MSS constraints) or merged before transmission. Similarly, the receiver may read multiple messages in a single operation, leading to:

- Packet Coalescing: Multiple application layer messages are merged into a single-byte stream for reception (e.g., sending "Hello" followed by "World" may result in the receiver receiving "HelloWorld").
- Packet Fragmentation: A single application layer message is received as multiple fragments within the byte stream (e.g., sending "12,345" might result in receiving "12" followed by "345").

The primary causes of packet coalescing and fragmentation include:

- MSS Constraints: When application layer data exceeds the Maximum Segment Size (MSS), TCP fragments it into multiple segments. For example, with MTU = 1500 bytes, MSS $\approx$ 1460 bytes. An application layer packet of 2000 bytes would be split into two segments: 1460 + 540 bytes.
- Operating System Buffering Mechanisms: The sender may consolidate data from multiple write operations into a single TCP segment for transmission. Similarly, when the receiver calls read(), it may return multiple segments in a single operation.

Since TCP itself does not handle message boundaries, they must be explicitly defined within the application layer protocol. Common approaches include:

1. Fixed-Length Messages: Each message has a fixed length (e.g., sending 1024 bytes per transmission, padding with spaces or fill characters if shorter).

2. Delimiter-Based (E.G., \r\n, \0): Append a special delimiter at the end of each message (e.g., HTTP protocol uses \r\n\r\n to separate headers and body, or custom \0 as an end marker).
3. Custom message structures, such as TLV structures.

2.5 TCP Optimization

2.5.1 TCP Fast Open

TCP Fast Open (TFO) [15] is a critical optimization mechanism in the TCP protocol designed to enhance transmission efficiency by reducing connection establishment latency. Its core principle allows clients to carry application data during the initial handshake phase (SYN packet), thereby skipping one round-trip time (RTT) required in the traditional three-way handshake.

When sending the SYN packet, the client includes a Cookie Request option, requesting the server to generate an encrypted Fast Open Cookie. After verifying the client's IP legitimacy, the server generates a Cookie (typically 16 bytes) containing the client's IP and port information, returning it to the client via a SYN-ACK packet. The client then caches this Cookie.

When reconnecting, the client includes the cached Cookie and application data (e.g., an HTTP GET request). The server validates the cookie's validity; if valid, it processes the data directly and sends a SYN-ACK confirmation. This allows response data transmission to begin before the client completes its ACK, enabling "0-RTT" data exchange.

TFO is documented in RFC 7413 (2014). With increasing deployment, it may enter the formal standardization process in the future. TCP Fast Open significantly reduces short-connection latency by revolutionizing the connection establishment process, demonstrating powerful optimization value, especially in scenarios like HTTP. Despite security and compatibility challenges, its low deployment cost and significant effectiveness within the existing TCP ecosystem make it a crucial means for enhancing network performance.

2.5.2 TCP Selective Acknowledgment (SACK)

TCP's early cumulative acknowledgment mechanism proved inefficient during packet loss, as the receiver could only indicate the "last continuously received segment position" to the sender. This forced the sender to retransmit segments that had already arrived successfully. The selective acknowledgment (SACK) mechanism allows the receiver to precisely specify in ACK packets which data blocks have been received and which remain missing. This enables the sender to retransmit only the missing segments, significantly improving bandwidth utilization and transmission performance in high-packet-loss environments. SACK is widely deployed and remains a core optimization technique in modern TCP.

2.5.3 BBR Congestion Control Algorithm

Traditional congestion control algorithms like Reno and CUBIC primarily rely on packet loss or RTT variations to assess network conditions, often resulting in underutilized link bandwidth or excessively long queues. Google's BBR (Bottleneck Bandwidth and Round-trip propagation time) algorithm directly estimates bottleneck bandwidth and minimum RTT to adjust transmission rates. This significantly boosts throughput and reduces latency on high-bandwidth, long-RTT links. BBR is now supported in the Linux kernel and is progressively being adopted in real-world Internet services, representing a major direction in TCP evolution.

2.6 MIN-NC-TCP Protocol: TCP Optimization with Integrated Network Coding

2.6.1 Overview of Network Coding

Network coding is a technique that combines routing with encoding, enabling nodes to forward received packets after linear or nonlinear combination. Its core advantage lies in cross-temporal and cross-traffic redundancy utilization, which masks random packet loss in wireless links. Network coding has evolved into a significant potential approach for operating communication networks, particularly wireless networks. Its greatest benefit lies in its ability to mix data across time and traffic streams. This enables stable and efficient data transmission in lossy wireless networks.

Traditional TCP experiences significant performance degradation under lossy channels because it equates packet loss with congestion, leading to excessive congestion window shrinkage and reduced link utilization. To address TCP's performance degradation in lossy wireless networks and identify a feasible path for practical network coding deployment.

Traditional TCP interprets packet loss as a congestion signal, causing excessive congestion window shrinkage and steep throughput drops in wireless environments. While link layer retransmissions partially mask losses, their cross-layer interactions introduce complexity that may reduce overall system efficiency.

Randomized linear network coding provides redundancy through cross-temporal and cross-stream data mixing, masking packet loss for more stable and efficient transmission. However, existing methods primarily rely on "batch processing (generation coding)," which is incompatible with TCP's sliding window mechanism.

Implementing network coding in the actual Internet requires maintaining gradual deployment and end-to-end compatibility. Therefore, a sliding window method highly similar to TCP mechanisms should be developed—one that preserves TCP's flow control and congestion control principles while leveraging the redundancy advantages of network coding.

2.6.2 MIN-NC-TCP Architecture

Network Coding TCP (NC-TCP) is a TCP protocol integrated with network coding under the MIN network [16]. Its core concept involves introducing network coding into the traditional Transmission Control Protocol (TCP) while achieving performance improvements with minimal modifications to the existing protocol stack. The primary objective of this protocol is to mask packet loss in TCP through random linear coding. To this end, several key modifications have been made to the original protocol mechanisms.

First, the sender no longer transmits raw packets directly but instead sends a random linear combination of packets within the congestion window. While network coding offers significant advantages in masking packet loss, it also introduces challenges to the acknowledgment mechanism. Traditional TCP operates on strictly ordered raw packet units, allowing sequence numbers to be directly used for acknowledgment. In NC-TCP, however, information units are abstracted as "degrees of freedom." After multiple original packets are jointly encoded, these degrees of freedom lack inherent ordering, eliminating direct basis for acknowledgment. To resolve this, the concept of "seen packets" is introduced. This establishes a logical sequence for degrees of freedom that aligns with the original packet sequence numbers, enabling reliable acknowledgment.

At the receiver, when a new linear combination arrives, the protocol determines whether this transmission makes any previously "unseen" packet visible. It then sends the sequence number of this "latest seen" packet as an acknowledgment back to the sender. This approach allows the receiver to eventually "see" all original packets sequentially and complete decoding, while enabling the sender to seamlessly integrate with traditional TCP mechanisms based on these acknowledgments. By transmitting random linear combinations and employing an acknowledgment mechanism based on "seen packets," TCP logically masks packet loss.

Given the typically large coding domain, each newly received combination has a high probability of making the next unseen packet visible. Thus, even if a preceding combination is lost, subsequent combinations compensate for its effect.

From TCP's perspective, this resembles degrees of freedom queuing in a virtual queue until the channel permits their smooth transmission. Consequently, unlike TCP-Reno, duplicate acknowledgments do not occur; instead, each acknowledgment guarantees a congestion window slide. In other words, link loss introduces only an additional delay to TCP, manifested as an increase in the effective round-trip time (RTT). Effective RTT is defined as: the time consumed by the network to reliably deliver a freedom of degree (including delays caused by coding redundancy), plus the time required for the return acknowledgment. Clearly, this effective RTT exceeds the actual network delay under lossless transmission. As the link loss rate increases, the effective RTT lengthens accordingly. Although TCP throughput typically inversely correlates with RTT, within the MIN-NC-TCP protocol, a larger RTT prevents congestion window shrinkage triggered by packet loss. It also provides extended redundancy within timer timeout windows for data transmission, effectively masking and offsetting the impact of traditional packet loss.

However, this mechanism introduces a new challenge: how to implement congestion control in such an environment? Since NC-TCP masks packet loss through encoding, congestion control methods like TCP-Reno, which rely on packet loss detection, become inapplicable. We observe that congestion manifests primarily as RTT growth, necessitating congestion state inference based on round-trip time variations.

Guided by this insight, we adopt TCP-Vegas as the congestion control algorithm. TCP-Vegas employs an active detection approach, anticipating potential congestion by predicting network buffer occupancy before packet loss occurs. Its core mechanism involves using RTT to estimate the discrepancy between the expected transmission rate and the actual rate. When buffers gradually fill up and cause RTT to rise, Vegas interprets this as a congestion signal, subsequently adjusting the congestion window and transmission rate.

In the MIN-NC-TCP protocol, to ensure the correct operation of the Vegas algorithm, we must guarantee it uses valid RTT based on degrees-of-freedom acknowledgments, which include virtual queueing delays introduced by encoding. In other words, RTT should still be measured as the time interval from a segment's transmission to the return of its acknowledgment. The sender records the transmission time for each packet. When the corresponding acknowledgment arrives, it compares this time with the timestamp to calculate the RTT, thus requiring no modification to the original RTT measurement mechanism.

Figure 2.11 illustrates an example of encoding and acknowledgment. As illustrated in the figure, assume a congestion window size of 4. At time $t = 0$, TCP sends 4 packets to the network encoding layer, which transforms them into 4 linear combinations for transmission. The first transmission makes the first packet visible. The second and third transmissions are lost, while the fourth transmission makes the third packet visible. For RTT estimation, the second, third, and fourth transmissions can all be considered attempts to deliver the third packet. Consequently, the round-trip time for the third packet is defined as the duration from $t = 0$ until the successful receipt of ACK = 3.

2.6.3 MIN-NC-TCP Protocol Implementation Mechanism

The transmitter module receives packets from the TCP layer and stores them in an encoding buffer representing the encoding window. These packets remain in

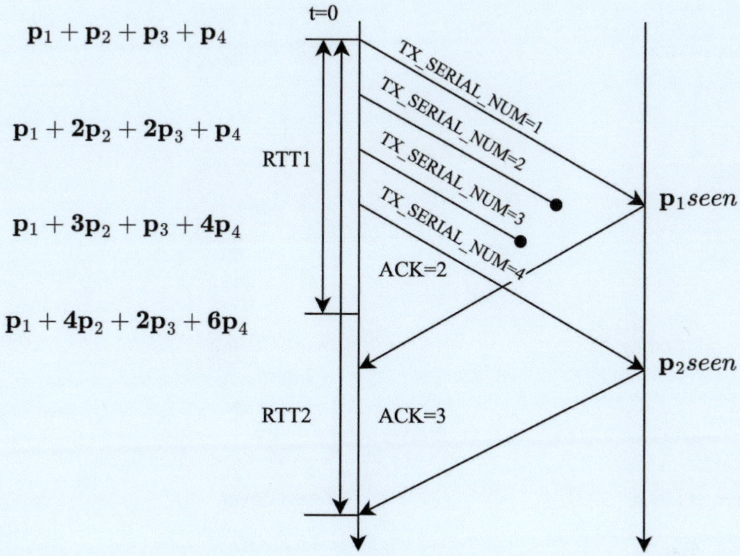

Fig. 2.11 Encoding and acknowledgment example

the encoding window until acknowledged by the receiver. The transmitter then generates and sends randomly selected linear combinations of packets from the encoding window. The coefficients within the linear combination are transmitted via the encoded packet header. Figure 2.12 shows the network coding within the protocol stack.

For each packet arriving from the TCP layer, after undergoing coding within the coding window, the resulting coded packets are delivered to the IP layer at a fixed rate. A new parameter R is introduced, representing the redundancy parameter, which determines both the number and transmission rate of currently sent coded packets. The average rate at which each linear combination of encoded packets is sent to the network is a constant factor determined by R, not the rate dictated by traditional TCP congestion window mechanisms. This adapts to compensate for channel packet loss rates and matches the actual TCP packet transmission rate to the receiver. If redundancy is too low, packet loss causes the data rate reaching the receiver to mismatch the sender's rate. Consequently, the TCP layer cannot effectively mask packet loss, leading to numerous timeouts and low throughput. Conversely, excessive redundancy is also detrimental: it limits the transmission rate to the encoding's inherent speed and may congest the network by sending too many linear combinations. The ideal redundancy value is maintained at R, which is the reciprocal of the probability of successfully receiving an encoded packet at the receiver. Consequently, in practical applications, the value of R should be dynamically adjusted based on the packet loss rate, potentially utilizing estimated round-trip times.

Upon receiving a linear combination, the receiver module first retrieves the encoding coefficients from the encoded packet header and adds these coefficients

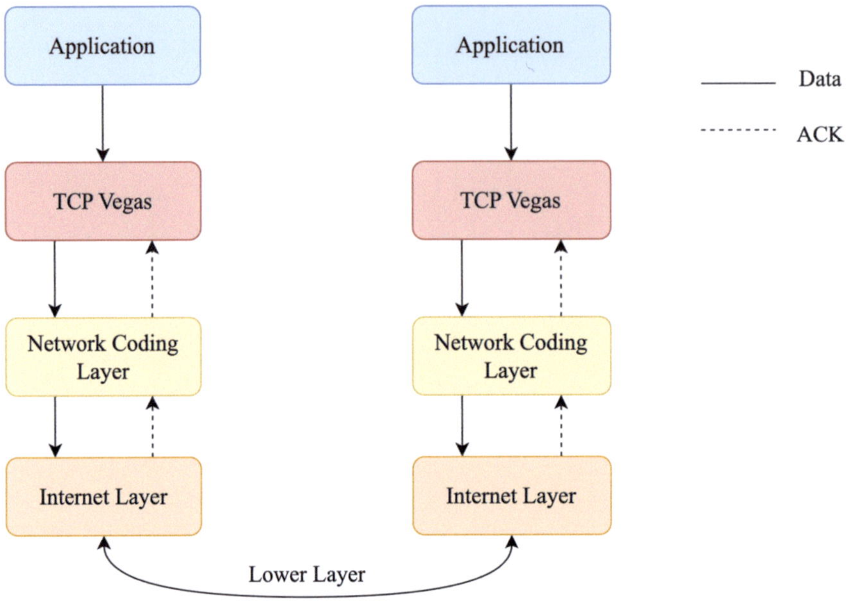

Fig. 2.12 Network encoding in the protocol stack

to the basis matrix of the knowledge space. Next, Gaussian elimination is performed to identify the most recently observed packet, enabling its confirmation. The receiver module also maintains a cache of linear combinations for undecoded packets. Once these packets are decoded, the receiver module transmits them to the TCP link and clears the corresponding linear combinations from the cache.

Next, we describe the specific algorithms involved in the network coding layer within the node using pseudocode. We illustrate this using a simple example of a point-to-point unidirectional TCP stream transmission.

1. Sender: The sender's network encoding layer must respond to two types of events—the arrival of packets from the upper-layer TCP and the arrival of acknowledgments (ACKs) from the receiver received via the lower-layer IP.

    (a) Set variable NUM to 0.
    (b) Wait state: Perform the following acknowledgment operations if the events below occur; otherwise, wait.
    (c) A packet arrives from the TCP layer:
        (i) If it is a control packet for link management, forward it to the IP layer and return to the waiting state.
        (ii) If it is a data packet and it is not in the current encoding window, add it to the encoding window.
        (iii) NUM = NUM + R (R is the redundancy factor).
        (iv) Repeat the following code [NUM] times: ([NUM] denotes the integer part of NUM's current value):Within the encoding window, combine

all current packets using a specific algorithm to generate a random linear packet combination. Combine the network coding header containing random linear combination coefficients with the randomly generated linear packet combination from the encoding window. Pass this encoded packet to the IP layer.

(v) NUM = The fractional part of NUM.

(vi) Return to waiting state.

(d) An acknowledgment ACK from the receiver arrives at the IP layer:

Remove the acknowledged original packet from the encoding cache and forward this acknowledgment to the sender's TCP layer.

2. Receiver: At the receiver end, the algorithm similarly responds to two types of events—the arrival of packets from the sender received from the IP layer, and the arrival of acknowledgments (ACKs) from the receiver's TCP layer.

(1) Waiting State: Perform the following acknowledgment operations if the events below occur; otherwise, wait.

(2) Receive an acknowledgment ACK from the TCP layer: If this ACK is a control packet for link management, forward it to the IP layer and return to the waiting state; otherwise, ignore the ACK signal.

(3) Receive an encoded packet from the sender delivered by the IP layer:

(i) Remove the network encoding header and retrieve the encoding vector.

(ii) Add this coding vector as a new row to the coding coefficient matrix and update the seen packet set using Gaussian elimination.

(iii) Add the payload to the decoding buffer and perform Gaussian elimination on the buffer contents. If any raw packet is decoded during this process, forward it to the TCP layer and remove it from the decoding buffer.

(iv) Generate a new TCP acknowledgment (ACK) with a sequence number matching the latest unseen packet.

Since the NC layer is positioned between TCP and IP, to ensure the added protocol layer remains transparent to others, we set the encoding module's input and output buffers to match the current TCP sliding window value.

The decoding module's input and output buffers are set to the current TCP receive window value. The initial value of the TCP sliding window is set to 64 KB calculated based on IP packets not exceeding 1.5 KB in length, allowing storage of at least 40 segments. The number of segments involved in encoding should not be excessive, as this would significantly complicate decoding. The decoding window of the decoding module corresponds to the encoding window of the encoding module; hence, its size is also set to 64 KB.

2.7 MIN-SANC-TCP Protocol: Adaptive Redundancy-Based Fused Network Coding TCP

2.7.1 Basic Architecture of the MIN-SANC-TCP Protocol

As mentioned in the previous subsection, network coding is a technique that enables the combined forwarding of packets across time and data streams. In recent years, it has been regarded as a potential method to enhance the reliability of wireless networks and lossy networks. Its advantage lies in mitigating packet loss by transmitting redundant combined packets, thereby improving link utilization and end-to-end throughput.

However, the gradual deployment of network coding in the Internet still faces challenges: On the one hand, the reliability and congestion control mechanisms of traditional TCP heavily rely on in-order acknowledgments, which are directly incompatible with the "combined packet/degree of freedom" semantics; on the other hand, excessive modifications to the protocol stack would compromise compatibility with existing networks and increase deployment costs.

Self-Adaptive Network Coding TCP (SANC-TCP) under the MIN network was proposed precisely in this context [17]. It introduces a lightweight network coding layer between the Transport and network layers, resolving the conflict between coding semantics and TCP flow control by extending the ACK mechanism. This represents an optimization of the Network Coding TCP (NC-TCP) protocol under the MIN network.

Figure 2.13 shows a schematic diagram of the MIN-SANC-TCP protocol in the network-layered model. In the MIN-SANC-TCP protocol:

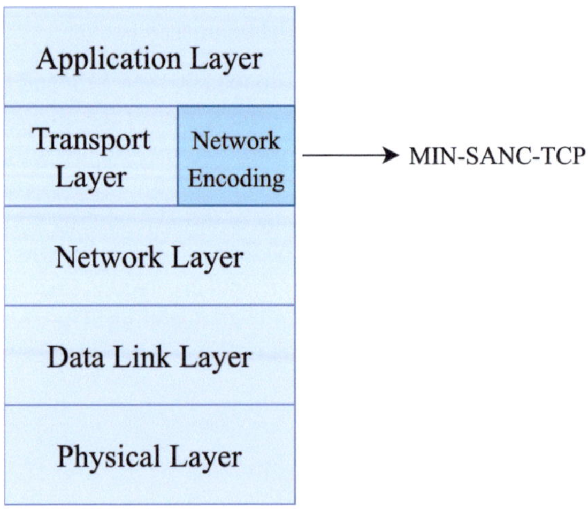

Fig. 2.13 Schematic diagram of the MIN-SANC-TCP protocol in the network-layered model

1. The sender no longer transmits raw packets directly but performs random linear combinations of packets within the current congestion window;
2. The receiver operates on "Degrees of Freedom (DoF)"—each linearly independent combined packet.
3. Once the receiver acquires DoFs equal to the window size, it can reconstruct all original packets via Gaussian elimination.
4. The acknowledgment mechanism evolves from "receiving a raw packet" to "seeing a packet (Seen Packet)," meaning that the receiver sends an ACK even if it hasn't fully decoded the original packet, as long as sufficient DoFs allow it to "see" that packet.

This mechanism preserves TCP's end-to-end principle: reliability still relies on acknowledgment feedback, and the congestion window remains ACK-driven. However, the underlying "acknowledgment unit" shifts from raw packets to degrees of freedom, enabling seamless integration with network coding.

2.7.2 MIN-SANC-TCP Packet Structure

To achieve adaptive redundancy adjustment, SANC-TCP adds a few new fields to the packet header:

Figure 2.14 shows the packet format of the SANC-TCP protocol. Encoded data packet header (NC-Header):

- Encoding Coefficient Vector γ: Identifies the linear relationship of this composite packet.
- pktID: Globally incrementing sequence number of the encoded packet.

  (a) ACK Extension Fields:

- diff_loss: Estimated incremental decoding gap at the receiver, i.e., $loss_{new} - loss_{old}$.
- echo_pktID: Indicates which encoded packet triggered this ACK.

This design is extremely lightweight, requiring only two integer fields within the ACK to convey the receiver's network status and requirements.

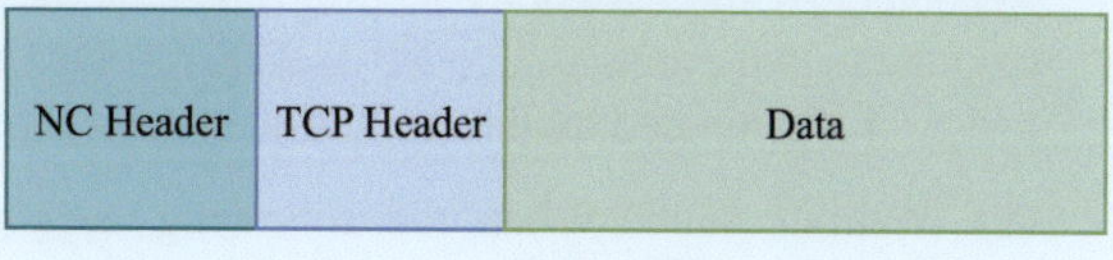

Fig. 2.14 SANC-TCP protocol packet format

2.7.3 Adaptive Adjustment of Redundancy Coefficient in MIN-SANC-TCP Protocol

The traditional NC-TCP protocol employs a fixed redundancy coefficient R, meaning that the sender transmits a fixed number of redundant packets after every specified number of original packets. However, in real wireless environments, packet loss rates fluctuate significantly over time, rendering a fixed R ineffective.

SANC-TCP introduces an adaptive control law based on the window scale. The receiver calculates:

$$\mathrm{loss}_{\mathrm{new}} = k_{\max} - k_{\mathrm{seen}},\ \mathrm{diff}_{\mathrm{loss}} = \mathrm{loss}_{\mathrm{new}} - \mathrm{loss}_{\mathrm{old}} \tag{2.9}$$

and writes diff_loss and echo_pktID into the ACK.

$$R_{\mathrm{new}} = \max\left(1, R_{\mathrm{old}} + 2 \cdot \tfrac{\mathrm{diff}_{\mathrm{loss}}}{L} + \tfrac{\mathrm{diff}_{\mathrm{loss}_{\mathrm{old}}}}{L}\right). \tag{2.10}$$

Upon receiving the ACK, the sender updates the redundancy factor if the trigger condition is met:

$$\text{echo pktID} \geq W + L \cdot R_{\mathrm{old}}, \tag{2.11}$$

where L is the update step size (e.g., 10), then:

Simultaneously update the state variable:

$$W \leftarrow \text{echo pktID, diff\_ loss\_ old} \leftarrow \mathrm{diff}_{\mathrm{loss}}, R_{\mathrm{old}} \leftarrow R_{\mathrm{new}}. \tag{2.12}$$

This allows the redundancy factor to adjust dynamically with packet loss rates: increasing R during high loss and decreasing it during low loss, maintaining near-optimal performance.

2.7.4 MIN-SANC-TCP Protocol Operation Flow

1. Receiver: At the network encoding layer of the receiver, the algorithm must respond to two events—encoded packets received from the sender at the IP layer and ACKs generated by the current receiver at the transport layer.
   (1) Waiting State: When the following events occur, react as described; otherwise, continue waiting.
   (2) Receive an ACK generated by the receiver: If this ACK is for a connection establishment packet, pass it to the IP layer and return to the waiting state. Otherwise, discard this ACK.

(3) Receive an encoded packet from the sender. The NC header contains the encoding coefficient vector γ and the variable pktID, which uniquely identifies the current encoded packet ID.
   (a) Remove the network encoding header from the encoded packet and extract the encoding coefficient vector.
   (b) Add this coding coefficient vector as a new row to the coefficient matrix in the network coding layer. Update the number of "seen" packets via Gaussian elimination.
   (c) Send the newly arrived coded packet to the decoding buffer and perform the Gaussian elimination process corresponding to step b. If any original packet is decoded, pass it to the receiver's TCP layer and delete the corresponding coded packet from the decoding buffer.
   (d) Calculate the value of the variable loss_new, which equals the difference between the maximum packet index in the coefficient matrix and the maximum sequence number of "seen" packets. Compute the difference between the current loss_new and the previous loss_old, i.e., diff_loss = loss_new – loss_old. Assign the loss_new value to loss_old, i.e., loss_old = loss_new. Extract the variable pktID from the encoded packet header and assign it to the variable echo_pktID in the receiver's network coding layer: echo_pktID = pktID;
   (e) Generate a new ACK packet with a sequence number equal to the latest unacknowledged original packet's sequence number. Embed diff_loss and echo_pktID into this ACK's header.

2. Sender: At the sender's network coding layer, the algorithm must also respond to two events—raw packets received from the sender's transport control layer and ACKs received from the receiver.

   (1) Set the value of variable NUM to 0.
   (2) Wait State: If any of the following events occur, perform the corresponding action. Otherwise, continue waiting.
   (3) Receive a raw packet from the sender's transport control layer:
      (a) If this packet is for connection establishment control, pass it to the IP layer and return to the waiting state.
      (b) If this packet is not for connection establishment control and is not in the encoding window, add it to the encoding window.
      (c) Set NUM = NUM + R (where R is the redundancy factor).
      (d) Execute the following actions NUM times:
         i. Combine all packets in the encoding window to generate a random linear encoded packet.
         ii. Append a network coding header containing the random encoding coefficient vector and the variable pktID indicating the current packet number.
         iii. Pass this encoded packet to the network layer.
      (e) Assign the fractional part of variable NUM to variable NUM;
      (f) Return to waiting state.

(4) Upon receiving an ACK from the receiver, forward it to the receiver's network coding layer. The NC header now contains the variable diff_loss, indicating the difference between the current total lost packets and the total lost packets at the last R value adjustment, and the variable echo_pktID, indicating the packet ID of the encoded packet whose arrival at the receiver generated this ACK packet.
   (a) Extract the echo_pktID variable from the header to determine if the redundancy coefficient R should be adjusted:
      (i) If echo_pktID equals $W + 10*R$_old or if echo_pktID exceeds $W + 10*R$_old for the first time, prepare to adjust R. Here, W is the echo_pktID value corresponding to the last R adjustment.
      (ii) Extract the diff_loss value from the header and assign it to the variable diff_loss_new in the sender's encoding layer.
      (iii) Calculate the value of R_new: R_new = R_old + 2*(diff_loss_new/10.0) + diff_loss_old/10.0.
      (iv) Record the current variable values in the encoding layer: R_old = R_new; diff_loss_old = diff_loss_new; $W = W + 10*R$_new.
      (v) Otherwise, directly enter state b;
   (b) Remove the acknowledged original packet from the encoding buffer and pass this ACK to the sender's transmission control layer.

The core value of SANC-TCP lies in its ability to seamlessly integrate the redundancy advantages of network coding with TCP's congestion control mechanisms, achieving a compatible and efficient transmission method with minimal alteration to TCP's original mechanisms. By introducing lightweight extensions and adaptive redundancy adjustment mechanisms into the protocol stack, SANC-TCP effectively masks packet loss over wireless and lossy links, maintains stable throughput, and demonstrates excellent fairness and scalability in multi-stream contention. It also maintains low deployment and implementation costs, providing a viable path for practical network coding applications.

2.8 MIN-TCP Protocol

2.8.1 Basic Architecture of the MIN-TCP Protocol

The architecture of the MIN-TCP protocol stack is illustrated in Fig. 2.15. At the application layer, its core is a universal interface layer. MIN applications leverage the function interfaces provided by this layer to easily implement critical operations such as connection listening, establishment, and data read/write. The transport layer protocol stack handles actual connection management, state maintenance, and network communication tasks, serving as the central hub for ensuring reliable data transmission. Figure 2.15 shows the architecture of MIN-TCP.

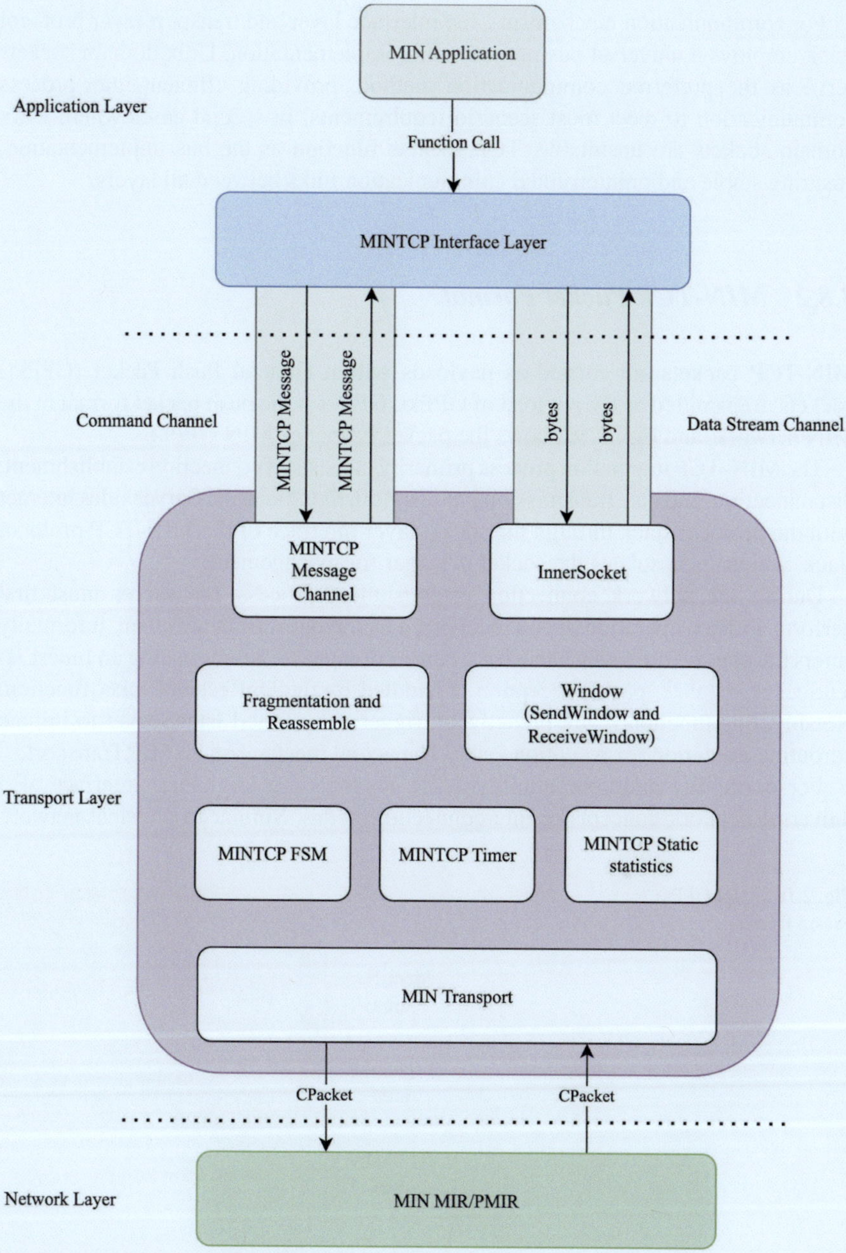

Fig. 2.15 MIN-TCP architecture diagram

For communication mechanisms, the interface layer and transport layer protocol stack employs a universal bus programming implementation. Unix domain sockets serve as the preferred communication method, providing efficient inter-process communication to meet most scenario requirements. In special cases where Unix domain sockets are unsuitable, TCP sockets function as the bus implementation, ensuring stable and uninterrupted communication links between all layers.

2.8.2 MIN-TCP Packet Format

MIN-TCP packets are carried as payloads within General Push Packet (GPPkt) packets, transmitted as the payload of GPPkt. GPPkt is the push packet format in the MIN network, and Fig. 2.16 shows the packet format of MIN GPPkt.

The MIN-TCP interaction process primarily consists of connection establishment, disconnection, and data transmission phases. Both the Client and Server sides interact with the protocol stack through the socket layer interface of the MIN-TCP protocol stack, which encapsulates the socket manager for management.

During the network connection establishment process, the server must first perform a Listen operation. Upon receiving a Dial request from the client, it formally enters the classic three-way handshake connection phase. After creating an InnerListenSocket instance, packet reception is handled by the OnReceivePacket function. Notably, this function is not proactively triggered by InnerListenSocket to initiate coroutine execution for reception tasks. The actual mechanism is: MIRTransport.

For portability and compatibility, MIR abstracts the LogicFace interface as a universal network concept for interconnecting nodes. Similar to physical network

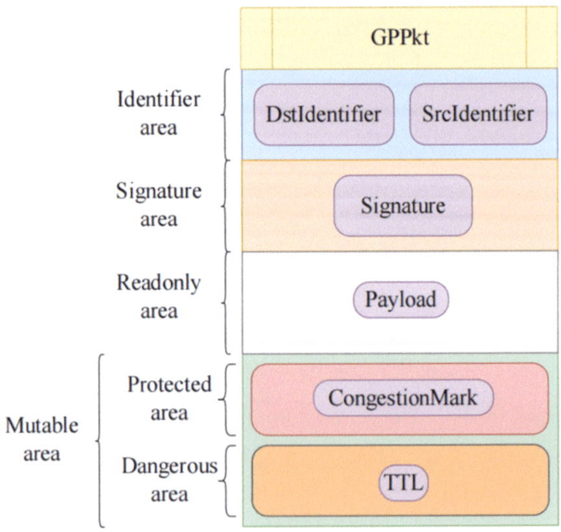

Fig. 2.16 MIN GPPkt packet format

interfaces, it primarily handles MIN network packet transmission. This unified abstraction allows upper-layer MIR modules (e.g., forwarding modules) to process standardized MIN packets without concerning themselves with underlying protocol differences. The LogicFace can utilize different underlying communication channels: logical network interfaces, Unix, TCP. After registering the monitoring signal with the MIR system, the MIR TransportComponent initiates a LogicFace-type packet reception coroutine. This coroutine invokes the OnReceivePacket function via a callback mechanism, precisely delivering the received packet to the InnerListenSocket for subsequent processing, ensuring the operational integrity of the data transmission link.

Upon successful dialing, both the Client and Server sides establish a Bytechannel via SocketManager. All data transmission occurs through this Bytechannel. Acting as an intermediary, SocketManager relays data between both sides, ensuring data reliability and ownership control during the relay process.

2.8.3 MIN-TCP Reliable Transmission and Congestion Control

This section details the reliable transmission mechanism mentioned above.

TCP achieves reliable transmission through acknowledgment numbers, and MIN-TCP follows suit. When a packet is sent, the sender must receive an acknowledgment number from the peer to confirm that the packet was correctly and completely delivered.

After establishing a connection via the three-way handshake, MIN-TCP receives a packet and passes it to InnerSocket's dealReceivePacket for processing. It uses ReceiveWindow's ReceivePacket to calculate the ACK and then calls SendAck to acknowledge receipt to the sender.

ReceivePacket primarily handles ACK calculation, buffering packets within the window, and processing ordered packets. The structure of the receive window is shown below. Both the nextSeq and maxSeq markers are measured in bytes, and each packet has a different length. Figure 2.17 shows the MIN-TCP receive window.

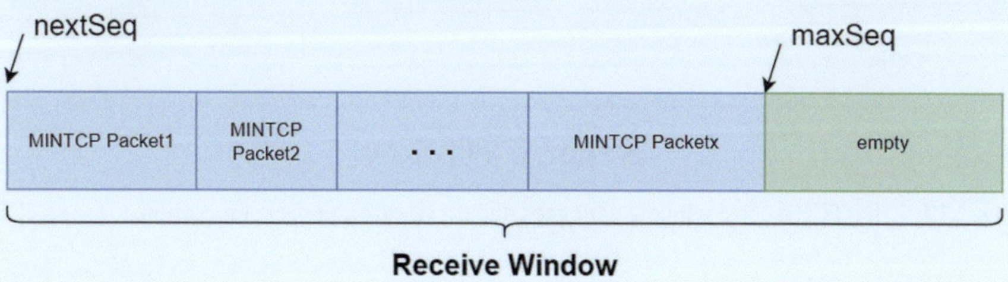

Fig. 2.17 MIN-TCP receive window

The processing flow for receiving ordered packets is as follows. A sliding window operation is performed to extract all sequentially arriving packets and pass them to the socket layer for processing, and Fig. 2.18 shows the MIN-TCP processing flow for in-order packet reception.

The above assumes an in-order arrival scenario. However, in actual network conditions, packets may not arrive as expected, leading to a "gap" in the window. Note that only header gaps occur here. If a packet with a header is received, it is guaranteed to be in order and is immediately handed over to the interface layer for processing. In this state, the receiver will respond with the next sequence it previously requested, and Fig. 2.19 shows the MIN-TCP receive window with gaps caused by out-of-order packet reception.

Congestion control is primarily implemented through window adjustment algorithms. MIN-TCP currently implements two window adjustment algorithms: Reno and Cubic. Both algorithms were introduced in Sect. 2.3.4 and will not be repeated here.

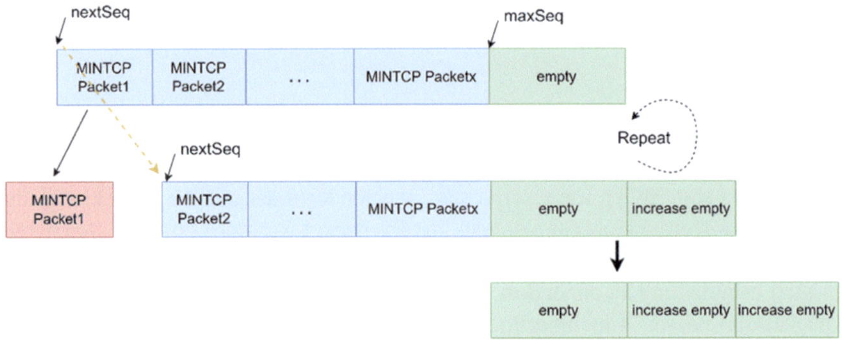

Fig. 2.18 MIN-TCP processing flow for in-order packet reception

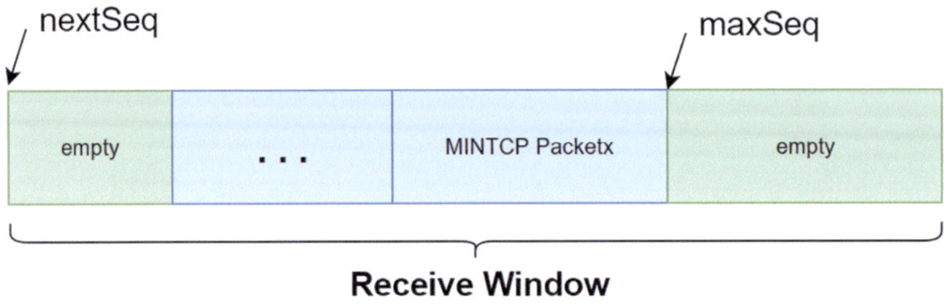

Fig. 2.19 MIN-TCP receive window with gaps due to out-of-order packet reception

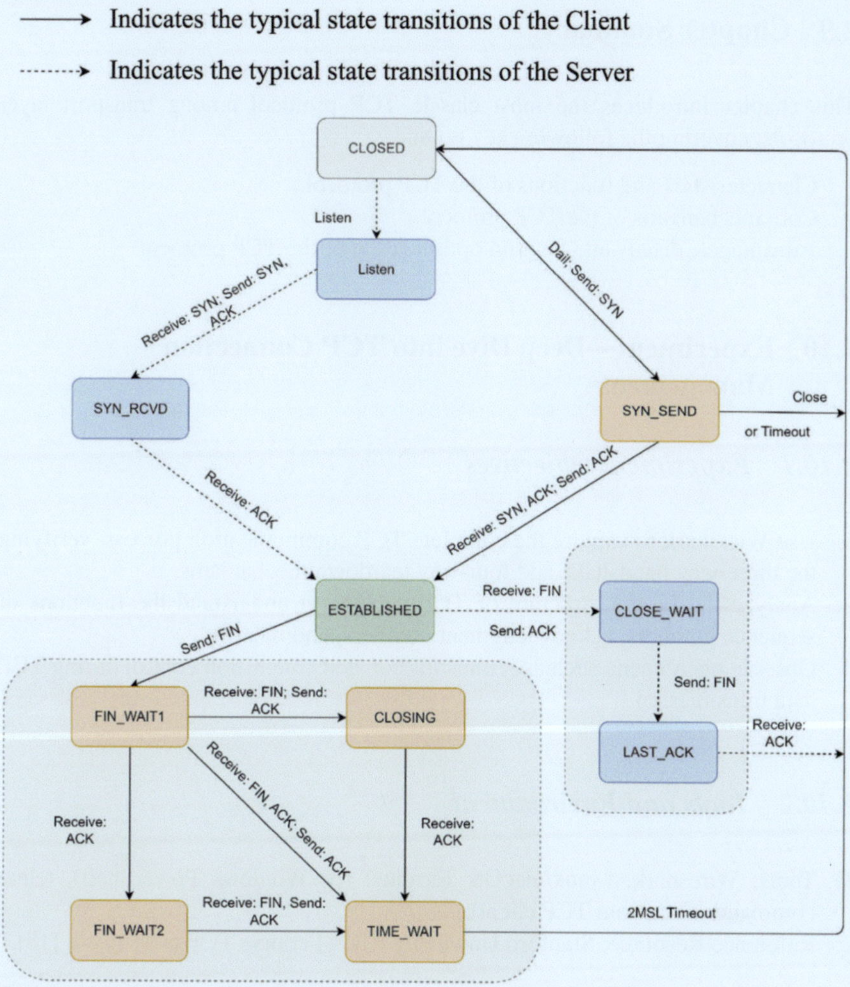

Fig. 2.20 MIN-TCP state transition flowchart

2.8.4 *MIN-TCP Connection State Transitions*

MIN-TCP state transitions are divided into two entities: the client and the server. The server provides services to the client. It transitions from the CLOSED state to the Listen state via the socket layer's listen function to await service requests from the client. After the client calls the dial function to initiate a handshake request, it enters the SYN_SEND state. Upon receiving the handshake request, the server transitions to the SYN_RCVD state. When the server subsequently receives the client's ACK, the connection is established, and data communication commences. Upon completing data transmission, both the server and client enter the connection termination phase. The server transitions through CLOSE_WAIT and LAST_ACK states, while the client progresses through FIN_WAIT1, FIN_WAIT2, CLOSING, and TIME_WAIT states. Figure 2.20 shows the state transition flowchart of MIN-TCP.

2.9 Chapter Summary

This chapter introduces the most classic TCP protocol among transport layer protocols, covering the following key points:

1. Characteristics and functions of the TCP protocol.
2. Core mechanisms of the TCP protocol.
3. Advantages, disadvantages, and optimization of the TCP protocol.

2.10 Experiment—Deep Dive into TCP Connection Management

2.10.1 Experiment Objectives

1. Use Wireshark to capture the complete TCP communication process, verifying the three-way handshake and four-way teardown mechanisms.
2. Analyze the header structure of TCP packets to understand the functions of sequence numbers, acknowledgment numbers, and flag bits.
3. Observe phenomena such as retransmission and congestion control during TCP data transmission.

2.10.2 Tools and Environment

1. Tools: Wireshark, Linux/macOS Terminal (or Windows PowerShell), telnet command (or custom TCP client).
2. Reference Resource: Stanford University CS144 course TCP experiment [18].

2.10.3 Experimental Procedure

1. Prepare TCP Connection Scenario
   (1) Launch Wireshark, select the current network adapter, and start capturing. Set the filter condition to tcp.
   (2) Open a terminal and establish a TCP connection using the telnet command (using connection to Baidu's HTTP service as an example) (Fig. 2.21):
   ```
   telnet baidu.com 80
   ```
   (3) After successful connection, enter a simple HTTP request (press Enter three times to send) (Fig. 2.22):
   ```
   GET / HTTP/1.1
   ```
   (First Enter)

```
zhemingbao@MacBook-Pro-2 ~ % telnet baidu.com 80
Trying 39.156.70.37...
Connected to baidu.com.
Escape character is '^]'.
```

Fig. 2.21 Telnet TCP connection to Baidu

`Host: baidu.com`
(Second Enter)
(Third Enter)

(4) After receiving the server response, enter quit to close the connection (Fig. 2.23).

2. Analyzing the Three-Way Handshake

(1) In the Wireshark capture results, locate the three packets from the connection establishment phase:

(a) First Packet: SYN packet sent by the client (SYN flag set), recording the sequence number (Seq) (Fig. 2.24).

```
zhemingbao@MacBook-Pro-6 ~ % telnet baidu.com 80
Trying 39.156.70.37...
Connected to baidu.com.
Escape character is '^]'.
GET / HTTP/1.1
Host: baidu.com
```

Fig. 2.22 Manually initiating an HTTP request

```
zhemingbao@MacBook-Pro-6 ~ % telnet baidu.com 80
Trying 39.156.70.37...
Connected to baidu.com.
Escape character is '^]'.
GET / HTTP/1.1
Host: baidu.com

HTTP/1.1 200 OK
Content-Length: 81
Content-Type: text/html
Server: bfe
Date: Sun, 31 Aug 2025 02:10:15 GMT

<html>
<meta http-equiv="refresh" content="0;url=http://www.baidu.com/">
</html>
```

Fig. 2.23 Viewing HTTP response

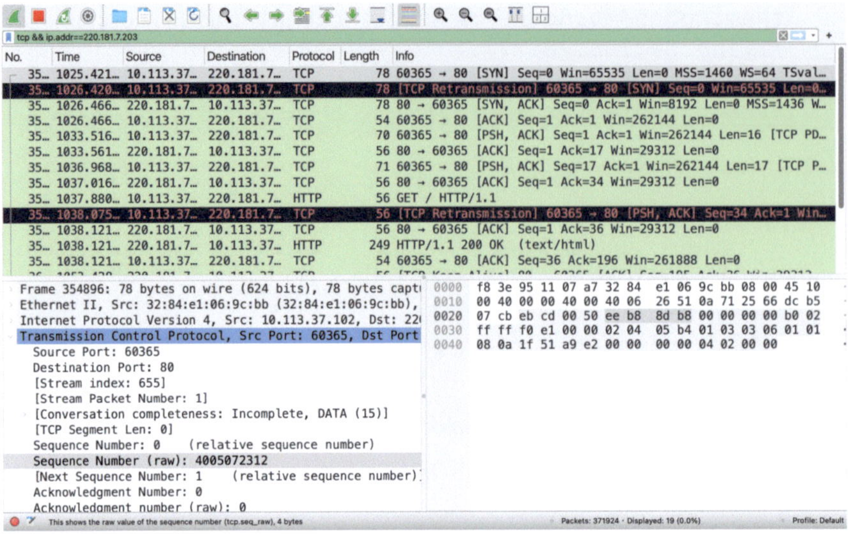

Fig. 2.24 Recording Seq

(b) Second Packet: The server's SYN + ACK response (flags SYN, ACK). The acknowledgment number (Ack) should be Seq + 1 from the first packet and includes the server's Seq (Fig. 2.25).

(c) Third Packet: The client's ACK response (flag ACK). The acknowledgment number should be the server's Seq + 1.

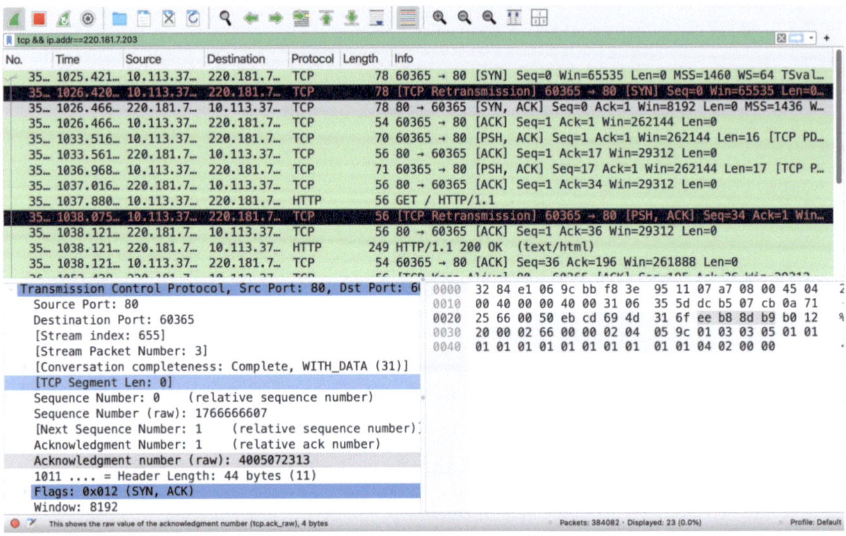

Fig. 2.25 Observing Ack = Seq + 1

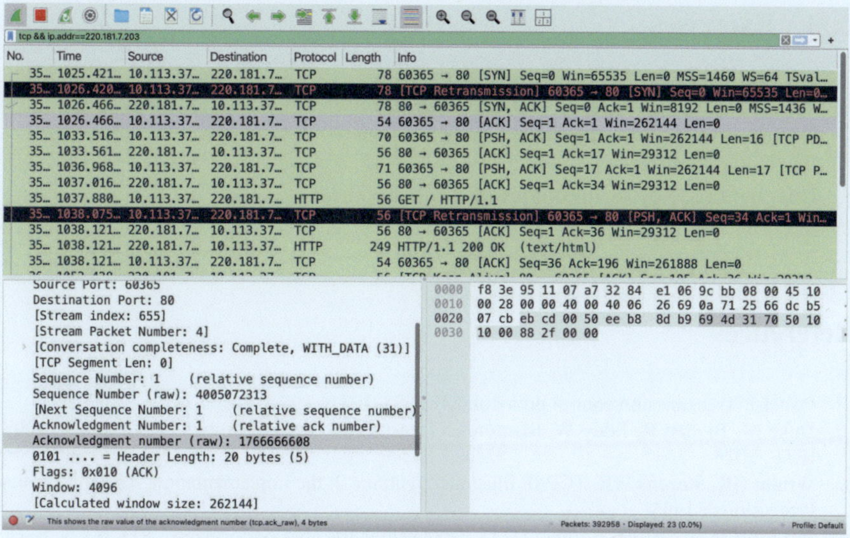

Fig. 2.26 Packet capture related to the experiment

Packets related to the experiment can be filtered using the "tcp && ip.addr ==" command, as shown (Fig. 2.26).

(2) Capture screenshots of the three-way handshake packet details, annotating key fields (Seq, Ack, Flags).

3. Analyze Data Transmission and the Four-Way Handshake

 (1) Locate the TCP packets corresponding to HTTP requests and responses, observing the Seq increment pattern in the data segment (each packet's Seq equals the previous packet's Seq plus the data length).
 (2) Identify the four packets during the connection termination phase:
  (a) Client sends FIN packet (FIN, ACK).
  (b) Server replies with ACK packet (ACK).
  (c) Server sends FIN packet (FIN, ACK).
  (d) Client replies with ACK packet (ACK).
 (3) Measure the total duration from connection establishment to closure, analyzing the time proportion for each phase.

2.10.4 Experiment Summary

This experiment visually verified the actual process of TCP three-way handshake and four-way teardown, demonstrating the role of sequence numbers and acknowledgments in reliable transmission.

2.11 Exercises

1. Briefly describe the fundamental characteristics of the TCP protocol.
2. Briefly describe the difference between flow control and congestion control in the TCP protocol.
3. List the three key technologies of the TCP protocol.

References

1. Postel J. Transmission control protocol. RFC 793, IETF; 1981.
2. Duke M, Braden R, Eddy W, Blanton E. Transmission control protocol (TCP). RFC 9293, IETF; 2023.
3. Wright GR, Stevens WR. TCP/IP illustrated, volume 2: the implementation. Addison-Wesley Professional; 1995.
4. Jacobson V, Braden R, Borman D. TCP extensions for high performance. RFC 1323, IETF; 1992.
5. Mathis M, Mahdavi J, Floyd S, Romanow A. TCP selective acknowledgment options. RFC 2018, IETF; 1996.
6. Allman M, Paxson V, Stevens W. TCP congestion control. RFC 2581, IETF; 1999.
7. Tanenbaum AS, Wetherall DJ. Computer networks. 5th ed. Pearson; 2010.
8. Kurose JF, Ross KW. Computer networking: a top-down approach. 8th ed. Pearson; 2021.
9. Jacobson V. Congestion avoidance and control. ACM SIGCOMM Comput Commun Rev. 1988;18(4):314–29.
10. Allman M, Paxson V, Blanton E. TCP congestion control. RFC 5681, IETF; 2009.
11. Floyd S, Henderson T. The NewReno modification to TCP's fast recovery algorithm. RFC 2582, IETF; 1999.
12. Ha S, Rhee I, Xu L. CUBIC: a new TCP-friendly high-speed TCP variant. ACM SIGOPS Oper Syst Rev. 2008;42(5):64–74.
13. Rhee I, Xu L. CUBIC for fast long-distance networks. RFC 8312; 2018.
14. Paxson V, Allman M, Chu J, et al. Computing TCP's retransmission timer. RFC 6298; 2011.
15. Cheng Y, Chu J, Radhakrishnan S, Jain A. TCP fast open. RFC 7413; 2014.
16. Fan X, Li H, Pan K.A dynamic self-adapting algorithm of redundancy parameter in TCP-NC. In: 2012 IEEE 14th international conference on communication technology. IEEE, 2012. p. 1276–1280.
17. Song S, Li H, Pan K, Liu J, Li SYR. Self-adaptive TCP protocol combined with network coding scheme. In: International conference on systems and networks communications (ICSNC). 2011. p. 20–25.
18. Stanford University. CS144: Introduction to computer networking—Lab 3: an internet router [EB/OL]. 2025. https://cs144.github.io. Accessed 14 Sept 2025.

Chapter 3
User Datagram Protocol

After a detailed examination of TCP's reliability mechanisms, connection-oriented behavior, and the overheads they entail, this chapter turns to applications that are sensitive to latency and protocol overhead; in such contexts, the User Datagram Protocol (UDP) offers a lighter-weight, lower-latency alternative.

In real-time scenarios such as videoconferencing, online gaming, and livestreaming, the speed and efficiency of the User Datagram Protocol (UDP) make it irreplaceable. For applications demanding ultimate efficiency and low latency, UDP offers a minimalist alternative.

This chapter explores UDP as a lightweight, connectionless transport layer protocol, detailing its core characteristics and minimal header structure. This chapter delves into UDP's strengths and weaknesses (fast but unreliable) and how application-layer protocols like QUIC and RTP can optimize it. Finally, a hands-on experiment implementing UDP client–server communication and exercises comparing TCP and UDP help students apply theoretical knowledge to real-world scenarios.

3.1 Introduction to UDP

The User Datagram Protocol (UDP) is one of the core transport layer protocols in the Internet Protocol Suite. First defined in RFC 768 in 1980, it shares the responsibility of end-to-end data transmission across networks with TCP. Unlike TCP's reliability and complex control mechanisms, UDP is renowned for its simple and efficient design, making it particularly suitable for scenarios demanding high real-time performance and tolerating minor data loss [1].

H. Li and Z. Bao, *Transport Layer for Computer Networks*,
https://doi.org/10.1007/978-981-95-7374-5_3

3.1.1 Fundamental Characteristics of UDP

This section details the core features of UDP. Figure 3.1 shows the UDP transmission protocol.

- **Connectionless**: UDP transmits data without establishing connections. In live streaming scenarios, broadcasters must deliver video streams to thousands of viewers in real time. Using TCP would require establishing connections with each viewer, consuming significant system resources and time, thereby increasing streaming latency. With UDP, the broadcaster can directly encapsulate video data into datagrams for transmission. As long as viewers are ready to receive, they can obtain data in real time, enabling a low-latency streaming experience. Technically, connectionless operation means UDP avoids the three-way handshake for connection establishment and the four-way handshake for disconnection required by TCP. This reduces network interactions and accelerates initial data transmission speeds.
- **Unreliable Transmission**: UDP's unreliable transmission is not a flaw but a deliberate design choice for specific scenarios. Unlike TCP's reliable transmission mechanism, UDP does not actively confirm delivery or retransmit datagrams after

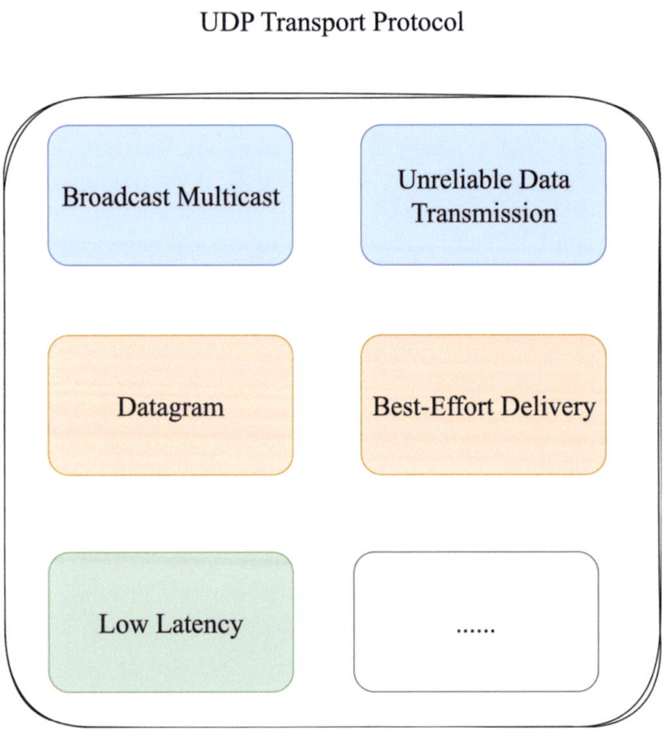

Fig. 3.1 UDP transmission protocol

sending. When an application sends data via UDP, it simply encapsulates the data into datagrams and pushes them onto the network. UDP bears no responsibility for whether the data arrives accurately, error-free, or in sequence at the receiving end. For instance, in online gaming scenarios, player commands (such as movement or shooting) must be transmitted rapidly to the server. Even if one or two commands are occasionally lost, the player's experience remains largely unaffected, as the game visuals dynamically adjust based on subsequent commands. Moreover, in complex and fluctuating network environments, relying on TCP for retransmissions could introduce significant delays due to acknowledgment waits and retransmission attempts, thereby compromising the game's real-time interactivity. However, this unreliability introduces risks. In scenarios demanding high data accuracy—such as file transfers or financial transaction data—UDP's unreliable transmission may cause data loss or errors, potentially leading to severe consequences. Therefore, when using UDP, application developers must design data validation and retransmission mechanisms at the application layer to ensure data reliability based on business requirements.

- **Datagram-Oriented**: UDP's datagram-oriented nature defines its unique data processing approach. Data is transmitted as independent datagrams, each containing complete header information including source port number, destination port number, data length, and checksum. These function like discrete packages, operating independently of one another. The size of data written by the application directly correlates with the final datagram size. If the application writes data exceeding the underlying network's Maximum Transmission Unit (MTU), UDP fragments the data into multiple datagrams for transmission. Conversely, smaller data writes are encapsulated into a single datagram. The receiving end reads complete datagrams at a time, unable to perform continuous byte-stream reads like TCP. For example, in a voice call application, each segment of captured voice data is encapsulated into a datagram for transmission. Upon receiving the datagrams, the receiver reconstructs and plays back the voice data in sequence. However, due to UDP's unreliability, datagrams may be lost or arrive out of order. This necessitates corresponding measures at the application layer, such as caching and sorting, to ensure the continuity and integrity of voice playback.
- **Supports Broadcast and Multicast**: UDP's support for broadcast and multicast makes it indispensable in one-to-many data transmission scenarios. Broadcast refers to sending datagrams to all hosts within the same network. For example, in a local area network (LAN), certain devices' auto-discovery features rely on UDP broadcasts. When a new printer joins the LAN, it can broadcast its device information and service address via UDP. Other hosts in the LAN receive these broadcast datagrams, detect the new printer's presence, and proceed with connection configuration. Multicast involves sending datagrams to a specific group of hosts that join the same multicast group to receive data. In video conferencing systems, the presenter's audio and video data can be sent via UDP multicast to the multicast group where participants reside. Only participants who have joined that multicast group receive the data. This approach achieves efficient one-to-many data transmission while avoiding unnecessary data delivery to irrelevant

hosts, thereby conserving network bandwidth. Compared to unicast, broadcast and multicast significantly enhance data transmission efficiency and reduce server load pressure. They find extensive applications in network management, multimedia transmission, and other fields.

In summary, UDP's characteristics—connectionless operation, unreliable transmission, datagram-oriented nature, and support for one-to-many communication—provide irreplaceable advantages in applications demanding high real-time performance. However, UDP's simplicity also means it lacks built-in reliability guarantees. Consequently, when using UDP, the application layer often needs to implement supplementary mechanisms tailored to specific requirements to balance reliability and efficiency.

3.1.2 Primary Functions of UDP

Despite its extremely minimalist design, the UDP protocol embodies the "less is more" philosophy. This lightweight architecture provides upper-layer applications with high flexibility, enabling developers to implement customized functional extensions at the application layer according to specific requirements. UDP's core functions can generally be summarized in three aspects, each optimized for specific network communication needs.

- **End-to-End Data Transmission**: UDP provides applications with fundamental end-to-end transport services. Unlike TCP, UDP does not modify or reassemble application-layer data, strictly preserving the original data boundaries. This means that if the application layer sends multiple independent packets, the receiver will receive exactly the same multiple independent packets without the packet-sticking phenomenon that can occur in TCP. This characteristic makes UDP particularly suitable for transmitting discrete, independent message units such as DNS queries or SNMP traps.
- **Checksum Mechanism**: UDP's checksum covers the protocol header, pseudo-header, and actual data content, effectively detecting most bit errors occurring during transmission. Though seemingly simple, this mechanism provides remarkably reliable error detection. It is noteworthy that the checksum field is optional in the UDP specification. However, in practical applications, the vast majority of implementations enable the checksum feature for data integrity considerations. When an error is detected, UDP handles it directly—discarding the erroneous datagram without attempting any form of recovery or retransmission. This "fail fast" design philosophy aligns closely with UDP's overall lightweight nature.
- **Broadcast and Multicast Support**: This is a key feature distinguishing UDP from TCP and a crucial reason for its irreplaceability in certain scenarios. Broadcast functionality allows a host to send data to all other hosts within the same subnet without needing to know specific recipients. Multicast offers greater flexibility,

enabling hosts to join specific multicast groups and receive only data intended for that group. Both capabilities prove invaluable in scenarios requiring one-to-many communication, such as video conferencing systems, online game state synchronization, and real-time market data push in financial markets. In these applications, UDP's multicast capabilities significantly reduce network bandwidth consumption and enhance overall system scalability.

It is noteworthy that while these UDP features are simple, they collectively form an exceptionally flexible foundational communication platform. Upper-layer applications can leverage these foundational capabilities to construct various complex communication patterns. For instance, while UDP itself offers no reliability guarantees, the application layer can implement custom reliable transport protocols on top of UDP by adding sequence numbers, acknowledgment mechanisms, retransmission timers, and similar techniques. This flexibility makes UDP the foundation for many specialized application protocols, such as the Real-Time Transport Protocol (RTP) and the Trivial File Transfer Protocol (TFTP).

3.2 UDP Header Structure Analysis

The UDP header is only 8 bytes long yet contains all the control information required for basic data transmission. This minimalist design offers significant advantages, particularly when handling large volumes of short datagrams, as reduced header overhead substantially improves network utilization. Figure 3.2 shows the structure of the UDP header, composed of four 16-bit fields:

- **Source Port**: Identifies the application process port number of the sender. In some unidirectional communication scenarios, this field is often set to 0, indicating no need for return messages. However, in bidirectional communication, correctly setting the source port allows the receiver to clearly identify the target port for responses.
- **Destination Port**: Specifies the application process on the receiving host to which the datagram should be delivered. This is a critical field for inter-process communication. The combination of source and destination ports effectively defines a

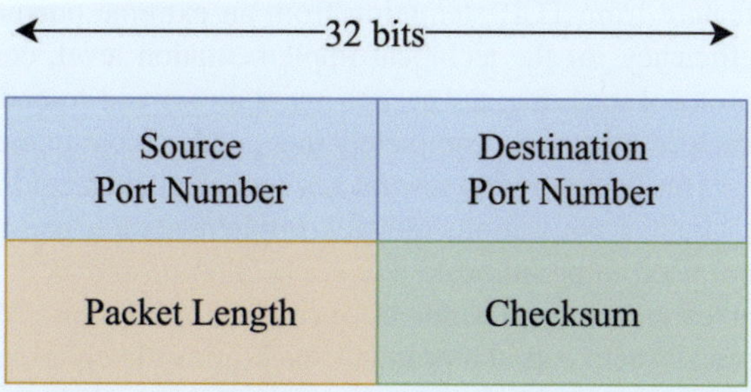

Fig. 3.2 UDP header structure

logical communication endpoint, establishing the foundation for UDP to facilitate inter-process communication at the transport layer.

- **Length**: Represents the total length of the UDP datagram, including the 8-byte header and data portion. The minimum value is 8 bytes (header only, no data), while the theoretical maximum is 65,535 bytes. However, in practical networks, the effective length of a datagram is typically constrained by the Maximum Transmission Unit (MTU) of the underlying protocol, such as the common 1500 bytes in IPv4. The presence of the Length field also enables the receiver to detect whether a datagram has been truncated, providing useful information for fault diagnosis.
- **Checksum**: Provides error detection functionality, serving as UDP's sole data integrity assurance mechanism. When calculating the checksum, UDP introduces a "Pseudo Header" structure containing information such as the source IP address, destination IP address, protocol number, and UDP length. This establishes a loosely coupled relationship between the transport layer and the network layer, significantly enhancing the accuracy of error detection. It should be noted that while the original RFC 768 treated the checksum as optional, RFC 1122 mandates its implementation and default activation; in IPv6 environments, the checksum is even mandatory [1].

From an implementation perspective, the simplicity of the UDP header delivers several key performance advantages: First, header parsing and processing incur minimal overhead, making UDP highly suitable for resource-constrained environments like embedded systems. Second, the fixed header length simplifies buffer management and reduces the risk of memory fragmentation. Finally, its alignment-friendly design (all fields are 16-byte aligned) enhances processing efficiency on modern CPU architectures. Collectively, these characteristics make UDP an ideal choice for high-performance network applications.

3.3 Core Mechanisms of UDP

3.3.1 Connectionless Transmission Model

UDP's connectionless transmission model is its most fundamental distinguishing feature from TCP, stemming from an extreme pursuit of network communication efficiency. At the technical implementation level, connectionless means the UDP protocol stack does not need to maintain any end-to-end connection state information; each datagram is a completely independent communication unit (Fig. 3.3).

This design yields several key technical characteristics:

First, from a protocol stack implementation perspective, the UDP sender does not need to pre-allocate any connection resources or maintain complex state variables such as send windows or congestion windows. When an application invokes a send system call, the protocol stack immediately encapsulates the data into a UDP

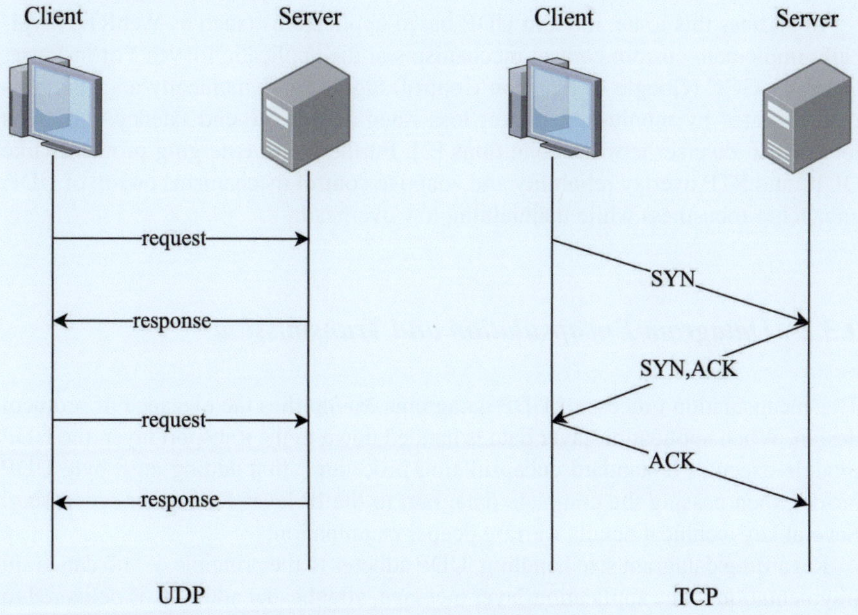

Fig. 3.3 Comparison of UDP and TCP connection establishment

datagram and hands it off to the IP layer for transmission. This process involves no additional protocol interactions. This instantaneous transmission capability enables UDP to achieve initial transmission delays as low as microseconds, significantly outperforming the millisecond-level handshake delays typically required by TCP.

Second, on the receiver side, UDP employs a "best-effort" delivery strategy. The kernel-maintained UDP receive buffer uses simple FIFO queue management. When a new datagram arrives, the kernel checks if the destination port has a corresponding receiving socket. If found, the datagram is placed into that socket's receive queue; if not, the datagram is discarded outright and may trigger an ICMP port unreachable error. This process involves no flow control or congestion feedback mechanisms, maintaining extremely high processing efficiency.

From the perspective of network programming interfaces, UDP's connectionless nature offers developers greater flexibility. A single UDP socket can communicate with multiple peers simultaneously by simply specifying the destination address for each transmission. This characteristic is particularly crucial for multicast and broadcast applications. For instance, in a videoconferencing system, a single UDP socket can simultaneously send video streams to hundreds of participants, whereas TCP would require maintaining separate connections for each recipient.

However, the connectionless model also introduces challenges, most notably the absence of built-in flow control and congestion management mechanisms. When transmission rates exceed the receiver's processing capacity or the network's carrying capacity, datagrams can be lost on a large scale.

To address this issue, modern UDP-based applications (such as WebRTC) typically implement custom control mechanisms at the application layer. For instance, Google's GCC (Google Congestion Control) algorithm dynamically adjusts transmission rates by monitoring packet loss rates and end-to-end latency variations to adapt to diverse network conditions [2]. Furthermore, emerging protocols like QUIC and RTP overlay reliability and adaptive control mechanisms on top of UDP, enhancing robustness while maintaining low overhead.

3.3.2 Datagram Encapsulation and Transmission

The encapsulation process of UDP datagrams exemplifies the elegance of protocol design. When application-layer data is handed down to the transport layer, the UDP module executes a standard encapsulation procedure: first adding an 8-byte UDP header, then passing the complete datagram to the IP layer for further processing. Several key technical details warrant deeper examination:

Regarding datagram size handling, UDP adheres to the principle of "no datagram fragmentation." The application-layer message, after header addition, is delivered to the IP layer as a single entity. If the message exceeds the Maximum Transmission Unit (MTU) of the underlying link, IP handles fragmentation.

This stands in stark contrast to TCP's stream-oriented transmission: TCP segments application-layer data into appropriately sized segments based on the network's MTU, whereas UDP preserves the boundaries of application data units. This characteristic makes UDP particularly well-suited for transmitting discrete application-layer protocol messages, such as DNS queries and responses, as the receiver can fully reconstruct the original application-layer data units. However, it is important to note that in IPv6, routers no longer perform intermediate fragmentation. Instead, the sending host is responsible for fragmentation, requiring applications to pay greater attention to MTU adaptation during design [3].

Regarding path selection, UDP relies entirely on IP-layer routing mechanisms. An interesting phenomenon arises because UDP maintains no connection state: different datagrams within the same data stream may traverse distinct network paths, potentially causing out-of-order delivery in multi-path network environments. To address this, advanced UDP applications (such as the QUIC protocol) implement intelligent path discovery and selection algorithms at the application layer.

From an implementation optimization perspective, modern operating systems incorporate extensive performance enhancements for UDP datagram processing. For instance, the Linux kernel's UDP implementation utilizes zero-copy techniques. When applications transmit large data chunks, the kernel can directly reference user-space buffers, eliminating unnecessary data copying. On the receiving end, efficient hash algorithms manage socket lookups, ensuring rapid target socket identification even under high concurrency.

3.3.3 Error Detection Mechanism

Although UDP's error detection mechanism is simple, its design embodies pragmatic engineering wisdom. The checksum field serves as the sole data integrity safeguard in the UDP protocol, and its implementation principle and practical effectiveness warrant in-depth analysis:

In terms of calculation scope, the UDP checksum employs an innovative "pseudo-header" design. This pseudo-header incorporates critical IP layer information (source IP address, destination IP address, protocol type, and UDP length), enabling the checksum to verify the entire transmission path's integrity. This design cleverly achieves cross-validation between the transport layer and network layer, detecting misdelivery issues caused by routing errors. For instance, if a datagram is routed to the wrong host due to an incorrect routing table, the mismatched IP addresses in the pseudo-header will cause the checksum to fail.

Regarding the checksum algorithm, UDP employs the same 16-bit two's complement sum algorithm as the IP protocol. While computationally simple, this algorithm demonstrates remarkable effectiveness in detecting random errors. In practical network environments, the probability of undetected bit errors during transmission is extremely low, largely due to the presence of CRC checks at the underlying link layer (e.g., Ethernet).

From a protocol evolution perspective, the handling of UDP checksums has undergone an interesting transformation. The original RFC 768 designated the checksum as an optional field, permitting its disabling for performance gains in environments with low reliability requirements. However, as network attack methods evolved, subsequent RFC 1122 explicitly mandated the implementation and default activation of checksum functionality [4]. This shift reflects heightened cybersecurity awareness and underscores that even simple error-detection mechanisms play a crucial role in defending against fundamental network attacks.

When encountering a checksum failure, UDP adopts a "silent drop" strategy. This seemingly passive approach is deeply rational: first, in networks with low error rates, correcting a single packet error offers limited value; second, omitting error reports avoids generating additional network traffic; finally, this approach aligns with UDP's overarching stateless design philosophy. Upper-layer applications requiring higher reliability can implement more sophisticated error detection and recovery mechanisms at the application layer.

From a performance optimization perspective, modern CPU architectures provide hardware acceleration support for UDP checksum computation. Most network interface cards (NICs) support checksum offloading, enabling checksum calculation and verification at the hardware level, significantly reducing CPU load. Operating system kernels also implement highly optimized checksum computation routines, utilizing SIMD instruction sets for parallel processing. This ensures that checksum computation does not become a performance bottleneck, even in high-bandwidth scenarios.

3.4 Analysis of UDP's Advantages and Disadvantages

3.4.1 *Efficiency and Low Latency*

UDP's efficiency and low latency stem from its streamlined protocol design and unique transmission mechanism. In the network transmission process, the traditional TCP protocol requires establishing a connection through a three-way handshake.

During this process, the client and server must exchange at least three round-trip packets to synchronize their initial sequence numbers, confirm each other's reachability, and negotiate transmission parameters. After the connection is established, a connection state machine must be maintained to continuously track the sending and acknowledgment of packets, which undoubtedly increases system resource overhead and network interaction costs. UDP, however, operates in a connectionless mode. The sender does not need to pre-negotiate with the receiver; it directly encapsulates data into datagrams and pushes them onto the network. The datagram header contains only four fields: source port number, destination port number, length, and checksum, totaling 8 bytes. This significantly reduces transmission overhead compared to TCP's header, which has a fixed minimum overhead of at least 20 bytes (excluding option fields).

From a data-processing perspective, UDP does not execute complex flow-control or congestion-control algorithms. During data transmission, the TCP protocol dynamically adjusts the send window size based on network conditions and employs mechanisms like slow start and congestion avoidance to prevent network congestion. However, these mechanisms introduce additional computational overhead and waiting time. UDP imposes no such constraints. The sender transmits data directly at the application's generation rate, bypassing connection establishment, window adjustment, and retransmission timer management. This significantly reduces processing latency in data transmission.

At the network device processing level, the connectionless nature also simplifies router operations. Routers need not maintain connection states for each UDP stream; instead, they forward packets based solely on the destination IP address in the datagram header, thereby enhancing data forwarding efficiency. Additionally, UDP supports datagram fragmentation and reassembly. When data exceeds the Maximum Transmission Unit (MTU) of a link, it can be automatically fragmented at the network layer. The receiver then reassembles the fragments based on fragment information. This process does not rely on an end-to-end acknowledgment mechanism like TCP, further ensuring transmission efficiency.

3.4.2 Unreliability and Lack of Flow Control

UDP's unreliability fundamentally stems from its connectionless design philosophy and absence of acknowledgment and retransmission mechanisms. During data transmission, the UDP sender transmits datagrams without actively tracking their delivery status or awaiting acknowledgment from the receiver.

Upon receiving a datagram, the receiver performs only basic error detection via the checksum field. If the checksum verification fails, the datagram is discarded without notifying the sender. Under this mechanism, datagrams may be lost during transmission due to link failures, router congestion, or other issues, yet the sender remains unaware. This prevents data from reaching the receiver intact. For applications demanding high data integrity—such as file transfers or database backups—UDP's unreliability can cause data loss or corruption, disrupting normal operations.

Furthermore, UDP lacks a flow control mechanism to dynamically adjust transmission rates based on the receiver's processing capacity and network conditions. In TCP, the receiver signals available buffer space to the sender via a sliding window mechanism, enabling the sender to adjust its transmission window for flow control.

Conversely, UDP senders rely entirely on application-layer control logic; without specific handling, they may transmit data at a constant rate. When the receiver's processing capacity is insufficient or network congestion occurs, datagrams accumulate in the receiver's buffer. Once the buffer overflows, data is discarded. This issue is particularly pronounced in video streaming. If a server continuously sends video data at a high bitrate while the client has limited network bandwidth or insufficient device performance, it can cause video stuttering or even prevent playback entirely. Additionally, the absence of flow control in UDP can exacerbate network congestion. The unordered transmission of large volumes of UDP datagrams may exhaust network bandwidth resources, disrupting the normal operation of other network applications.

3.4.3 Transmission Security Issues

UDP's transmission security issues primarily stem from its connectionless nature and lack of built-in security mechanisms. Since UDP requires no connection establishment before communication, senders can arbitrarily construct datagrams and transmit them to target addresses, making it difficult for receivers to effectively verify sender identities. This allows attackers to easily spoof source IP addresses and flood target hosts with malicious datagrams, launching UDP flood attacks (UDP Flood Attack). In such attacks, the target host's network interfaces and operating system resources become exhausted by the flood of invalid datagrams, preventing normal services from responding. Additionally, UDP datagrams are transmitted unencrypted by default, with data content exposed in plaintext. Attackers can use network sniffing tools to intercept and view the transmitted raw data, posing significant information leakage risks.

Furthermore, while UDP incorporates a checksum field for error detection, this mechanism can only identify partial bit errors and does not guarantee data integrity. The checksum employs a 16-bit binary complement sum operation, which carries a certain false-positive rate. When multiple bits fail simultaneously and cancel each other out, the checksum may fail to detect data tampering. Attackers can exploit this vulnerability by intercepting datagrams, modifying their contents, recalculating the checksum, and then forwarding them.

The receiving end finds it difficult to detect that the data has been altered. Furthermore, UDP's broadcast and multicast capabilities introduce security risks. Attackers can exploit UDP broadcasts to flood all hosts on a local network with massive amounts of junk datagrams, causing network congestion. Alternatively, they may impersonate legitimate members to join multicast groups and transmit malicious data, disrupting normal communication among other group members. Due to UDP's inherent lack of effective security mechanisms, practical implementations typically require additional security measures—such as encryption, authentication, and access control—deployed at the application or network layer to ensure secure data transmission.

3.5 Optimization and Development of UDP

3.5.1 QUIC Protocol

QUIC (Quick UDP Internet Connections), a next-generation transport layer protocol redesigned on top of UDP, stems from a deep analysis and improvement of traditional transport protocols' limitations. For a long time, the TCP protocol ensured reliability through mechanisms like the "three-way handshake" and "four-way handshake." However, in environments with high latency or frequent network handoffs, the overhead of establishing and maintaining connections became a performance bottleneck. While UDP offers low latency and lightweight characteristics, it lacks reliability and security support, making it difficult to meet the demands of complex applications. QUIC achieves cross-layer integration on top of UDP, deeply integrating transport control, encryption mechanisms, and connection management to build an efficient, reliable, and secure transport system. It has become the default transport protocol for HTTP/3 [5]. Figure 3.4 shows the application of QUIC in HTTP/3.

From a protocol stack architecture perspective, QUIC breaks the strict boundaries of traditional layering by vertically integrating transport layer functions on top of UDP. It tightly binds TLS 1.3 security features to the connection establishment process, completing encryption parameter negotiation and identity authentication directly within the initial handshake packets. This compresses the 3–4 RTTs (round-trip times) required by the traditional "TCP + TLS" combination down to 1 RTT, and even enables 0-RTT connection establishment during session recovery. This

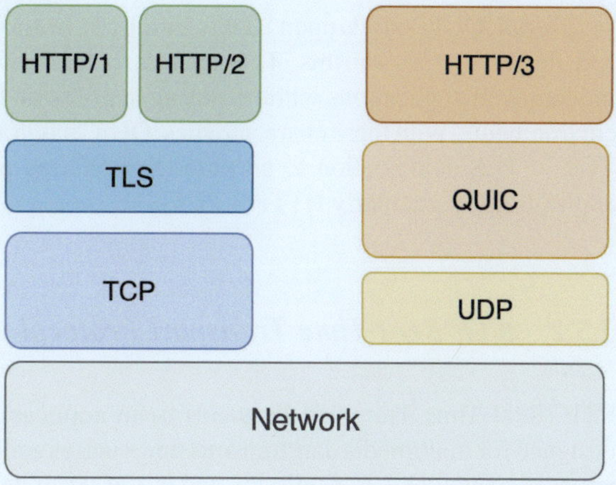

Fig. 3.4 Application of QUIC in HTTP/3

design effectively reduces startup latency and minimizes performance overhead from redundant processing across layers, balancing security with efficiency.

Regarding reliability assurance, QUIC introduces a revolutionary innovation to traditional acknowledgment and retransmission mechanisms. Unlike TCP's byte-based acknowledgment approach, QUIC employs a packet-based batch acknowledgment strategy. The receiver transmits multiple acknowledgment ranges within a single ACK frame, such as "Packets 1–10 and 15–20 received." The sender precisely locates lost data based on this information, avoiding misjudged retransmissions caused by single-ACK loss in TCP.

Additionally, QUIC incorporates version negotiation and connection migration mechanisms. When network conditions change (e.g., switching between Wi-Fi and cellular networks), devices can rapidly reuse existing connection states via the Connection ID, updating only underlying network path information. This effectively resolves TCP's requirement to re-establish connections during network transitions. Furthermore, QUIC's packet loss detection mechanism combines timestamp and jitter analysis. By recording packet transmission and reception times, it dynamically calculates network latency trends. Coupled with Selective Acknowledgment (SACK) technology, this enables precise packet loss localization and efficient retransmission.

For secure transmission, QUIC builds a comprehensive protection system centered on TLS 1.3. The protocol employs elliptic curve cryptography (ECC) for key exchange, significantly reducing computational overhead compared to traditional RSA algorithms while maintaining equivalent security strength, thereby enhancing key negotiation efficiency. Additionally, QUIC encrypts all transmitted data end-to-end, including handshake messages, application data, and connection management control frames, effectively defending against man-in-the-middle attacks, data eavesdropping, and tampering. Notably, QUIC incorporates a session recovery mechanism. By caching session keys, it avoids repeating the full key negotiation process during quick reconnections, further reducing transmission latency.

Overall, QUIC builds upon UDP's simplicity by incorporating reliability, security, and flexibility mechanisms. This enables it to meet the low-latency demands of modern web applications while ensuring stability and security in complex network environments. With these characteristics, QUIC has gradually replaced the traditional TCP + TLS combination to become the preferred transport protocol for internet applications, particularly HTTP/3 [6, 6].

3.5.2 RTP Real-Time Transport Protocol

RTP (Real-Time Transport Protocol) is an application-layer protocol specifically designed for multimedia data transmission, such as audio and video. It aims to address issues like unreliable transmission and out-of-order delivery inherent in UDP during real-time scenarios [8]. In real-time communication, audio and video data demand strict requirements for time synchronization and sequence integrity, which traditional UDP struggles to guarantee reliably. RTP builds upon UDP by defining standardized packet formats and control mechanisms, establishing an efficient and dependable transmission framework for real-time data.

RTP's packet structure is designed around "time synchronization" and "data ordering." Its core header consists of a fixed 12-byte field, with key elements including:

- Version: Identifies the protocol version to ensure compatibility between different systems;
- Sequence Number: Increments with each sent packet, allowing the receiver to reorder out-of-sequence packets and restore the sequence of video frames;
- Timestamp: Records sampling time in clock ticks (e.g., a 44.1 kHz sampling rate represents 1/44100 s per tick), enabling audio–video synchronization during playback;
- Payload Type: Identifies the specific encoding format (e.g., PCM audio, H.264 video), enabling the receiver to invoke the corresponding decoder based on this field.

Additionally, RTP supports an extensible header mechanism, facilitating the addition of supplementary information in specific scenarios (e.g., VR perspective identifiers, AI annotation data).

To achieve finer-grained transmission control, RTP incorporates RTCP (Real-Time Control Protocol) as an auxiliary protocol. RTCP periodically sends control packets to synchronize session member states and provide transmission quality feedback. Sender Reports (SR) contain metrics like packet count, bytes transmitted, and timestamps, enabling receivers to calculate transmission rates and data generation timestamps. Receiver Reports (RR) provide feedback on reception status, including metrics like packet loss rate and jitter. The sender dynamically adjusts transmission strategies based on this feedback. For instance, when network congestion causes packet loss to increase, the sender may reduce video encoding bitrate or activate Forward Error Correction (FEC) mechanisms.

For packet-loss handling, RTP integrates forward error correction with retransmission mechanisms to accommodate scenarios with varying real-time requirements. Forward error correction technology adds redundant information (e.g., Reed-Solomon encoding) to the original data, enabling the receiver to recover the original content using redundant data when some packets are lost. For instance, in VoIP voice calls, adding 10–20% redundant data allows for imperceptible recovery when the packet-loss rate is below this threshold, avoiding increased delays caused by retransmissions. For scenarios tolerating some delay (e.g., videoconferencing), RTP employs a retransmission mechanism based on RTCP feedback. The receiver reports lost packet sequence numbers, allowing the sender to prioritize retransmission of critical frames, ensuring video continuity.

Furthermore, RTP's extensibility design provides a foundation for the protocol's ongoing evolution. The protocol supports header extension mechanisms, enabling developers to add custom fields tailored to specific application needs. For instance, in virtual reality (VR) video transmission, headers can be extended to carry viewpoint information. Simultaneously, RTP collaborates with protocols like SIP (Session Initiation Protocol) and RTSP (Real-Time Streaming Protocol) to form comprehensive real-time communication solutions widely deployed in online education, telemedicine, video surveillance, and other fields. Through continuous optimization and innovation, RTP drives the advancement of real-time multimedia transmission technology, serving as a crucial enabler for reliable real-time delivery over UDP.

Looking ahead, the proliferation of emerging technologies like 5G and IoT will generate increasingly complex and diverse real-time multimedia transmission demands, presenting both challenges and opportunities for the RTP protocol. On the one hand, it must further optimize time synchronization and packet loss handling strategies within higher-bandwidth, lower-latency network environments. On the other hand, deep integration with technologies like edge computing and artificial intelligence to achieve smarter transmission control will become a key direction for RTP's continued evolution. Through persistent exploration and refinement, RTP is poised to deliver greater value in more innovative scenarios, continuously enhancing the UDP-based real-time transmission ecosystem.

3.6 Chapter Summary

This chapter introduces the UDP protocol within transport layer protocols, covering the following key aspects:

1. Characteristics and functions of the UDP protocol.
2. Core mechanisms of the UDP protocol.
3. Advantages, disadvantages, and optimization strategies for the UDP protocol.

3.7 Experiment—UDP Communication Code Practice

3.7.1 Experiment Objectives

1. Implement UDP client–server communication using the Go programming language.
2. Understand UDP's connectionless and unreliable transmission characteristics.
3. Compare the differences between UDP and TCP in programming implementation.

3.7.2 Tools and Environment

1. Tools: Go 1.20 or later, terminal, Wireshark.
2. Reference Resources: Official Go networking documentation.

3.7.3 Experiment Steps

1. Write UDP server code
   Create udp_server.go to implement UDP server functionality:

Program 3.1 UDP Server

```
package main
import (
	"log"
	"net"
	"time"
)
func main() {
	// Listen on UDP port 9000
	addr, err:= net.ResolveUDPAddr("udp", ":9000")
	if err != nil {
		log.Fatalf("Failed to resolve address:%v", err)
	}
	conn, err:= net.ListenUDP("udp", addr)
	if err != nil {
		log.Fatalf("Monitoring failed:%v", err)
	}
	defer conn.Close()
	log.Println("UDP server started, listening on port 9000...")
	buf:= make([]byte, 1024)
	for {
```

```
        // Receive client data
        n, clientAddr, err:= conn.ReadFromUDP(buf)
        if err != nil {
            log.Printf("Failed to receive data:%v", err)
            continue
        }
        data:= buf[:n]
        log.Printf("Received data from %s: %s", clientAddr, string(data))
        // Reply to client (simulate 100ms delay))
        time.Sleep(100 * time.Millisecond)
        resp:= []byte("The server has received:" + string(data))
        _, err = conn.WriteToUDP(resp, clientAddr)
        if err != nil {
            log.Printf("Response sending failed:%v", err)
        }
    }
}
```

2. Write UDP client code

   Create udp_client.go to implement UDP client functionality:

Program 3.2 UDP Client

```
package main

import (
    "log"
    "net"
    "os"
    "time"
)

func main() {
    if len(os.Args) < 2 {
        log.Fatal("Please enter the message to send, e.g.: go run udp_client.go 'hello'")
    }
    // Connect to server
    serverAddr, err:= net.ResolveUDPAddr("udp", "localhost:9000")
    if err != nil {
        log.Fatalf("Failed to resolve server address: %v", err)
    }
    conn, err:= net.DialUDP("udp", nil, serverAddr)
    if err != nil {
        log.Fatalf("Failed to connect to server: %v", err)
    }
```

```go
	defer conn.Close()

	// Send data
	msg:= os.Args[1]
	_, err = conn.Write([]byte(msg))
	if err != nil {
		log.Fatalf("Failed to send data: %v", err)
	}
	log.Printf("Sent: %s", msg)

	// Set receive timeout (2 seconds)
	conn.SetReadDeadline(time.Now().Add(2 * time.Second))

	// Receive response
	buf:= make([]byte, 1024)
	n, _, err:= conn.ReadFromUDP(buf)
	if err != nil {
		log.Fatalf("Failed to receive response: %v", err)
	}
	log.Printf("Received response: %s", buf[:n])
}
```

3. Run and test

   (1) Start the server (Fig. 3.5):

   ```
   go run udp_server.go
   ```

   (2) Open a new terminal, start the client, and send a message (Fig. 3.6):

   ```
   go run udp_client.go Hello
   ```

   (3) Observe the server and client outputs to confirm successful communication (Fig. 3.7).

```
PS C:\code> go run udp_server.go
2025/10/30 22:26:13 UDP server started, listening on port 9000...
```

Fig. 3.5 Starting the UDP server

```
PS C:\code> go run udp_server.go
2025/10/30 22:26:13 UDP server started, listening on port 9000...
2025/10/30 22:29:35 Received data from 127.0.0.1:60172: Hello
```

Fig. 3.6 Starting the client and sending a message

```
PS C:\code> go run udp_client.go Hello
2025/10/30 22:29:35 Sent: Hello
2025/10/30 22:29:35 Received response: The server has received:Hello
```

Fig. 3.7 Observing server output

(4) Launch Wireshark, filter for 'udp.port == 9000', and capture and analyze the header structure of UDP packets (source port, destination port, length, checksum).

4. Verifying UDP's Unreliability

(1) While the server is running, abruptly terminate the server process. Then restart the client to send messages and observe whether the client receives an error prompt (the client remains unaware, only experiencing timeout failures).
(2) Launch 10 clients simultaneously to send messages (scripting can automate this). Observe whether the server misses any data (packet loss may occur due to UDP's connectionless nature).

3.7.4 Experiment Summary

By implementing a UDP client/server, we gained an understanding of UDP's connectionless and acknowledgment-free characteristics.

3.8 Exercises

1. Briefly describe the fundamental characteristics of the UDP protocol.
2. Briefly describe the differences between TCP and UDP protocols.

References

1. Postel J. User Datagram Protocol. RFC 768; 1980.
2. Holmer S, Lundin H, Carlucci G, De Cicco L, Mascolo S. A Google congestion control algorithm for real-time communication. IETF Draft, IETF; 2015.
3. Deering S, Hinden R. Internet protocol, version 6 (IPv6) specification. RFC 8200, IETF; 2017.
4. Braden R, Postel J. Requirements for internet hosts—communication layers. RFC 1122, IETF; 1989.
5. Iyengar J, Thomson M. QUIC: a UDP-based multiplexed and secure transport. RFC 9000, IETF; 2021.
6. Thomson M, Turner S. Using TLS to secure QUIC[R]. RFC 9001, IETF; 2021.

7. Kurose JF, Ross KW. Computer networking: a top-down approach. 8th ed. London: Pearson; 2021.
8. Schulzrinne H, Casner S, Frederick R, et al. RTP: a transport protocol for real-time applications. RFC 3550, IETF; 2003.

Chapter 4
The QUIC Protocol

Building on the previous chapter's examination of UDP's lightweight design and its limitations in reliability and advanced transport capabilities, this chapter turns to a new protocol engineered to retain UDP's agility while addressing the shortcomings of traditional transport mechanisms.

As internet demands outgrow TCP's limitations—particularly in latency and head-of-line blocking—the industry requires a transformation. The QUIC protocol emerges as the next-generation transport layer protocol for the Internet.

This chapter delves into QUIC, a modern transport protocol built atop UDP. This chapter details QUIC's key features, including its 0-RTT/1-RTT connection establishment, head-of-line blocking-free stream multiplexing, and integrated TLS 1.3 encryption. It analyzes core mechanisms such as QUIC packet headers, stream-level flow control, and pluggable congestion control. Finally, it introduces the design principles and advantages of MIN-QUIC. A hands-on experiment implementing stream multiplexing using QUIC helps students grasp the protocol's design philosophy and high-performance benefits.

4.1 Introduction to QUIC

Since the rise of the internet in the 1990s, primary internet traffic transmission has relied on protocols such as IPv4, TCP, SSL/TLS, DNS, and HTTP. However, the evolution of these protocols has been relatively slow, with major improvements primarily focused on TCP congestion control algorithms and upgrades to SSL/TLS protocol cipher suites. As communication technology advances, network interaction scenarios have grown increasingly complex, while transmitted content has become larger and more diverse.

H. Li and Z. Bao, *Transport Layer for Computer Networks*,
https://doi.org/10.1007/978-981-95-7374-5_4

Numerous conflicts exist between the traditional internet architecture and emerging user demands. The rigidity of the internet architecture presents a challenging problem, encompassing both the inflexibility of intermediate devices and protocol rigidity. The inflexibility of intermediate devices stems primarily from TCP traffic's long-term dominance across the internet, leading to many network devices being specifically engineered to handle TCP traffic.

For instance, some firewalls permit only TCP traffic on ports 80 and 443, while certain NAT gateways require modifying transport layer headers during network address translation. These specialized devices make optimizing or modifying TCP protocols exceptionally difficult and may prevent non-TCP traffic from transmitting properly. Protocol rigidity stems from TCP being implemented at the operating system kernel level, necessitating kernel updates for any TCP optimization or enhancement. This makes updating the TCP protocol stack exceptionally difficult.

For transport layer protocols, issues like lengthy connection-establishment handshakes and head-of-line blocking degrade user experience. HTTP/1.0, HTTP/1.1, and HTTP/2 all rely on TCP for transmission and TLS for encryption. However, establishing a TCP connection requires a three-way handshake, and TLS also necessitates its own handshake. Even with optimizations, a single connection handshake requires at least one RTT (Round-Trip Time) to complete, introducing a 1 RTT delay. This handshake latency significantly impacts user experience, particularly in short-connection scenarios, and cannot be eliminated.

Head-of-line blocking occurs in protocols like TCP and TLS when a packet is lost or delayed. All preceding packets must wait for retransmission or acknowledgment, blocking subsequent packets and degrading overall connection efficiency and performance. This blocking problem is particularly pronounced in high-latency, high-packet-loss networks, compromising the real-time nature and stability of network transmission.

Against this backdrop, Google introduced the QUIC protocol, an abbreviation for Quick UDP Internet Connections (standardized by the IETF) [1]. QUIC integrates TLS (Transport Layer Security) 1.3 directly into the transport layer, eliminating the traditional layering between TCP and TLS and enabling secure session establishment within a single handshake.

QUIC utilizes UDP as its underlying transport protocol. Although QUIC is built on UDP, it defines its own cryptographic handshake and connection state independent of the operating system. This design avoids TCP's kernel-level constraints, but QUIC still performs a secure handshake rather than eliminating it. At the application layer, QUIC achieves reliability comparable to TCP and security akin to TLS. QUIC provides its own transport-layer multiplexing mechanism and serves as the foundation of HTTP/3, rather than HTTP/2. This effectively enhances network transmission efficiency and performance. Furthermore, QUIC bypasses limitations imposed by operating systems and intermediary devices. As long as both client and server applications support QUIC, they can leverage it for efficient network transmission.

QUIC incorporates several innovative technologies. For instance, it performs encryption and authentication during connection establishment to minimize round-trip delays. Additionally, it employs multiplexing over a single connection, providing dedicated streams for each request/response to enhance data transfer efficiency. QUIC packet protection encrypts and authenticates the payload and most header fields, except for a small set of bits required for routing and version negotiation, such as the first byte of Long Headers and length-prefixed connection IDs. To avoid retransmission ambiguity, it uses unique packet numbers and leverages explicit signaling in ACKs for precise round-trip delay measurement. Furthermore, QUIC identifies connections using connection IDs instead of IP quintuplets, enabling connections to migrate across IP addresses. QUIC also provides flow control to prevent individual streams from exhausting the receiver's buffers. Figure 4.1 shows the QUIC transport protocol.

Being UDP-based, QUIC bypasses limitations of traditional kernel implementations and intermediary devices. Deployment is achievable whenever both client and

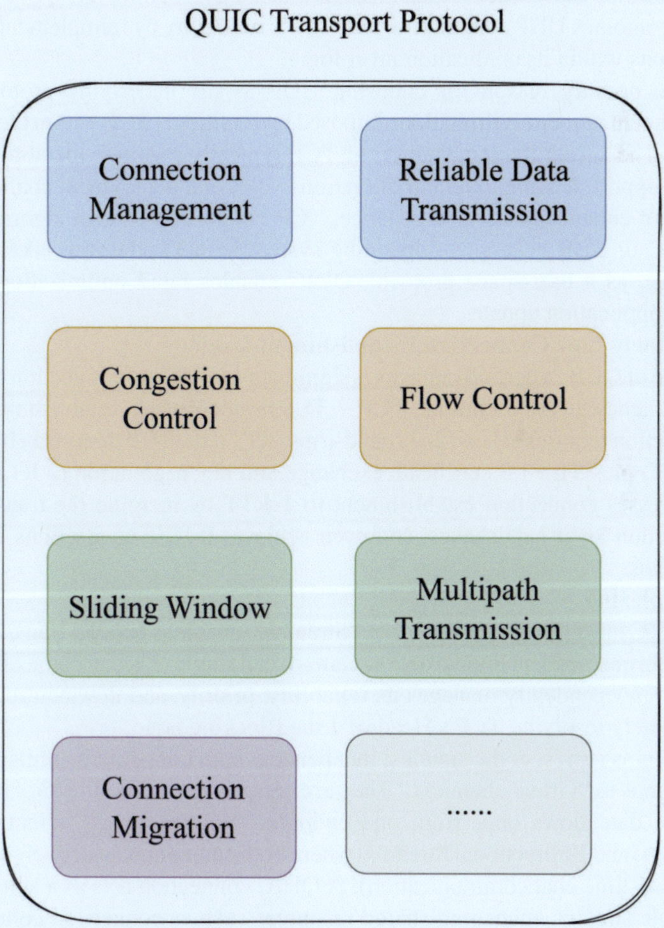

Fig. 4.1 QUIC transport protocol

server applications support QUIC. More significantly, the IETF has standardized QUIC as the underlying transport protocol for HTTP/3, establishing it as a critical infrastructure for the future of the Internet [2].

4.1.1 Fundamental Characteristics of QUIC

1. **Efficient Transmission Architecture Based on UDP**

   QUIC (Quick UDP Internet Connections) is a novel transport protocol introduced by Google in 2012. Its core design philosophy is to build an efficient, reliable, and secure transport layer framework using the UDP protocol. Traditionally, UDP is regarded as an unreliable transport protocol lacking flow control, congestion control, and packet retransmission mechanisms. However, QUIC successfully combines UDP's flexibility with TCP's reliability by reimplementing these functions within its application layer logic.

   The primary reason for choosing UDP as the underlying protocol is to circumvent numerous limitations imposed by traditional TCP within the protocol stack. The kernel implementation of TCP typically requires operating system-level support, leading to lengthy iteration cycles and deployment challenges for protocol enhancements. For instance, TCP congestion control algorithms like CUBIC or BBR necessitate operating system kernel updates to take effect. In contrast, as a user-space protocol, QUIC enables rapid optimization through direct application updates.
2. **Extremely Low Connection Establishment Latency**

   One of QUIC's core advantages is significantly reducing connection establishment latency. In the traditional TCP + TLS protocol stack, establishing a secure connection requires at least 2–3 round-trips (RTT): the TCP three-way handshake (1 RTT) plus TLS 1.2 certificate exchange and key negotiation (2 RTT). QUIC compresses connection establishment to 1 RTT by merging the transport and encryption layer handshakes, and even achieves 0-RTT connections in certain scenarios.
3. **Multiplexing**

   QUIC introduces the concept of "Streams," enabling parallel transmission of multiple independent logical data streams over a single physical connection. Each stream independently manages its reliability, priority, and flow control, thereby completely resolving TCP's Head-of-Line Blocking issue.

   Streams represent the smallest independent data transmission units in QUIC, analogous to "virtual channels." They are categorized as Unidirectional Streams (where data flows only from one endpoint to another, e.g., client-to-server requests) and Bidirectional Streams (where both endpoints can actively send data, e.g., real-time chat communication). A QUIC connection acts as a container for multiple streams, managing shared resources such as congestion control state, encryption keys, and connection migration identifiers. All streams share the same

UDP port and encryption context. Underlying this, frame multiplexing encapsulates data from different streams within a single UDP packet, enabling "multiple streams over a single connection."

While HTTP/2 also supports multiplexing, it relies on the underlying TCP protocol. TCP's byte-stream model requires data to arrive strictly in sequence. If any TCP packet is lost, all subsequent data (even from different HTTP streams) becomes blocked. In contrast, QUIC implements multiplexing at the transport layer. Packet loss affects only the current stream, allowing data from other streams to continue processing.

4. **No Head-of-Line Blocking**

   Head-of-Line Blocking (HOL Blocking) is a major performance bottleneck in traditional TCP. When a packet is lost in the TCP channel, the receiver must wait for its retransmission before passing subsequent data to the application layer. This strict sequentially causes severe performance degradation in high-loss or high-latency networks.

   QUIC operates over UDP, eliminating TCP's head-of-line blocking. Its stream-based transmission ensures data frames for each stream can arrive out of order, with the receiver reassembling data per stream. Packet-level out-of-order processing: QUIC packets may contain frames from multiple streams, allowing the receiver to immediately process frames unaffected by packet loss.

   Head-of-Line Blocking (HOL Blocking) is a major performance bottleneck in traditional TCP. When a packet is lost in the TCP channel, the receiver must wait for its retransmission before passing subsequent data to the application layer. This strict sequentially causes severe performance degradation in high-loss or high-latency networks.

   QUIC operates over UDP, eliminating TCP's head-of-line blocking. Its stream-based transmission ensures data frames for each stream can arrive out of order, with the receiver reassembling data per stream. Packet-level out-of-order processing: QUIC packets may contain frames from multiple streams, allowing the receiver to immediately process frames unaffected by packet loss.

5. **Improved Congestion Control**

   QUIC employs a pluggable congestion control mechanism. This approach breaks free from the rigid kernel-level constraints of traditional TCP, enabling flexible algorithm replacement and dynamic optimization through its pluggable architecture. This ensures efficient bandwidth utilization and low-latency transmission across diverse network scenarios.

   TCP congestion control is implemented in kernel mode, requiring system parameters to alter algorithms. In contrast, QUIC's congestion control operates in user mode, granting greater flexibility. Typically running in user space (e.g., Chrome browser, Cloudflare proxy nodes), the QUIC protocol stack allows developers to bypass OS kernel constraints for rapid iteration of congestion control algorithms. Beyond algorithms like CUIBIC, BRR, and RENO, developers can implement novel algorithms tailored to specific scenarios.

6. **Connection Migration**

   Traditional TCP connections heavily rely on the quadruple (source IP, source port, destination IP, destination port). When a client's IP or port changes (e.g., switching from Wi-Fi to cellular), TCP connections must be reestablished. QUIC introduces a Connection ID to enable true connection migration. This mechanism decouples connections from network addresses, allowing QUIC connections to seamlessly migrate across network environments without reconnecting.

   Each endpoint selects its own Connection IDs, which are opaque identifiers without any requirement for global uniqueness, and may issue multiple CIDs through NEW_CONNECTION_ID frames. Even if the client IP or port changes, the server can still recognize it as the same connection as long as the Connection ID remains unchanged. This mechanism is particularly critical for mobile devices, ensuring uninterrupted video streaming during network switches in certain scenarios.

4.1.2 Key Features of QUIC

Building upon UDP's connectionless and fast transmission framework, the QUIC protocol innovatively implements core TCP reliability features while achieving significant breakthroughs in performance and flexibility. Currently, QUIC serves as the default transport layer foundation for HTTP/3. Its design aims not only to replace the traditional TCP + TLS + HTTP/2 protocol stack but also to deliver lower latency and higher robustness in complex network environments [3]. The following sections detail its capabilities across four key areas: reliable transmission, flow control, congestion control, and multiplexing:

1. **Reliable Transmission**

   QUIC achieves reliable transmission over UDP. Each packet is assigned a unique, strictly incrementing sequence number, even when retransmitted. This unique numbering ensures that if Packet N is lost, its retransmitted counterpart will have a sequence number greater than N. This design eliminates TCP's "retransmission ambiguity" issue, enabling more precise RTT (Round-Trip Time) calculation and optimizing timeout retransmission strategies.

   Each QUIC packet carries a monotonically increasing Packet Number, but this value is not a fixed 64-bit field on the wire; instead, the sender encodes it using 1, 2, or 4 bytes as indicated by the Packet Number Length bits in the packet header, while the full packet number is reconstructed internally to maintain strict ordering. Upon reception, the endpoint reconstructs the packet number space, allowing it to buffer and process packets that arrive out of order, and uses ACK frames—which report the largest acknowledged packet number along with any missing ranges—to accurately detect packet loss without retransmission ambiguity.
2. **Flow Control**

   Similar to TCP flow control, QUIC's flow control is one of its core features. It aims to balance sender and receiver processing capabilities through a layered, dynamic window management mechanism, preventing data overload or resource contention while enhancing transmission efficiency and reliability.

QUIC operates over UDP, which lacks built-in flow control. Consequently, QUIC implements its own flow control mechanism. While the sliding window conditions differ slightly from TCP, data within the same stream must remain ordered to ensure reliable transmission. Therefore, packet loss within a single stream prevents the window from sliding.

QUIC's sliding window operates on two levels:

Connection-level window: The MAX_DATA frame limits the maximum unacknowledged data across the entire connection (e.g., an initial window of 1 MB).

Stream-level window: Each stream (e.g., video stream, control command stream) independently limits data volume via the MAX_STREAM_DATA frame (e.g., an initial 512 KB per stream).

3. **Congestion Control**

QUIC's congestion control is a core design feature, dynamically adjusting data transmission rates to balance network load, maximize throughput, reduce latency, and prevent network congestion failures. Compared to traditional TCP, QUIC's congestion control offers greater flexibility and adaptability, performing particularly well in complex network environments (e.g., high packet loss, high latency, multipath). QUIC's congestion control continuously monitors network conditions (bandwidth, latency, packet loss rate) to dynamically adjust data transmission rates, preventing network overload. Its core objectives are maximizing throughput while maintaining network fairness (bandwidth sharing among streams) and low latency. With the adoption of HTTP/3, QUIC congestion control is propelling the internet transport layer into a new era of "adaptive and intelligent" operation.

4. **Multiplexing**

QUIC's multiplexing is one of its core features. By transmitting multiple independent logical data streams (Streams) concurrently over a single physical connection, it significantly enhances transmission efficiency, reduces latency, and resolves the traditional TCP head-of-line blocking issue.

HTTP/1.1 establishes a separate TCP connection for each request, leading to a connection explosion (e.g., browsers default to 6 concurrent connections). While HTTP/2 supports multiplexing, it relies on the maintenance overhead of persistent connections.

In QUIC, all requests (e.g., multiple resources in HTTP/3) are transmitted through multiple streams over a single QUIC connection, reducing handshake overhead and memory consumption. HTTP/3 leverages QUIC's multiplexing as its underlying foundation, mapping each resource request (HTML, CSS, JS, images) to a dedicated stream for true parallel transmission. Currently, many RPC protocols utilize HTTP/2 multiplexing at their core. With QUIC's growing adoption, we anticipate the emergence of various protocols built upon HTTP/3 in future.

4.2 QUIC Header Structure Analysis

HTTP/3 messages are carried as payload inside QUIC STREAM frames; HTTP/3 frames (including headers encoded via QPACK) are placed inside stream payloads. Figure 4.2 shows the HTTP/3 header.

QUIC packets are encapsulated within UDP datagrams. Each QUIC packet begins with a Packet Header, which specifies how the packet should be interpreted, protected, and associated with a particular connection. QUIC defines two types of packet headers: Long Headers and Short Headers. Long Headers are used during connection establishment and version negotiation, while Short Headers are used for most packets after the handshake is complete.

1. **Packet Header**

   In QUIC protocol datagrams, each packet begins with a Packet Header that describes critical information such as packet type, connection identifier, and sequence number. Depending on the usage phase, QUIC packet headers come in two forms: Long Header and Short Header. The Long Header is primarily used for connection establishment and version negotiation, while the Short Header is used for regular data transmission after connection establishment. Figure 4.3 shows the QUIC packet header.

   Long Header packets are used during the initial stages of a connection, when version negotiation, cryptographic handshake, or address validation is taking place. A Long Header packet begins with a fixed-format first byte, followed by version information and length-prefixed connection IDs.

   (1) Header Form (1 bit): Always set to 1 to indicate a Long Header.
   (2) Fixed Bit (1 bit): Always set to 1 to indicate a valid QUIC packet.
   (3) Long Packet Type (2 bits): Defines the long header type, e.g.:

   - 0x00: Initial Packet, carrying initial encrypted data and TLS ClientHello.
   - 0x01: 0-RTT Packet, used to send early data during session resumption.
   - 0x02: Handshake Packet, used to transmit TLS handshake data.

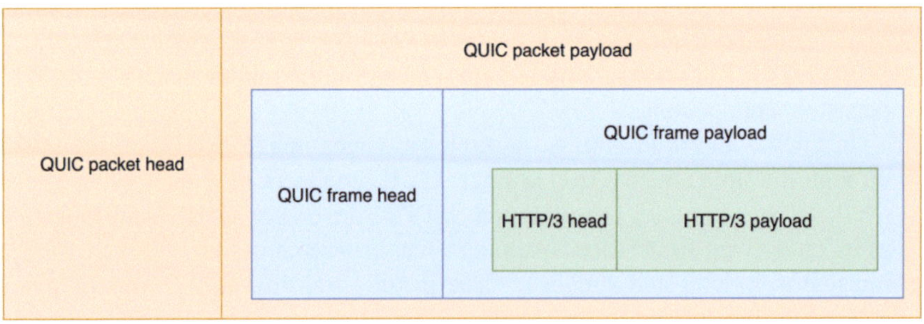

Fig. 4.2 HTTP3 header

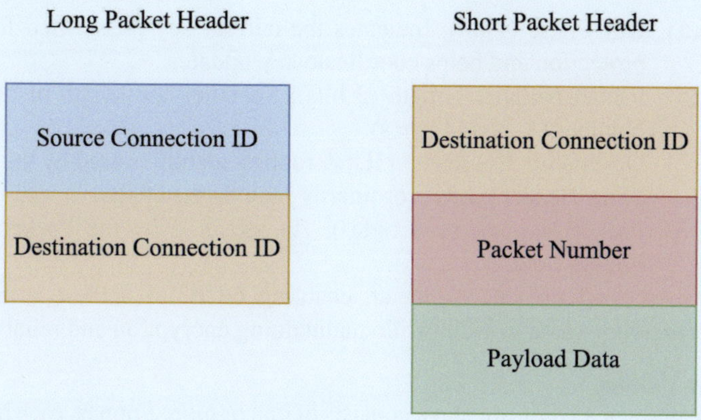

Fig. 4.3 QUIC packet header

- 0x03: Retry Packet, used for server address verification.

(4) Reserved Bits (Reserved, 2 bits): Unused, default set to 0.
(5) Packet Number Length (2 bits): Encodes the byte length of the Packet Number (1, 2, or 4 bytes).
(6) Version (4 bytes): Identifies the QUIC protocol version, e.g., 0 × 00,000,001 denotes IETF QUIC v1.
(7) Destination Connection ID (DCID, variable length): Recipient's connection identifier for unique connection identification.
(8) Source Connection ID (SCID, variable length): Sender's connection identifier.
(9) Packet Number (1–4 bytes): Sequence number assigned to the packet, supporting out-of-order reassembly and packet loss detection. QUIC design allows flexible selection of sequence number length to balance space overhead and robustness across different network environments.
(10) **Destination Connection ID Length (1 byte)** followed by the **Destination Connection ID**.
(11) **Source Connection ID Length (1 byte)** followed by the **Source Connection ID**.

During initial connection, the client sends an Initial Packet containing the long header, carrying the TLS Client Hello and initial encrypted data.

Once the handshake completes, QUIC endpoints switch to the Short Header format for nearly all packets. Short Header packets are more compact and optimized for encrypted data transmission.

(1) Header Form (1 bit): Always set to 0 for Short Header.
(2) Fixed Bit (1 bit): Always set to 1.
(3) Spin Bit (1 bit): Optional latency-measurement bit; its use is path-dependent.
(4) Reserved Bits (2 bits): Must be set to 00.

(5) Key Phase (1 bit): Indicates the current key phase used for packet protection and helps coordinate key updates.
(6) Packet Number Length (2 bits): Specifies the length of the Packet Number (1, 2, or 4 bytes).
(7) Destination Connection ID: A routing identifier used by the receiver; Short Header packets ordinarily include the DCID.
(8) Packet Number (1–4 bytes): As specified by the Packet Number Length field.

Short-head reduces overhead, enabling QUIC to achieve transmission efficiency close to UDP while maintaining encryption and reliability.

2. **Frame Header**

The body of a QUIC message consists of one or more Frames, each beginning with a Frame Header that indicates the frame type and carries necessary control information. QUIC's design philosophy is "frames as transport units, packets as encapsulation containers." Common frame types include:

STREAM Frame: Carries application data, supports multiplexing, and includes stream ID, offset, and payload.
ACK Frame: Contains acknowledgments from the receiver, including the highest acknowledged sequence number and missing range, used for packet loss detection and RTT estimation.
CRYPTO Frame: Transmits TLS handshake data, equivalent to carrying TLS messages within QUIC.
MAX_DATA and MAX_STREAM_DATA Frame: Used for flow control, limiting the maximum data volume for the entire connection and a single stream, respectively.

Additionally, QUIC defines frame types like PING and NEW_CONNECTION_ID to maintain connection activity and support connection migration.

In summary, QUIC's Packet Header provides an efficient and flexible mechanism for packet identification and connection management, while the Frame Header delivers rich control and data-carrying capabilities. These two components complement each other, enabling QUIC to inherit TCP's reliability advantages while overcoming its scalability and latency limitations.

4.3 Core Mechanisms of QUIC

4.3.1 Connection Establishment and Recovery

One of the core objectives of the QUIC protocol is to optimize the connection establishment and recovery process, reducing latency and enhancing network adaptability. Compared to the traditional TCP/TLS combination, QUIC deeply integrates encryption and authentication mechanisms during connection establishment while supporting more efficient connection recovery capabilities. Figure 4.4 shows the QUIC initial connection process. Figure 4.5 shows the QUIC subsequent connection process.

1. Connection Establishment

   QUIC's initial connection establishment is based on TLS 1.3, typically completed in one round-trip (1-RTT), and supports 0-RTT acceleration by leveraging prior session state to expedite the recovery process. Figure 4.6 shows the 1-RTT initial handshake process.

   (1) 1-RTT Initial Handshake

   During the initial connection establishment, the client initiates the handshake with an Initial packet containing a TLS ClientHello message and necessary QUIC transport parameters. The ClientHello carries random numbers, key exchange parameters, supported ciphersuites, and the client's

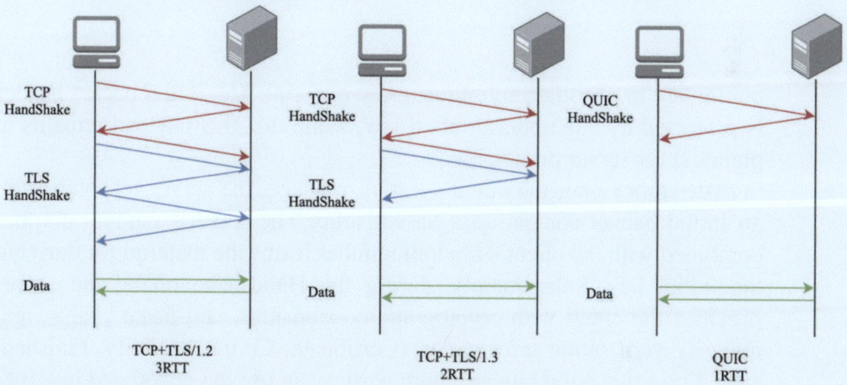

Fig. 4.4 QUIC initial connection

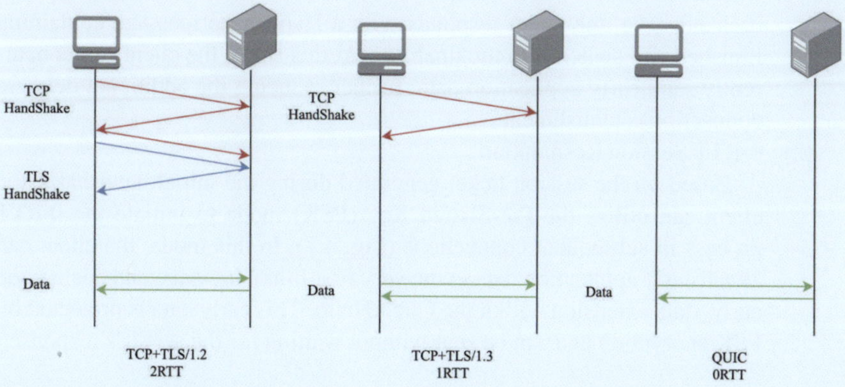

Fig. 4.5 QUIC subsequent connection

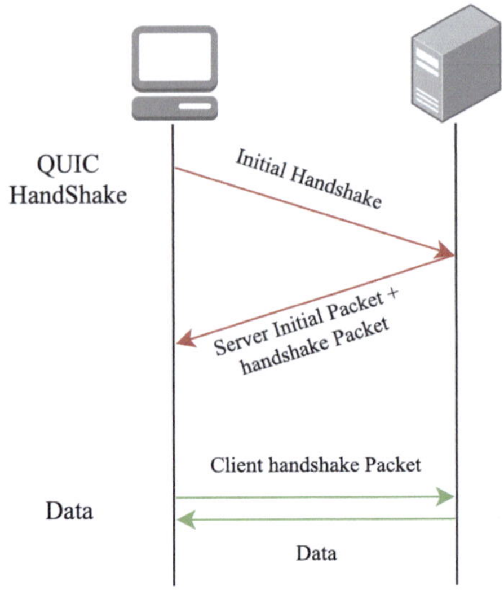

Fig. 4.6 1-RTT initial handshake

public key to negotiate subsequent key material. The initial packet header is protected by a temporary initial key, while the TLS payload remains in plaintext for server processing.

After processing the client's initial message, the server responds with an Initial packet containing a ServerHello. The server's random number combined with the client's random number forms the material for deriving the initial key. Subsequently, during the Handshake phase, the server provides the client with cryptographic extensions, certificate chains, and integrity verification information (Certificate, CertificateVerify, Finished, etc.). From this point onward, both parties can use the negotiated intermediate key for encrypted communication.

During the handshake, the server also sends session tickets to the client, which can be stored for future fast recovery. After the server completes its handshake, the client responds with a Handshake message containing Finished and switches to the final key. At this stage, the client can concurrently send early application data, further reducing the additional delay in connection establishment.

(2) 0-RTT Session Resumption

Based on the session ticket generated during the initial handshake, the client can utilize the Pre-Shared Key (PSK) mode to initiate the 0-RTT process in subsequent connections (Fig. 4.7). In this mode, the client can attach early application data to the very first Initial message and declare the early_data extension within the ClientHello. This early data is protected by PSK encryption and can be sent without waiting for the server's response.

Fig. 4.7 0-RTT session resumption

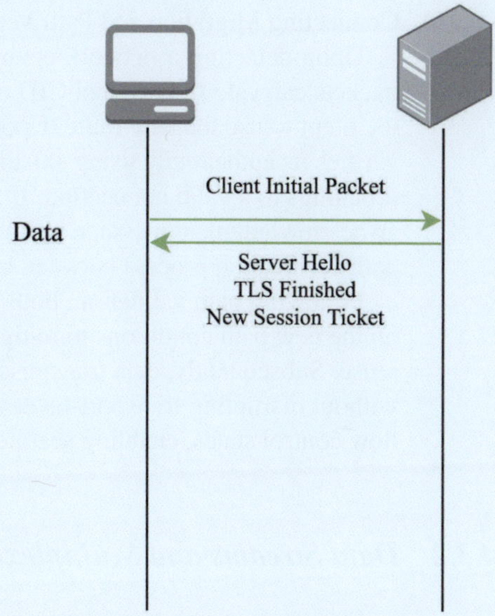

Upon receiving the ClientHello containing the ticket, the server validates the ticket's validity and the PSK's legitimacy. If validation succeeds, the server directly restores the corresponding encryption context and accepts the early data, but only for idempotent requests to prevent replay attacks. Subsequently, the server uses a new random number to derive updated key material and completes the transmission of the Finished message. Upon receiving the server's confirmation, the client switches to the final key, concluding the handshake.

2. Connection Recovery

Traditional TCP connections rely on a quadruple to identify connection state. When a client's access path changes (e.g., IP or port alteration), the original connection becomes unusable and must be reestablished. QUIC eliminates this limitation by introducing a path-independent Connection ID (CID), enabling connections to persist after network path changes and supporting seamless migration.

(1) The Function of the Connection ID

During the handshake phase, both parties negotiate multiple randomly generated CIDs as logical identifiers for the connection. This identifier is independent of the underlying address and can be switched using the NEW_CONNECTION_ID frame when necessary. The server does not need to maintain a state mapping based on the quadruple; instead, it identifies the connection context using the CID provided by the client. This prevents connections from being reset due to path changes.

(2) Connecting Migration and Path Verification

Upon detecting a network environment change, the client sends probe packets carrying the original CID over the new path to signal to the server its intent to use the new route. Upon receiving the probe packet, the server verifies its authenticity using existing key material and determines whether it belongs to a valid connection. If verification succeeds, the server returns an acknowledgment message via the new path, completing the bidirectional path verification process between both parties.

Following path validation, both parties update the ephemeral key based on the new path conditions to mitigate risks associated with cross-path key reuse. Subsequently, data transmission resumes over the new network path without disrupting transport-layer context such as congestion windows or flow control states, enabling seamless service migration.

4.3.2 Data Streams and Multiplexing

QUIC employs a design featuring data streams and multiplexing, enabling a single QUIC connection to simultaneously carry multiple independent logical channels. This mechanism effectively eliminates the head-of-line blocking issue that frequently occurs in traditional TCP during multiplexing scenarios, thereby significantly improving transmission efficiency.

In QUIC, a stream is an independent logical unit used to transmit application-layer data, such as different HTTP requests, responses, or server-pushed content. As shown in Fig. 4.8, multiple streams can coexist within a single QUIC connection without interfering with each other. Data within each stream must be kept in order and arrive sequentially, but data fragments from different streams can be transmitted in parallel and interleaved.

Streams are categorized as Unidirectional Streams, where data flows only from the initiating end (e.g., client sends requests, server sends server-push), and Bidirectional Streams, where data flows bidirectionally between both ends (e.g., HTTP request-response pairs). Either connection endpoint can establish either type of stream. Streams can transmit data in parallel, interleaved, and can be canceled.

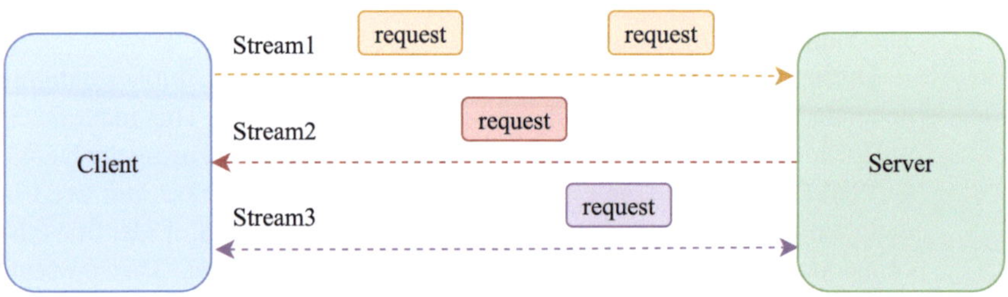

Fig. 4.8 QUIC stream

Stream IDs are encoded as QUIC variable-length integers (variant). The low-order two bits indicate initiator and direction (bit0 = initiator, bit1 = direction), but stream IDs are not fixed to 62 bits. The least significant two bits of the stream ID identify the stream type (unidirectional or bidirectional) and the stream initiator. The least significant bit (0 × 1) of the stream ID identifies the initiator: clients initiate even-numbered streams (least significant bit 0), while servers initiate odd-numbered streams (least significant bit 1). The second bit (0 × 2) identifies unidirectional/bidirectional streams. Stream IDs use QUIC variable-length integers. The least significant bit (0 × 1) identifies the initiator (0 = client, 1 = server), and the second bit (0 × 2) identifies directionality (0 = bidirectional, 1 = unidirectional).

4.3.3 Flow Control and Window Mechanism

QUIC operates over UDP, which lacks built-in flow control. Consequently, QUIC implements its own flow control mechanism. While the sliding window conditions differ slightly from TCP, data within the same stream must remain ordered to ensure reliable transmission. Therefore, packet loss within a single stream prevents the window from sliding. In TCP, the left boundary of the receive window only advances when all preceding segments have been received. If subsequent bytes are received while preceding ones remain unacknowledged, the window does not move. In QUIC, the left boundary's advancement depends on the maximum number of out-of-order bytes received.

QUIC implements two levels of flow control: Stream-level and Connection-level. These two levels work together to ensure stable and efficient data transmission.

Figure 4.9 shows stream-level flow control. Stream-level flow control forms the foundational layer of QUIC's flow control mechanism. In QUIC, a Stream can be simply understood as an HTTP request. Each Stream maintains an independent sliding window, enabling distinct flow control for each Stream. This design prevents a single Stream from consuming the entire connection's receive buffer. For instance, in a website accessed by multiple users simultaneously, each user's request can be treated as an independent Stream. Without stream-level flow control, a single user could initiate numerous requests, monopolizing a large portion of the receive buffer resources and thereby impacting the processing of other users' requests. By setting an independent sliding window for each stream, the system can allocate receive buffer resources reasonably based on each stream's actual demand and network conditions. This ensures that data transmission for each stream remains within controllable limits, preventing performance degradation of the entire connection due to excessive usage by a single stream.

Connection-level flow control, however, operates from the perspective of the entire connection, limiting the total combined byte count of all streams within it. Its purpose is to prevent the sender from exceeding the connection's buffer capacity. In a busy network server where numerous streams transmit data simultaneously, without connection-level flow control, the sender might send data unrestrainedly, filling the

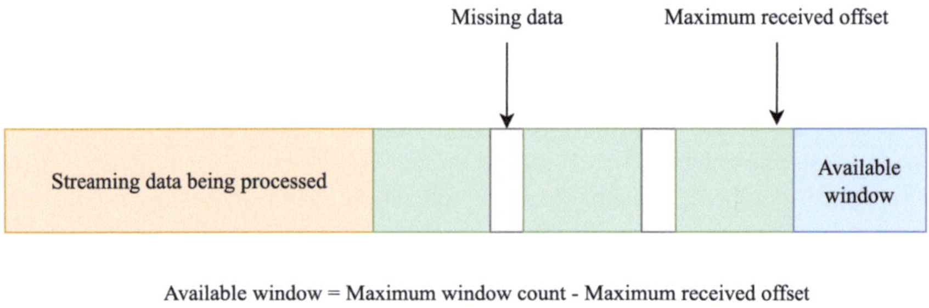

Fig. 4.9 Stream-level flow control

receiver's buffer and causing issues like data loss or transmission delays. By implementing connection-level flow control, the system monitors the aggregate data transmission across all streams. When approaching the connection's buffer capacity, it promptly notifies the sender to reduce data transmission, ensuring stable connection operation and preventing transmission failures caused by buffer overflow.

QUIC's flow control and window mechanisms are designed with full consideration for UDP-based transmission characteristics and practical network communication needs. Through dual-level flow control (Stream and Connection) and an independent Stream sliding window mechanism, it achieves efficient and reliable data transmission. Compared to HTTP/2's flow control mechanism, QUIC offers significant advantages in concurrent performance and resource utilization, providing a more powerful and flexible transmission solution for modern network applications. As network technologies continue to evolve, these characteristics of QUIC are poised for broader adoption across more domains, driving network communication toward higher performance and greater stability.

4.3.4 Congestion Control

The congestion control mechanism of the QUIC protocol is central to its efficient transmission performance. It aims to prevent network congestion caused by excessive data transmission through dynamic adjustment of the data sending rate. This enhances network bandwidth utilization, reduces data loss, and optimizes transmission performance. Building upon TCP's congestion control mechanism, QUIC has been optimized for low latency and efficient transmission, particularly in terms of flexibility, pluggability, and network adaptability.

1. **Fundamental Principles of Congestion Control**

   QUIC employs a congestion window to limit the sender's data transmission rate. The size of this window dynamically adjusts based on network feedback, ensuring the sender does not exceed the network's capacity. The sender can only gradually expand the congestion window to allow more data transmission after receiving an ACK confirmation. Its congestion control mechanism is based on four classic TCP algorithms: Slow Start, Congestion Avoidance, Fast Recovery, and Fast Retransmit.

- **Slow Start**: During the initial phase of a connection, QUIC's congestion window (CWND) begins at a small initial value. For each acknowledgment (ACK) received, the congestion window doubles, gradually increasing the transmission rate. This process can quickly identify the network's maximum bandwidth, but may also cause short-term network congestion.
- **Congestion Avoidance**: When QUIC detects network congestion signals (such as packet loss or increased latency), it enters the congestion avoidance phase. The congestion window growth rate slows down, preventing excessive transmission rate increases and thereby avoiding severe network congestion.
- **Fast Recovery**: Upon detecting packet loss, QUIC enters the fast recovery phase. It reduces the transmission rate by shrinking the congestion window and strives to quickly restore the transmission rate to pre-loss levels. Fast recovery enables QUIC to respond swiftly to packet loss events and minimize the impact of network congestion.
- **Fast Retransmit**: QUIC utilizes lost ACK detection to trigger its fast retransmit mechanism. Upon detecting three consecutive duplicate ACKs, the sender assumes a packet loss and immediately retransmits the missing packet without waiting for a timeout. This mechanism reduces retransmission delays and accelerates data recovery after packet loss.

2. **Supported Congestion Control Algorithms**

   QUIC defaults to the Cubic algorithm from TCP for congestion control and supports multiple alternative algorithms, including CubicBytes, Reno, RenoBytes, BBR (Bottleneck Bandwidth and Round-trip time), and PCC (Proportional Integral Controller). These algorithms can be flexibly selected based on varying network conditions and application requirements.

- **Cubic**: As QUIC's default algorithm, Cubic is suitable for high-bandwidth, high-latency networks. It prevents network congestion by employing an exponentially growing window function.
- **BBR**: The BBR algorithm dynamically adjusts the transmission rate by real-time estimation of bandwidth and latency. It is particularly well-suited for low-latency, high-bandwidth networks, enabling more efficient utilization of network resources.

3. **Plug-and-Play Flexibility of Congestion Control**

   QUIC's congestion control algorithms are pluggable, enabling the application layer to flexibly select, change, or disable different algorithms. This marks a significant departure from traditional TCP, whose congestion control requires operating system kernel support, resulting in lengthy update cycles and high deployment costs. QUIC allows applications to dynamically choose suitable algorithms based on network conditions, application needs, or big data analysis without service interruption.

- Application-Level Control: Different applications can utilize distinct congestion control algorithms based on their characteristics. Even a single server can employ different algorithms for different connections.
- No Operating System Support Required: QUIC's congestion control mechanism can be implemented directly at the application layer, eliminating the need for operating system or kernel upgrades and maintenance.
- Zero-Downtime Switching: QUIC can switch congestion control algorithms without service interruption, providing exceptional flexibility.

4. **Distinction Between Congestion Control and Flow Control**

   Congestion control and flow control are two independent yet collaborative mechanisms. While both limit data transmission, their focus and control targets differ:

   Flow control primarily protects the receiver, ensuring its buffers do not overflow. QUIC's flow control mechanism manages receiver buffer sizes through stream-level and connection-level flow control. The flow-level and connection-level traffic control windows are managed by the receiver, which periodically notifies the sender of the available window size. Traffic control focuses on the receiver's capacity and resources, ensuring the sender does not transmit excessive data beyond the receiver's processing capabilities.

   Unlike traffic control, congestion control aims to protect the network path by preventing network congestion caused by the sender transmitting data too rapidly. QUIC's congestion control adjusts the transmission rate by detecting packet loss and latency, preventing excessive data transmission that could cause network congestion. It focuses on the network's bandwidth and latency, ensuring data flow does not impose excessive load across the entire network path.

   In short, flow control protects the receiver's buffer, while congestion control safeguards the entire network path from congestion. These two mechanisms work together to ensure QUIC delivers stable and efficient transmission under varying network conditions.

4.3.5 Acknowledgment and Retransmission Mechanism

In the QUIC protocol, the acknowledgment and retransmission system serves as the core module ensuring reliable data transmission. It not only handles packet loss and reduces latency but also plays a crucial role in regulating network congestion and overall transmission performance. The design objective is to enable QUIC to maintain high efficiency and stability even in weak network environments.

1. Acknowledgment Mechanism

   QUIC uses ACK frames to report information about successfully received packets. Whenever the receiver acquires a new packet, it sends an ACK frame to inform the sender which packets have been received and which are still missing.

   QUIC's acknowledgment mechanism features the following characteristics:

(1) Batch Acknowledgment: ACK frames can carry multiple non-contiguous acknowledgment segments (up to 256), enabling the batch reporting of packet reception across multiple batches. Compared to TCP's segment-by-segment acknowledgment approach, QUIC's batch acknowledgment significantly reduces feedback overhead. This proves particularly effective in scenarios with network jitter or frequent packet loss, substantially improving acknowledgment efficiency.
(2) Rapid Acknowledgment: Upon receiving a data packet, QUIC immediately sends an ACK without waiting for the application layer to complete processing. This allows the sender to obtain the latest network status information in the shortest possible time, enabling rapid adjustments to congestion control strategies or transmission rates. Consequently, it reduces additional waiting caused by processing delays.
(3) Precise ACK Delay Calculation: The ACK frame explicitly records the delay introduced when the receiver sends an ACK (Ack Delay) and incorporates this into RTT calculations. Unlike TCP, which directly uses the arrival time of ACKs to estimate RTT, QUIC eliminates errors caused by ACK processing delays. This results in more accurate RTT measurements, leading to more stable congestion control and preventing over-transmission or bandwidth waste caused by inaccurate estimates.

2. Retransmission Mechanism

QUIC completely resolves the ambiguity issues in TCP retransmission through Packet Number and its stream-based design, enabling QUIC to efficiently and accurately identify and retransmit lost packets [4].

Within the design scope of the QUIC protocol, all transmitted packets—even those representing retransmissions of previously lost packets—are assigned a unique Packet Number that strictly follows a monotonically increasing sequence. This precise numbering strategy effectively circumvents the inherent ambiguity issues that can arise in traditional TCP protocols when retransmitted segments use identical sequence numbers.

Specifically, in a TCP environment, a lost packet retransmitted may carry the same sequence number as the original packet. This forces the receiver to face the dilemma of distinguishing whether the received packet is the initial transmission or a subsequent retransmission copy during parsing.

In contrast, the QUIC protocol assigns a unique and entirely new number to each packet. Even during retransmission, the new packet receives a fresh Packet Number. This fundamentally ensures accurate tracking of the data stream and guarantees clarity and reliability in subsequent processing stages.

QUIC employs a fast retransmission strategy for packet loss recovery that is similar to TCP but more efficient. When the sender receives multiple duplicate acknowledgments for the same data segment, it infers that the packet corresponding to that Packet Number is lost and immediately triggers a retransmission without relying on timeout events as recovery conditions. This mechanism significantly shortens the reaction interval between packet loss detection and compensation, avoiding the recovery lag caused by excessive RTO in traditional TCP.

After completing retransmissions, QUIC dynamically adjusts the transmission rate using its congestion control algorithm, enabling the transfer rate to quickly return to the stable state prior to packet loss. This recovery method is particularly effective on links with high packet loss rates or high latency, mitigating throughput fluctuations while maintaining link utilization. Compared to TCP, it offers faster bandwidth recovery and smoother performance.

Furthermore, QUIC introduces a stream offset structure based on offset values to ensure strict in-stream data reordering. Even when packets arrive out of order or undergo retransmission, the receiver can precisely locate data fragments using the offset, guaranteeing in-stream ordering without relying on connection-level sequence control. This mechanism effectively avoids the cross-segment out-of-order issues caused by retransmissions in TCP, enhancing the determinism and consistency of application-layer data processing.

3. Optimized Retransmission Mechanism versus TCP

   Compared to TCP, QUIC's retransmission mechanism avoids sequence number duplication and retransmission ambiguity through Packet Numbering. This enables more precise packet state tracking and reduces erroneous retransmissions. Its fast retransmission mechanism triggers retransmission after three duplicate ACKs without waiting for timeout counters, significantly accelerating recovery after packet loss. Additionally, QUIC's stream-based design and Stream Offset mechanism ensure data ordering, preventing the out-of-order delivery issues caused by retransmissions in traditional TCP and enhancing transmission stability.

4.4 QUIC Analysis

4.4.1 *Low Latency and Rapid Connection Establishment*

The QUIC protocol achieves revolutionary breakthroughs in low latency and connection establishment speed. Its core innovation lies in deeply integrating the encrypted handshake with transport layer negotiation, leveraging TLS 1.3's streamlined framework to achieve "zero round-trip time" (0-RTT) connection recovery. When a client has previously connected to a server, application data can be carried within the very first packet, reducing handshake latency by over three times compared to traditional TCP + TLS combinations. This mechanism is particularly suited for mobile network handover scenarios—when users reconnect after a brief disconnection in subway tunnels, QUIC can resume video streaming within hundreds of milliseconds, whereas TCP must repeat the entire handshake process. Its broader impact lies in advancing "instant web applications": for example, online document collaboration systems can synchronize editing changes in real time.

4.4.2 Transmission Reliability

Although QUIC is built on UDP, it ensures reliable data transmission by incorporating TCP-like retransmission mechanisms, flow control, and congestion management strategies, preventing data loss and out-of-order delivery. Simultaneously, QUIC integrates encryption as a core protocol component, employing modern cryptographic techniques to encrypt data during the connection establishment phase. This prevents data interception and tampering, providing end-to-end security protection for user data. This design not only guarantees transmission reliability but also enhances network communication security, effectively countering increasingly sophisticated cybersecurity threats.

4.4.3 Adaptability

QUIC's design emphasizes adaptability to dynamic network conditions, with its transmission behavior continuously adjusting based on link status. The protocol framework supports multiple congestion control algorithms, including BBR and CUBIC, enabling real-time selection or adjustment of the optimal control strategy based on metrics such as bandwidth, latency, and jitter. BBR significantly boosts throughput on high-bandwidth, high-speed links, while CUBIC offers more stable convergence characteristics in traditional internet environments. Through flexible support for different algorithms, QUIC maintains optimal transmission performance across heterogeneous networks.

Additionally, QUIC's Connection ID mechanism enables seamless migration across network paths. When endpoints experience address or port changes due to network handoffs, QUIC preserves the original session context without rebuilding connections, thereby avoiding connection interruptions and state resets common in TCP during such transitions.

For data scheduling, QUIC achieves finer-grained resource allocation through multiplexing and stream-level priority control. Streams operate independently, allowing application-defined service priorities to ensure critical tasks (e.g., media streaming) receive transmission resources first. This multi-stream architecture eliminates the contention and blocking common in traditional single-channel models, enabling efficient data distribution even under high concurrency.

4.4.4 Resolving Head-of-Line Blocking

Resolving head-of-line (HoL) blocking represents QUIC's most significant architectural breakthrough. Traditional TCP and HTTP/2 protocols are susceptible to HoL blocking during multiplexing, where packet loss in one stream can block all streams, degrading overall transmission efficiency [5]. QUIC completely eliminates this issue through its independent stream transmission mechanism. In QUIC, each data stream has its own unique identification and acknowledgment, with streams operating independently without interference. Consequently, even if packet loss occurs in one stream, only that stream is affected, while others continue transmitting normally. This design significantly enhances performance, especially in high-packet-loss scenarios.

4.4.5 Potential Compatibility Issues

Despite demonstrating significant advantages in performance and security, QUIC still faces several compatibility and environmental adaptation challenges during widespread deployment. First, certain enterprise-grade firewalls and NAT devices impose strict restrictions on UDP traffic. Under default policies, they often filter non-TCP traffic outright, preventing QUIC from establishing connections normally. Therefore, explicit allow rules for UDP port 443 are typically required in practical deployments; otherwise, intermediary devices may drop traffic, impacting reachability. Additionally, some legacy operating systems (e.g., Windows 7) lack system-level support for QUIC, forcing reliance on browser or application-layer protocol stacks for indirect implementation, which limits both compatibility and performance.

Second, QUIC's standardization history has resulted in some version fragmentation within its protocol family. Early Google QUIC and IETF-standardized QUIC are not entirely consistent in message formats, encryption details, and other aspects, introducing complexity for cross-platform interoperability. Concurrently, since QUIC encapsulates most control information within encrypted packet headers, traditional network analysis tools based on plaintext header structures struggle to directly identify and decode QUIC traffic. Operations teams require specialized decryption tools to perform debugging and monitoring.

Overall, QUIC provides a robust foundation for next-generation internet communications by reducing transmission latency, enhancing link robustness, and introducing a stronger security model. While localized challenges remain in deployment and diagnostics, QUIC is expected to see continued adoption across broader network and application environments as infrastructure evolves and the standardized ecosystem matures.

4.5 MIN-QUIC Protocol

MIN-QUIC is a transport protocol based on multi-identifier network architecture, enabling efficient and reliable data transmission in push-based communication within multi-identifier networks [6]. Inspired by the QUIC protocol, MIN-QUIC incorporates enhancements and innovations tailored to the characteristics of multi-identifier networks. It inherits several outstanding features from QUIC, such as fast handshake,

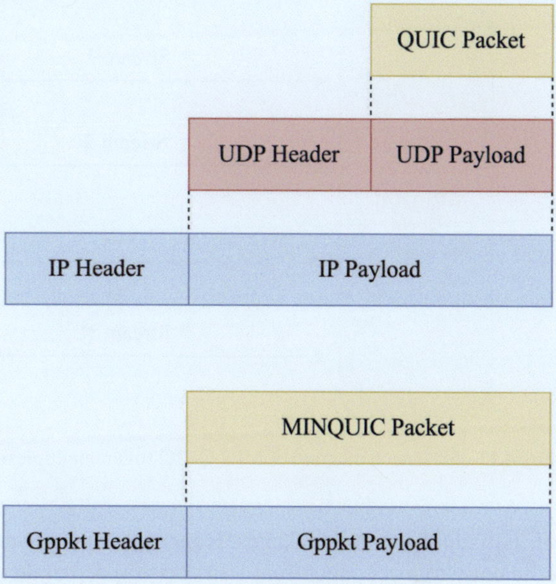

Fig. 4.10 Schematic comparison of MIN-QUIC and QUIC transport packets

multiplexing, pluggable congestion control, and encryption protection. Figure 4.10 shows a schematic comparison of MIN-QUIC and QUIC transport packets.

MIN-QUIC employs MIN packets as its transport layer. Within the MIN-QUIC protocol, two identifiers are required to determine communication endpoints: the local identifier and the peer identifier. The local identifier represents the sender's identity within the network, while the peer identifier denotes the communication partner's identity within the network.

To support session migration and multiplexing, MIN-QUIC introduces concepts analogous to QUIC's connection ID and stream ID: Session ID and Session Stream ID. The Session ID is a randomly generated value identifying a MIN-QUIC session. The Session Stream ID is an incrementing value that identifies the sequence number of a session stream within a session. Both the Session ID and Session Stream ID are carried as identification information within MIN-QUIC packets.

The MIN-QUIC protocol adopts the design of key components from the QUIC protocol, primarily including:

4.5.1 Stream Multiplexing in the MIN-QUIC Protocol

The stream multiplexing module transmits multiple data streams in parallel over a single transport layer connection. This significantly improves network resource utilization and overall data transfer rates while reducing latency and the impact

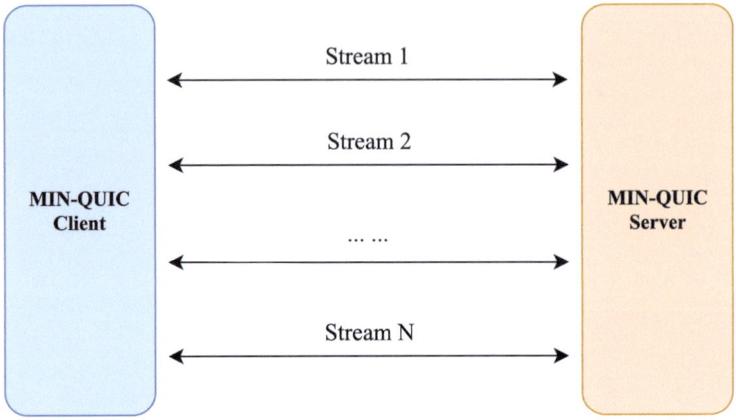

Fig. 4.11 Schematic diagram of MIN-QUIC stream multiplexing mechanism

of individual stream blockages. Consequently, network bandwidth is utilized more efficiently to meet concurrent transmission demands.

The data plane responsibilities in MIN-QUIC are carried out by streams.

The concept of a stream is relatively complex. At the lowest level, a stream is an ordered sequence of bytes from end to end. From a connection layer abstraction perspective, a stream is an independent data channel spanning endpoints. For example, TCP is a byte-stream-oriented protocol. This bidirectional byte stream constitutes a single stream. Since TCP maintains only one stream per connection, it is described as a single connection, single-stream transport layer protocol. In contrast, MIN-QUIC abstracts multiple streams over a single connection, making it a single connection, multi-stream transport layer protocol. This characteristic is known as stream multiplexing. A schematic illustration is shown in Fig. 4.11.

The data structure carrying streams in MIN-QUIC is the stream frame. The stream frame is the smallest unit of transmission. It consists of two parts: the Frame Header and the Frame Body. The Frame Header carries control and metadata for the stream, including Frame Type, Stream ID, Offset, Frame Length, and other parameters. The Frame Body carries the actual data content.

In MIN-QUIC, both the server and client must first establish a stream during the data transmission phase. The party initiating the stream sends a special stream frame called a Stream Creation Frame to create the stream. This Stream Creation Frame can carry data, after which the bidirectional communication channel is opened.

In QUIC, all streams are bidirectional by default. The application layer can implement unidirectional streams by restricting read or write operations on specific streams. Flows are uniquely identified by a 16-bit unsigned integer called the flow ID. To prevent flow ID conflicts between client and server-initiated flows, all client-created flows have a final bit set to 0, while server-created flows have the final bit set to 1. Both parties must generate flow IDs in ascending order.

4.5.2 MIN-QUIC Protocol Connection State Transitions

MIN-QUIC state transitions are divided into two entities: the Client and the Server (Table 4.1). The Server provides services to the Client, transitioning from the Closed state to the Listen state via the listen function call to monitor service requests from the Client. After the Client calls the Dial function to initiate a handshake or an encrypted handshake, it enters the SYN_SEND state. Figure 4.12 shows the MIN-QUIC connection state transition diagram.

Upon receiving the handshake request or encrypted handshake request, the Server transitions to the SYN_RCVD state, sends a SYN-ACK, and waits for the Client's ACK packet. Once the connection is successfully established, data communication commences. Upon completing data transmission, both the Server and Client enter the connection closure phase. The party initiating closure sends a Connection_Close message and transitions to the Closing state. The receiving party can terminate the connection upon receiving the Connection_Close message.

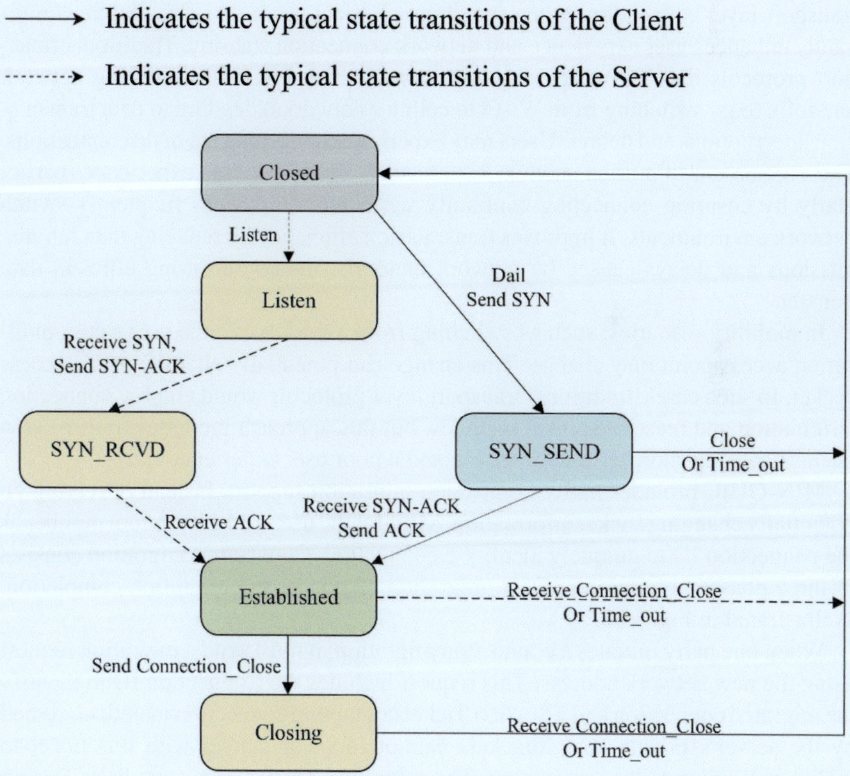

Fig. 4.12 MIN-QUIC connection state transition diagram

Table 4.1 MIN-QUIC state table

Serial number	Status name	Status description
1	Closed	Indicates the connection has been closed
2	Listen	Indicates listening, waiting for the other party to connect
3	SYN_SEND	Indicates actively establishing a connection, first handshake sent
4	SYN_ RCVD	Indicates passively establishing a connection, second handshake sent
5	Established	Indicates the connection has been established
6	Closing	Indicates actively terminating the connection, connection termination message sent

4.5.3 Connection Migration in the MIN-QUIC Protocol

The connection migration module enables devices to maintain uninterrupted transport-layer connections when switching physical networks. This feature significantly enhances user experience and network connection stability. Traditional transport protocols like TCP often require re-establishing connections during network handoffs (e.g., switching from Wi-Fi to cellular networks), leading to data transmission interruptions and delays. Users may experience noticeable lag or disconnections. The connection migration module significantly enhances user experience, particularly by ensuring connection continuity when mobile devices frequently switch network environments. It improves transmission efficiency by reducing data retransmissions and delays caused by network handoffs, thereby ensuring efficient data transfer.

In mobility scenarios, such as switching from Wi-Fi to 5G, the user's communication access point may change. This change can potentially alter the user's access socket. In such cases, traditional transport layer protocols would employ connection termination and reestablishment methods, but this approach increases transmission latency, causing short-term network lag and a poor user experience.

MIN-QUIC provides native connection migration support. Instead of relying on potentially changing socket information, MIN-QUIC uses a 64-bit random number as the connection ID to uniquely identify a connection. Connection migration consists of three phases: migration request, migration response, and migration completion, as illustrated in Fig. 4.13.

When one party initiates a connection migration, it must send a migration request using the new network address. This request includes the Connection ID to identify the migrated connection and a Session Ticket containing connection metadata, signed by the server's private key. Attackers cannot forge or tamper with this ticket to maliciously migrate the connection. The migration request can carry data. During the migration request phase, the initiator should continue listening on the old socket, as the other party may still send data to it. However, the initiator must not use the old socket to send data.

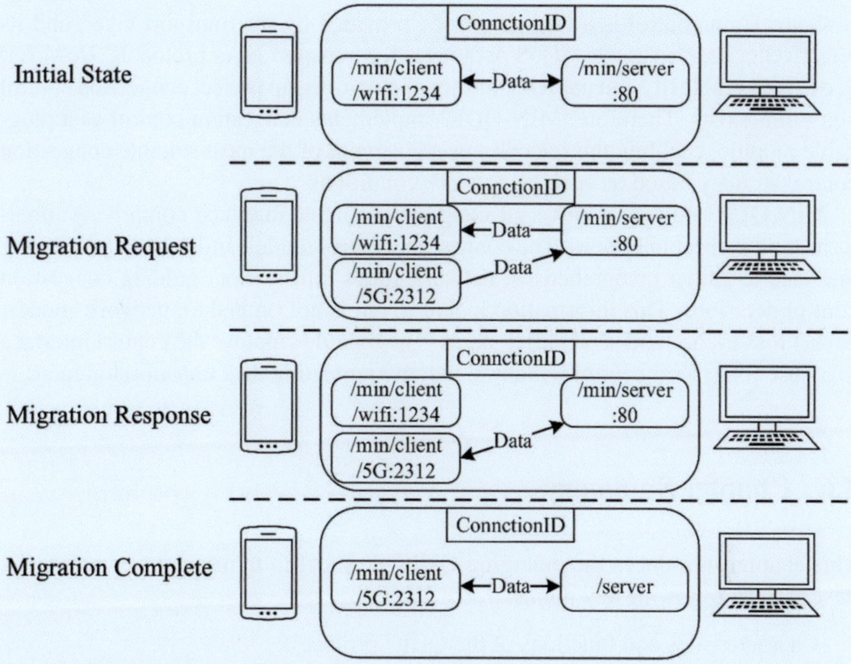

Fig. 4.13 MIN-QUIC connection migration diagram

The migration request must also include a signature. This signature serves as an encrypted proof of the new network address, generated using the private key of the original identity. The signature ensures the connection migration request originates from the original client and is not forged by a malicious third party. Since the private key is confidential, only the original communicating party can produce a valid signature. The server can verify the signature's authenticity using the public key. This mechanism safeguards communication entities during network address changes, preventing session hijacking risks.

4.5.4 Pluggable Congestion Control Modules in the MIN-QUIC Protocol

Pluggable congestion control modules enable network developers to select or customize appropriate congestion control algorithms based on specific scenarios, meeting diverse requirements. This design enhances the protocol's flexibility and scalability, allowing it to adapt to various network environments and optimize transmission performance.

Congestion control is a critical service provided by the transport layer, and its effectiveness serves as a key QoS parameter for transport layer protocols. However, due to the complexity and unpredictability of networks, no perfect congestion control algorithm exists. Therefore, MIN-QUIC implements congestion control as a pluggable module, enabling the selection or adjustment of the most suitable congestion control strategy based on specific network conditions.

MIN-QUIC defines a universal congestion control interface comprising monitoring and control interfaces. The congestion control module utilizes the monitoring interface to gather comprehensive network status information, guiding congestion control decisions. This information includes, but is not limited to, network latency, packet loss events, and send buffer status. The module employs the control interface to adjust congestion control windows, thereby regulating data transmission rates.

4.6 Chapter Summary

This chapter introduces the emerging QUIC protocol in transport layer protocols, covering the following key points:

1. Characteristics and functions of the QUIC protocol.
2. Core mechanisms of the QUIC protocol.
3. Advantages, disadvantages, and optimizations of the QUIC protocol.

4.7 Experiment—Practical End-to-End Communication Using QUIC

4.7.1 Experiment Objectives

1. Implement client–server communication based on the QUIC protocol.
2. Be able to perform simple modifications and extensions to the QUIC communication program.

4.7.2 Tools and Environment

1. Go Environment: Go 1.20 or later.
2. Code Repository: Official quic-go repository [7]. The quic-go version used in this experiment is 0.54.0.

4.7.3 Experiment Steps

1. Clone the code repository and download dependencies

```
git clone https://github.com/quic-go/quic-go.git
go mod tidy
cd quic-go/example
```

2. Run the default QUIC server code

   (1) Open terminal and run: go run main.go
   (2) Access URL: https://github.com/quic-go/quic-go/blob/master/example/main.go
   (3) Upon successful execution, the following will be displayed: listening on localhost:6121, as shown below (Fig. 4.14):

3. Run the default QUIC client code
   Open a new terminal (Fig. 4.15):

```
go run client/main.go https://localhost:6121/demo/tile
```

4. Code Modification

   (1) Modify the server's request handling logic to return custom JSON data:

Program 4.1 Modify Server Code

```
// Add the processing code to example/main.go
mux.HandleFunc("/demo/test", func(w http.ResponseWriter, r *http.Request) {
        w.Header().Set("Content-Type", "application/json")
```

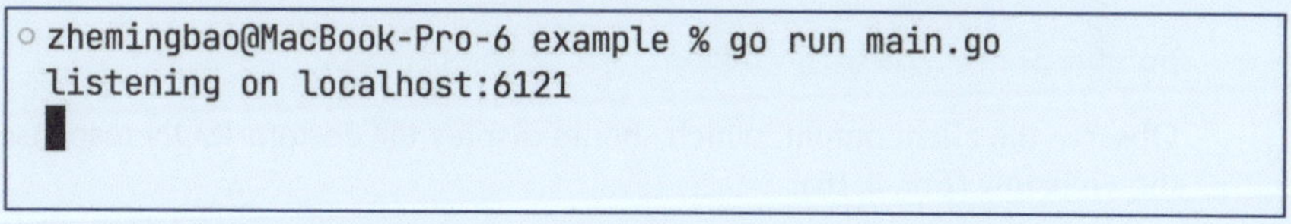

Fig. 4.14 QUIC server startup

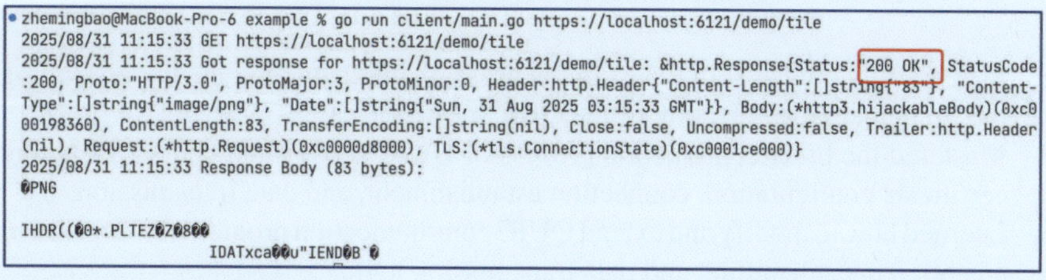

Fig. 4.15 QUIC client startup

```
• zhemingbao@MacBook-Pro-6 example % go run client/main.go https://localhost:6121/demo/test
2025/08/31 12:13:10 GET https://localhost:6121/demo/test
2025/08/31 12:13:10 Got response for https://localhost:6121/demo/test: &http.Response{Status:"200 OK", StatusCode
:200, Proto:"HTTP/3.0", ProtoMajor:3, ProtoMinor:0, Header:http.Header{"Cache-Control":[]string{"no-cache"}, "Con
tent-Length":[]string{"75"}, "Content-Type":[]string{"application/json"}, "Date":[]string{"Sun, 31 Aug 2025 04:13
:10 GMT"}}, Body:(*http3.hijackableBody)(0xc0000a8180), ContentLength:75, TransferEncoding:[]string(nil), Close:f
alse, Uncompressed:false, Trailer:http.Header(nil), Request:(*http.Request)(0xc000192000), TLS:(*tls.ConnectionSt
ate)(0xc0000d6000)}
2025/08/31 12:13:10 Response Body (75 bytes):
{"message":"Hello from QUIC server","path":"/demo/test","status":"success"}
```

Fig. 4.16 Custom output

```
        w.Header().Set("Cache-Control", "no-cache")
        response:= map[string]string{
                "status": "success",
                "message": "Hello from QUIC server",
                 "path": r.URL.Path,
        }
        jsonResponse, err:= json.Marshal(response)
        if err != nil {
                w.WriteHeader(http.StatusInternalServerError)
                w.Write([]byte("Internal Server Error"))
                return
        }
        w.WriteHeader(http.StatusOK)
        w.Write(jsonResponse)
})
```

(2) Verify the modification

Restart the server: go run main.go.

Run the modified client:

```
go run client/main.go https://localhost:6121
```

Observe the client output, which should display the custom JSON response as shown below (Fig. 4.16):

4.7.4 Experiment Summary

1. Successfully ran the HTTP/3 example program based on quic-go, understanding the fundamental application of the QUIC protocol.
2. Mastered the basic construction process of QUIC servers and clients, including certificate configuration, connection establishment, and data transmission.
3. Learned how to modify and extend QUIC communication programs to implement custom request handling and data transmission logic.

4.8 Exercises

1. Briefly describe the fundamental characteristics of the QUIC protocol.
2. List the advantages of the QUIC protocol over TCP.
3. List three key technologies of the QUIC protocol.

References

1. Iyengar J, Thomson M. QUIC: a UDP-based multiplexed and secure transport. RFC 9000, IETF; 2021.
2. Kurose JF, Ross KW. Computer networking: a top-down approach. 8th ed. London: Pearson; 2020.
3. Langley A, Riddoch A, Wilk A, et al. The QUIC transport protocol: design and Internet-scale deployment. In: Proceedings of the ACM SIGCOMM 2017 Conference. New York: ACM, 2017. p. 183–196.
4. Roskind J. QUIC: multiplexed stream transport over UDP. Google; 2013.
5. Jacobson V. Congestion avoidance and control. In: Proceedings of the ACM SIGCOMM 1988 conference. New York: ACM. 1988. p. 314–329.
6. Xiao M, Bai H, Li H, et al. A secure and efficient transport protocol for multi-identifier network. In: 2023 9th international conference on computer and communications (ICCC). IEEE; 2023. p. 1653–1659.
7. quic-go contributors. quic-go [EB/OL]. (2025). https://github.com/quic-go/quic-go. Accessed 05 Oct 2025.

Chapter 5
Transport Layer Security Protocol

Following the previous chapter's discussion of how QUIC enhances transport performance and security through integrated encryption and optimized handshakes, this chapter shifts the focus to the more fundamental and widely deployed security mechanism in network communications—the TLS protocol.

In data transmission, security is an indispensable cornerstone. The Transport Layer Security (TLS) protocol ensures the confidentiality and integrity of application-layer communications across the entire network, forming the core of modern internet security.

This chapter focuses on TLS, providing an in-depth explanation of its core security capabilities: data confidentiality, data integrity, and authentication. It details the TLS handshake, comparing traditional handshakes with the efficient 1-RTT and 0-RTT mechanisms in TLS 1.3. The chapter also addresses common security threats like man-in-the-middle attacks and replay attacks. Finally, a hands-on experiment analyzing TLS handshake packet captures helps students grasp TLS's critical role in protecting transmitted data.

5.1 Overview of Transport Layer Security

Transport Layer Security (TLS) is the de facto standard for secure internet communication, standardized by the Internet Engineering Task Force (IETF). It evolved from the Secure Sockets Layer (SSL) protocol originally proposed by Netscape in the 1990s. TLS was initially developed as a comprehensive enhancement of SSL 3.0 and has continuously incorporated advancements in modern cryptography in subsequent versions. It integrates multiple critical technologies—including symmetric encryption, message authentication codes (MAC), asymmetric encryption, digital signatures, and pseudorandom number generation—to ensure end-to-end secure communication in computer networks [1, 2].

H. Li and Z. Bao, *Transport Layer for Computer Networks*,
https://doi.org/10.1007/978-981-95-7374-5_5

The TLS protocol primarily provides three core security capabilities for network communication:

- **Data Encryption**: Protects transmitted content using symmetric encryption mechanisms to prevent eavesdropping on sensitive information;
- **Identity Authentication**: Verifies the identities of communicating parties using digital certificates and Public Key Infrastructure (PKI) mechanisms, ensuring connections are established between trusted entities;
- **Data Integrity**: Prevents data tampering or forgery during transmission through algorithms like MACs.

As a universal security layer, TLS can be layered over multiple application layer protocols. For instance, HTTP over TLS (HTTPS) is currently the most widely adopted secure web communication solution, while email protocols like SMTP, POP3, and IMAP typically rely on TLS to guarantee the confidentiality and integrity of email transmission. Additionally, high-security applications such as instant messaging, VoIP, and financial transaction systems all utilize TLS as their security infrastructure. With the release of TLS 1.3, the protocol has seen significant enhancements in handshake procedures, cryptographic suites, and forward secrecy, further boosting both performance and security [3].

The TLS protocol represents an evolution of the earlier SSL protocol, with each version continuously optimizing security and performance. The following table summarizes the key development features of major versions:

- **TLS 1.0 (1999)**

  Improved upon SSL 3.0, addressed known security vulnerabilities, and was the first version published as an IETF standard.
- **TLS 1.1 (2006)**

  Introduced stronger message authentication mechanisms and enhanced defenses against CBC mode attacks.
- **TLS 1.2 (2008)**

  Supported more flexible cryptographic algorithm negotiation, disabled insecure hash algorithms (such as MD5 and SHA-1) by default, recommended SHA-256 and higher hash functions, and introduced AEAD mode.
- **TLS 1.3 (2018)**

  Simplified the protocol, significantly reducing handshake latency. Removed numerous obsolete or security-risk features (like RSA key exchange and static DH), defaulting to more secure and efficient cipher suites such as ChaCha20-Poly1305 and AES-GCM. TLS 1.3 also eliminated support for non-forward-secure ciphers, comprehensively enhancing the confidentiality and performance of encrypted communications.

5.1.1 Data Confidentiality

Data confidentiality refers to the technical assurance that data transmitted during communication can only be read by authorized parties. Unauthorized third parties—such as hackers or man-in-the-middle attackers—cannot decipher the true information even if they intercept the communication content.

In the TLS protocol, data confidentiality is achieved through a combination of encryption algorithms and key management mechanisms. By encrypting data, even if information is intercepted during transmission, attackers find it difficult to decrypt and reconstruct it, effectively preventing data theft, information leaks, and content tampering. Figure 5.1 shows the TLS digital signature process.

1. **Hybrid Encryption System**

   TLS supports multiple encryption algorithms, which are categorized into symmetric and asymmetric types. Each plays a distinct role in achieving confidentiality, ensuring both security and efficiency.

   Asymmetric encryption is a crucial component of modern cybersecurity systems. Its core principle lies in leveraging mathematical challenges—such as integer factorization and the discrete logarithm problem—as the foundation for security, enabling the functional separation of public and private keys. Representative algorithms include RSA and elliptic curve-based ECDH/ECDHE. Asymmetric systems enable secure key negotiation between communicating parties without requiring pre-shared keys: the sender encrypts key material or handshake messages using the recipient's public key, ensuring only the corresponding private key holder can decrypt it. This safeguards key exchange from eavesdropping by intermediaries.

   Overall, asymmetric cryptography provides modern networks with verifiable identity and eavesdropping-resistant key exchange mechanisms, forming the foundation for establishing secure channels and trustworthy communication. Asymmetric encryption operates in two modes:

   (1) Public-Key Encryption, Private-Key Decryption: This ensures secure content transmission because content encrypted with a public key cannot

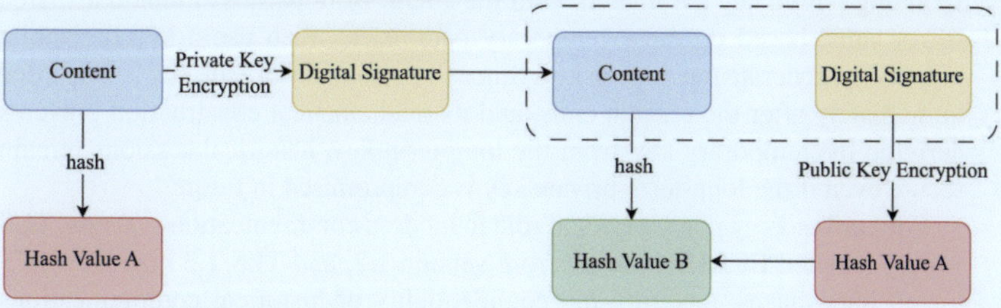

Fig. 5.1 TLS digital signature process

be decrypted by others. Only the holder of the private key can decrypt the actual content.

(2) Private-Key Encryption, Public-Key Decryption: This ensures messages cannot be forged. Since private keys must remain confidential, successful decryption of private-key-encrypted content using the public key verifies that the message originates from the private key holder.

Symmetric encryption is a cryptographic mechanism that uses a single key for both encryption and decryption operations. Its security typically relies on the size of the key space and the algorithm's structural resistance to analysis. Common symmetric encryption algorithms include AES and ChaCha20, which achieve efficient data encryption through structures such as Substitution-Permutation Networks (SPNs), linear superpositions, or stream ciphers. Compared to asymmetric encryption, symmetric encryption features lower computational complexity and higher throughput. Consequently, it is primarily employed in modern communication protocols to safeguard the confidentiality and integrity of vast amounts of application data.

Within security protocols such as TLS and QUIC, symmetric encryption is utilized for data encryption during the session phase. The required keys are generated during the handshake phase through asymmetric key exchange or key derivation mechanisms.

2. **Forward Secrecy**

Perfect Forward Secrecy (PFS) is a cryptographic property that ensures the independence of session keys. Its core objective is to prevent historical encrypted communications from being retroactively decrypted due to long-term key compromises. Specifically, PFS requires each session to generate an independent session key through an ephemeral key exchange, making it independent of the server's long-term private key or any permanently reusable secret values. This means that even if an attacker later obtains the server's private key, they cannot derive the encryption keys for past sessions and thus cannot decrypt recorded historical traffic.

In the TLS protocol, PFS is typically implemented using temporary Diffie–Hellman (DHE) or temporary Elliptic Curve Diffie–Hellman (ECDHE). The server generates a one-time key pair for each handshake and exchanges the corresponding public key parameters with the client. Both parties compute a shared secret value based on these temporary parameters, then use a key derivation function to generate the session key. Since the temporary private key is discarded immediately after the session ends, and its mathematical construction prevents deriving the temporary key from the long-term key, historical sessions remain secure even if the long-term private key is compromised in future.

Forward secrecy plays a critical role in modern communication systems. TLS widely adopted ECDHE starting from version 1.2, and TLS 1.3 mandates PFS for all handshakes, ensuring the confidentiality of historical communications throughout the system's lifecycle.

3. **Key Management**

   Key management serves as a critical foundation for the TLS protocol to ensure communication confidentiality and integrity. Its core objective is to securely generate, distribute, and maintain cryptographic keys during each session, thereby achieving session-level isolation and robust security. TLS's key management mechanism ensures that key generation and usage for each session meet security standards through the following approaches:

   Generating a Unique Session Key for Each Session: During each TLS handshake, the client and server generate a unique session key valid only for that session. This ensures that even if an attacker obtains a key for one session, they cannot decrypt data from future sessions.
   Utilization of secure random number generators: To guarantee the uniqueness and unpredictability of session keys, the TLS protocol relies on high-quality secure random number generators for key generation. These keys are derived from unpredictable random numbers, preventing key reuse and thereby enhancing security.

   The TLS protocol employs algorithms like Diffie–Hellman and Elliptic Curve Diffie–Hellman to guarantee forward secrecy. This ensures that even if one session key is compromised, it does not compromise the security of other sessions.

   Through these mechanisms, the TLS protocol generates secure, unique keys for each session, preventing key reuse risks and ensuring that every communication remains independently confidential.

5.1.2 Data Integrity

Within the TLS protocol framework, data integrity serves as a critical security attribute ensuring that messages remain unaltered, unfalsified, and unreused during transmission. Its core objective is to guarantee that the receiving end can verify the authenticity and unmodified state of the message. To achieve this, TLS constructs multi-layered integrity protection through cryptographic authentication mechanisms, sequence number management, and key derivation schemes.

In TLS 1.2 and earlier versions, record-level integrity relied on message authentication codes (MACs) based on shared keys, commonly implemented as HMAC-SHA variants. The sender calculates the MAC value for a message before encryption and appends it to the record. The receiver then recalculates the authentication code using the same key to verify the message's integrity. This method effectively detects bit-level tampering. However, its "MAC-then-Encrypt" structure previously exposed vulnerabilities to pattern attacks.

TLS 1.3 fundamentally reengineers integrity protection by adopting AEAD (Authenticated Encryption with Associated Data) algorithms such as AES-GCM and ChaCha20-Poly1305. AEAD binds encryption and authentication into a single atomic operation, generating an authentication tag to verify whether a record has been tampered with. Decryption failure indicates a failed integrity check, making the protocol more secure in implementation and reducing the overhead of additional MACs.

Additionally, TLS maintains monotonically increasing sequence numbers for each record to defend against replay attacks. These sequence numbers participate in verification as AEAD's associated data, preventing reuse of duplicated or forged records. For key derivation, TLS generates independent keys for encryption and integrity using PRF or HKDF, eliminating key dependencies between records or sessions to enhance resistance against attacks.

Overall, TLS's integrity assurance mechanisms achieve a higher level of cryptographic robustness in newer protocols, providing a solid foundation for end-to-end secure communication.

5.1.3 Authentication

The core objective of authentication is to ensure that communicating parties are indeed the expected entities, thereby preventing man-in-the-middle attacks and identity spoofing. The TLS protocol achieves this through Public Key Infrastructure (PKI) and digital certificates. Digital certificates are issued by trusted Certification Authorities (CAs) and contain the public key and identity information of the server or client.

During the TLS handshake, the server typically must present its digital certificate to the client. The client verifies the certificate's legitimacy and integrity, including:—The validity of the certificate chain (from the server certificate to intermediate CAs and the root certificate)—The correctness of the signature—Whether the domain name bound to the certificate matches the accessed server. Only after passing these checks does the client proceed to establish a secure connection.

Client authentication is optional but critical in high-security scenarios like financial transactions or enterprise VPNs. In this mode, the client must present a certificate signed by a trusted CA to the server. Only after the server validates this certificate can a mutually authenticated secure channel be established.

The certificate chain validation process typically relies on the trust anchor (root CA certificate) built into the operating system or browser. By sequentially verifying the certificate chain, TLS ensures the authenticity and trustworthiness of both communicating parties. TLS 1.3 optimizes the authentication mechanism during the handshake, reducing the number of handshake rounds and improving performance while maintaining strict requirements for certificate validation and identity authentication.

5.2 Transport Layer Security Protocol

5.2.1 How TLS Works

The core mechanism of the TLS protocol integrates multiple modern cryptographic techniques, including symmetric encryption, asymmetric encryption, and hash functions, to establish a secure and reliable data transmission channel. At the beginning of communication, the client and server must negotiate encryption parameters through a series of interactive steps—a process known as the TLS handshake.

According to the specifications in RFC 5246 (TLS 1.2) and RFC 8446 (TLS 1.3), upon completion of the handshake, both parties determine the encryption algorithms, shared keys, and session parameters for the current session based on the negotiated results, thereby initiating protected secure communication. TLS security is primarily manifested in the following three aspects:

1. **Data Confidentiality**

   During the handshake phase, both parties negotiate a shared session key through key exchange mechanisms (such as RSA, Diffie–Hellman, or Elliptic Curve Diffie–Hellman, ECDHE). TLS 1.3 fully adopts ECDHE based on elliptic curves for the handshake, ensuring forward secrecy. Once negotiated, subsequent communications encrypt data using efficient symmetric algorithms (e.g., AES-GCM, ChaCha20-Poly1305). Even if an attacker intercepts the ciphertext, decrypting and restoring the original content remains difficult without the key.
2. **Data Integrity**

   To prevent data tampering during transmission, TLS typically employs hash-based message authentication codes (MACs) like HMAC-SHA256 in TLS 1.2 and earlier versions. TLS 1.3 mandates the use of AEAD (Authenticated Encryption with Associated Data) mode, which combines encryption and integrity verification by generating an authentication tag directly from the encryption algorithm. The recipient verifies this tag to ensure data has not been maliciously altered or forged during transmission.
3. **Identity Authentication**

   TLS verifies the identities of communicating parties using a digital certificate mechanism. Digital certificates adhere to the ITU-T X.509 standard, issued and validated by trusted Certification Authorities (CAs). The most common scenario involves clients verifying server certificates to ensure the authenticity of their public keys and domain names. Certificate chain validation (from the server certificate to the root certificate) ensures the reliability of the trust relationship. In specific high-security scenarios, TLS also supports client certificate verification, enabling mutual authentication to further enhance security.

In summary, TLS achieves the three core security objectives of communication confidentiality, integrity, and identity authentication through handshake negotiation, key exchange, and multi-layer encryption mechanisms, providing a robust security foundation for modern internet applications.

5.2.2 TLS Handshake Process and Encryption Algorithms

The TLS handshake process involves four communications. Different key exchange algorithms result in distinct TLS handshake flows. Currently, two key exchange algorithms are commonly used: the RSA algorithm and the ECDHE algorithm.

Figure 5.2 shows the TLS handshake process. This subsection describes the TLS handshake process based on the RSA algorithm:

1. **ClientHello**

   During TLS protocol establishment, the ClientHello request initiated by the client marks the starting point of the secure communication connection. According to RFC 8446 specifications, the information sent by the client to the server at this stage carries the critical task of negotiating communication security parameters. First, the client explicitly lists the TLS protocol versions it supports. This information is crucial because different TLS protocol versions vary in functionality, security, and performance. For example, TLS 1.2 introduces stronger encryption algorithms and stricter security mechanisms, significantly enhancing resistance to security threats compared to earlier versions.

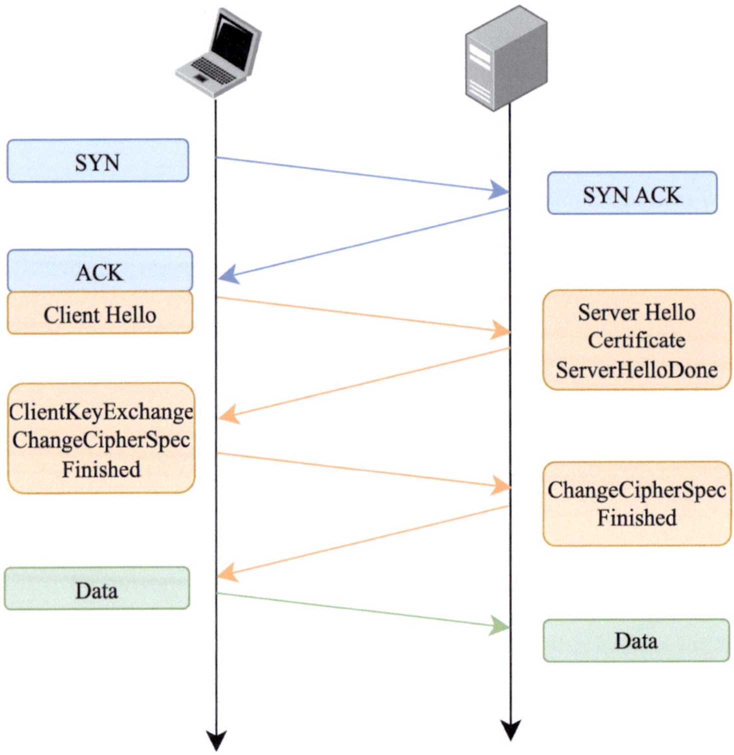

Fig. 5.2 TLS handshake process

TLS 1.3 further optimizes the handshake process, reducing connection establishment time and enhancing forward secrecy. The server must select an appropriate version from the client's provided list based on its own capabilities. If none of the client's supported versions are accepted by the server, the server will refuse the connection to avoid potential security risks.

The random number generated by the client (Client Random) plays an indispensable role in subsequent key generation. This random number is produced by the client using a specific random number generation algorithm, and its quality directly impacts the security of the final session key.

To ensure randomness, the client typically combines multiple entropy sources, such as system time and hardware noise, to generate a sufficiently long and unpredictable random value. Client Random, along with other random numbers obtained during subsequent interactions (Server Random and pre-master key), participates in the session key generation process. The combination of these three elements undergoes complex cryptographic operations to produce the session key used for encrypting and decrypting communication data. This multi-random-source approach significantly increases the difficulty for attackers to crack the key, thereby enhancing communication security.

The list of cipher suites supported by the client is another crucial component of the ClientHello request. A cipher suite is a combination of cryptographic algorithms, including key exchange algorithms, data encryption algorithms, and message authentication algorithms. For example, the common RSA encryption algorithm is often used for key exchange, AES (Advanced Encryption Standard) for data encryption, and SHA-256 for message authentication. Different cipher suites have varying strengths and weaknesses in terms of security and performance.

The client sends all supported cipher suites to the server in order of priority. The server selects a cipher suite from the list that is mutually supported and offers high security, based on its own configuration and security policies, to serve as the encryption scheme for this communication session. The selection of the cipher suite directly determines the encryption method and security strength of the data during communication. Therefore, during the negotiation process, both parties must carefully choose an appropriate cipher suite to strike a balance between security and performance.

2. **ServerHello**

After receiving the ClientHello request from the client, the server responds with a ServerHello message. This response process also strictly follows protocol specifications. First, the server verifies the TLS protocol versions supported by the client. Based on its own configuration and compatibility requirements, it selects a suitable version from the list provided by the client. If none of the client's supported versions meet the server's security and functionality needs, the server immediately terminates the connection to prevent communication using insecure or incompatible protocol versions. This version confirmation mechanism ensures both parties interact within the same protocol framework, avoiding security vulnerabilities and communication failures caused by version discrepancies.

The Server Random, generated by the server, is a crucial parameter for session key generation, similar to the Client Random. It is also produced using a reliable random number generation mechanism. Together with the Client Random and the subsequent pre-master key, it forms the foundational data for key generation. During random number generation, the server implements multiple security measures to ensure the randomness and unpredictability of the numbers, thereby enhancing the security of the session key. For instance, the server may utilize hardware random number generators or leverage random number interfaces provided by the operating system, combined with specific algorithms, to generate high-quality random numbers.

Confirming the cipher suite list is a critical step in the ServerHello phase. The server selects an appropriate cipher suite from the options provided by the client based on its own security policies and evaluation of the client's cipher suite list. During this selection process, the server prioritizes cipher suites that offer high security, good performance, and strong compatibility.

In a TLS 1.2 RSA handshake, the server's certificate is not included in the ServerHello message; it is sent in a separate Certificate handshake message. Issued by a trusted Certificate Authority (CA), this certificate contains critical information such as the server's public key, domain name details, validity period, and the CA's signature.

The server transmits this certificate to the client, which then validates it using its built-in CA root certificates. The verification process includes checking the certificate's validity period, ensuring the domain name matches the actual domain being accessed, and using the CA's public key to validate the authenticity of the certificate signature. If the certificate fails verification, the client will refuse to establish the connection, preventing communication with spoofed servers and effectively defending against security threats like man-in-the-middle attacks. The digital certificate mechanism provides a reliable means of identity authentication for the TLS protocol, ensuring secure communication between the client and legitimate servers.

3. **Client Response**

Upon receiving the server's ServerHello message, the client's primary task is to rigorously verify the authenticity of the server's digital certificate. The client utilizes the CA public keys embedded in the browser or operating system to validate the server certificate according to the X.509 certificate standard.

The X.509 certificate standard defines the certificate format and validation process. The client checks the certificate's signature validity to confirm issuance by a trusted CA. It also verifies the certificate's validity period to ensure it hasn't expired. Additionally, it matches the domain name information in the certificate with the actual domain being accessed to prevent domain spoofing attacks. If certificate validation succeeds, the client extracts the server's public key from the certificate for subsequent encryption operations. If validation fails, the client immediately terminates the connection and alerts the user to security risks.

After successful certificate validation, the client generates a new random number (pre-master key) and encrypts it using the public key extracted from the server certificate. The pre-master key is a critical parameter for generating the session key. Encrypting it with the server's public key ensures only the server possessing the corresponding private key can decrypt and obtain this random number. This encryption method guarantees the secure transmission of the pre-master key while enabling key exchange between client and server.

The Encryption Algorithm Change Notification is a critical message sent by the client to the server, signaling that subsequent communications will be encrypted using the negotiated encryption algorithm and session key. This notification ensures both parties agree on the encryption method at the start of the encrypted communication, preventing data transmission errors and security issues caused by mismatched encryption schemes.

The Client Handshake Complete notification serves as the client's summary of the entire handshake phase. Within this notification, the client performs a hash calculation on all data sent and received during the handshake process, generating a digest value. This digest is used by the server to verify the integrity of the handshake process, ensuring data has not been tampered with. By sending the Handshake Complete notification, the client indicates to the server that its handshake phase is complete and awaits the server's acknowledgment.

At this point, both the client and server possess three critical random numbers (Client Random, Server Random, pre-master key). Each party will independently compute the session key for this communication using the key generation algorithm specified within the negotiated cipher suite. The session key generation process involves complex cryptographic operations. The three random numbers are mixed and transformed to produce a symmetric key used for encrypting and decrypting data, ensuring secure subsequent communications.

4. **Server Response**

Upon receiving the encrypted pre-master key from the client, the server decrypts it using its private key to obtain the pre-master key. Combining this with the Server Random generated during the ServerHello phase and the received Client Random, the server calculates the session key for this communication using the key generation algorithm from the agreed cipher suite.

During key generation, the server strictly adheres to cryptographic standards to ensure the resulting session key possesses sufficient security and uniqueness. This session key will be used for encrypting and decrypting data throughout subsequent communications, with its security directly impacting the confidentiality and integrity of the exchanged content.

The server sends an Encrypted Communication Algorithm Change notification to the client, corresponding to the client's earlier notification. This explicitly informs the client that subsequent communications will be encrypted using the negotiated session key. This notification ensures both parties agree on the encryption method at the start of encrypted communication, preventing data transmission errors and security issues caused by mismatched encryption schemes.

The server's handshake completion notification also includes a digest of the entire handshake data, enabling the client to verify the integrity of the handshake process. By sending this notification, the server signals to the client that its handshake phase is complete, marking the conclusion of the entire TLS handshake process.

At this point, the entire TLS handshake phase is finalized, and the client and server transition into the encrypted communication phase. During encrypted communication, both parties use the generated session key to encrypt and decrypt application-layer data. Data transmission adheres to application-layer protocols like HTTP, but content is encrypted via the session key. This encrypted communication ensures data confidentiality and integrity during network transmission, effectively countering security threats such as data leaks and tampering, thereby providing users with a secure and reliable network communication environment.

5.2.3 Improvements and Advantages of TLS 1.3

1. **Limitations of TLS 1.2**

   Despite TLS 1.2's longstanding status as the mainstream protocol for secure internet communications, it still exhibits significant flaws in cryptographic algorithm selection, key exchange mechanisms, and protocol architecture. First, TLS 1.2 remains compatible with algorithms like MD5, SHA-1, RC4, and 3DES—all proven to have security vulnerabilities—exposing communications to risks such as hash collisions and key skew attacks. Second, the protocol permits RSA-based static key exchange, which lacks forward secrecy. Should a server's private key be compromised, all historical traffic becomes fully decryptable. Furthermore, the widely used CBC cipher mode in TLS 1.2 is vulnerable to padding oracle attacks (e.g., POODLE, BEAST), potentially enabling attackers to recover sensitive data. Performance-wise, TLS 1.2's full handshake typically requires 2-RTT, significantly impacting connection establishment speed in high-latency networks. Finally, the protocol defines an extensive array of cipher suites, whose complexity increases the risk of implementation errors and downgrade attacks.
2. **Improvements and Advantages of TLS 1.3**

   To address the aforementioned issues, TLS 1.3 systematically restructured the protocol architecture, achieving significant optimizations in cryptographic design, protocol security, and performance.

   (1) **Enhancing Cryptographic Security: Phasing Out Weak Algorithms Completely**

   TLS 1.3 completely removes weak algorithms such as RSA key exchange, CBC mode, SHA-1, and MD5. The protocol retains only ECDHE-based key exchange, mechanically enforcing forward secrecy for all sessions. Additionally, TLS 1.3 exclusively supports AEAD encryption algorithms (such as AES-GCM and ChaCha20-Poly1305), integrating confidentiality and integrity protection within a unified framework. This eliminates the structural vulnerability present in TLS 1.2's MAC-then-Encrypt mode.

(2) **Protocol Simplification: Reducing Attack Surface and Enhancing Robustness**

TLS 1.3 consolidates multiple handshake messages, significantly streamlining the message exchange process. For instance, messages such as ServerKeyExchange and ServerHelloDone are integrated into ServerHello, thereby reducing implementation complexity and parsing overhead. Additionally, the newly introduced supported_versions extension field effectively blocks protocol downgrade attacks, ensuring clients and servers negotiate using the highest available protocol version.

(3) **Performance Enhancements: 1-RTT Handshake and 0-RTT Acceleration**

In TLS 1.3, the handshake process is significantly streamlined and optimized. To reduce connection establishment latency, TLS 1.3 introduces the key_share extension in the ClientHello, enabling clients to proactively send key sharing parameters. This achieves a 1-RTT full handshake, significantly improving performance compared to TLS 1.2's 2-RTT requirement. Additionally, TLS 1.3 supports 0-RTT data transmission based on session tickets, allowing clients to send data before the first round-trip in session resumption scenarios, further enhancing interaction efficiency. The specific handshake process is illustrated in Fig. 5.3.

(a) **ClientHello:** The client sends the supported TLS version (1.3), a random (32 bytes), a list of cipher suites, and key extensions such as: key_share: Carries the client's temporary public key (e.g., ECDHE

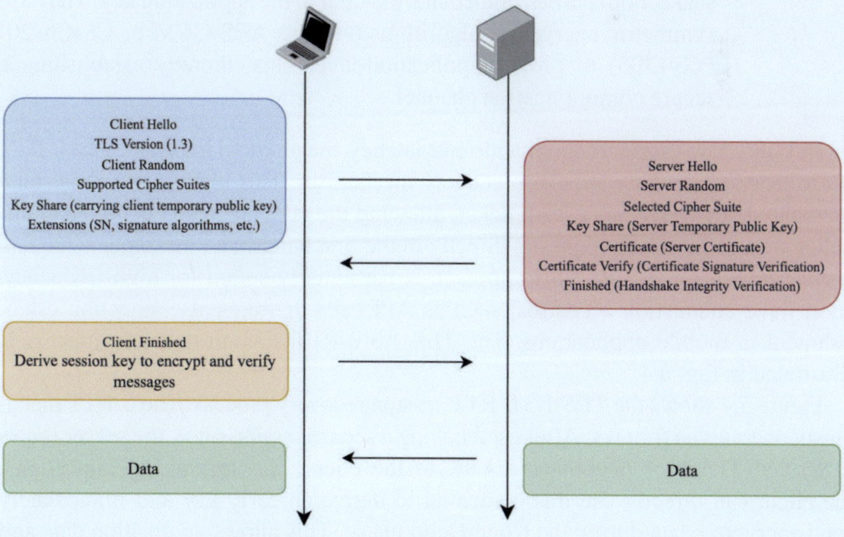

Fig. 5.3 TLS 1.3 handshake process

public key) to directly initiate key exchange. supported_versions: Declares the highest supported protocol version (to prevent downgrade attacks). signature_algorithms: Specifies supported signature algorithms (e.g., ECDSA, Ed25519).

(b) **ServerHello:** After receiving the ClientHello, the server sends the ServerHello, including cipher suites (e.g., TLS_AES_128_GCM_SHA256), server random, and key_share: the server's temporary public key, used to compute the shared secret with the client's public key. Certificate: Server certificate chain (X.509). CertificateVerify: Handshake message signed with the server's private key for client identity verification. Finished: Encrypted HMAC digest to verify handshake integrity.

(c) **Key Computation:** Client and server compute a shared secret using their respective ECDHE public keys. They then progressively generate keys for different phases via an HKDF-based key derivation function:

- Early secret (if using PSK or 0-RTT; otherwise empty);
- Handshake secret (derived from ECDHE output);
- Master secret (further derived to create the application key).

The resulting handshake key protects handshake messages, while the application key secures subsequent communications.

(d) **Client Finished:** The client verifies the server certificate and signature, and checks the integrity of the server's Finished message. The client then sends its own Finished message, confirming the handshake process is complete and unaltered.

(e) **Application Data Transmission:** After confirming a successful handshake, both parties immediately switch to the application key. They use symmetric encryption algorithms (such as AES-GCM or ChaCha20-Poly1305) to protect application-layer data, thereby establishing a secure communication channel.

In TLS 1.3, to further reduce handshake latency, the protocol introduces the 0-RTT (Zero Round Trip Time) session recovery mechanism. This mechanism relies on a pre-shared key (PSK) or session ticket, allowing the client to send encrypted application data (e.g., HTTP requests) directly in the first handshake message, achieving "zero-round-trip" startup. This approach is particularly suited for high-frequency, short-lived connection scenarios, such as API calls or frequent connection establishment in mobile applications. The TLS 1.3 0-RTT session recovery process is illustrated in Fig. 5.4:

Figure 5.4 shows the TLS 1.3 0-RTT session recovery process. The 0-RTT mechanism operates as follows: After establishing a secure session once, the server issues a Session Ticket or negotiates a PSK to the client. In subsequent connections, the client can directly use this credential to derive an early key and immediately send encrypted data during the ClientHello phase. This allows application data and

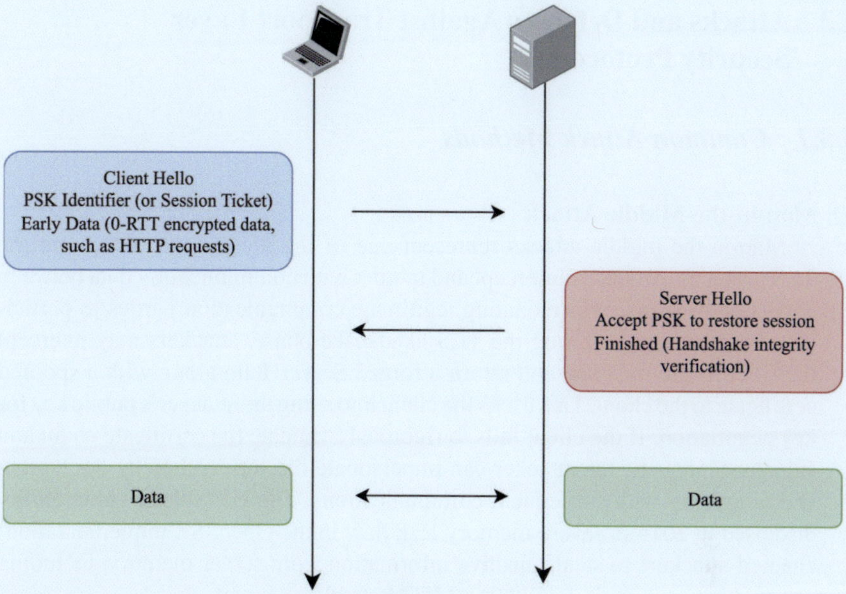

Fig. 5.4 TLS 1.3 0-RTT session recovery process

handshake messages to be transmitted in parallel, significantly reducing connection establishment latency. However, since 0-RTT data is susceptible to malicious replay attacks, the TLS 1.3 specification mandates that servers implement additional anti-replay protections at the application layer. These include restricting the scope of 0-RTT data usage and enabling idempotency checks. Consequently, 0-RTT is viewed as a trade-off mechanism between performance and security.

Currently, mainstream browsers (Chrome, Firefox, Safari) have enabled TLS 1.3 by default, and major operating systems and mobile platforms now fully support it. Major cloud service providers (Amazon AWS, Microsoft Azure, and Google Cloud) have fully deployed TLS 1.3 across core services, including load balancers, CDNs, and API gateways. This enables enterprise customers to benefit from enhanced security alongside reduced handshake latency and improved transmission performance.

5.3 Attacks and Defenses Against Transport Layer Security Protocols

5.3.1 Common Attack Methods

1. **Man-in-the-Middle Attack**

   Man-in-the-middle attacks represent one of the most severe threats to the TLS protocol. Attackers intercept and tamper with communication data between clients and servers, impersonating legitimate communication parties to participate in interactions. During the TLS handshake phase, attackers may intercept the ClientHello message and return a forged ServerHello along with a spoofed certificate to the client. This tricks the client into using the attacker's public key for key negotiation. If the client fails to rigorously validate the certificate chain and signature integrity, the attacker can impersonate the server, thereby decrypting and tampering with subsequent communications. The Heartbleed vulnerability disclosed in 2014 (a severe memory leak flaw in the OpenSSL implementation) enabled attackers to steal sensitive information from server memory, including private keys, indirectly facilitating MITM attacks.

   Defensive Measures: Strictly enforce digital certificate chain validation, trust only certificates issued by authoritative CAs, and regularly update the root certificate list embedded in operating systems or browsers. Additionally, Certificate Transparency (CT) and Online Certificate Status Protocol (OCSP) should be employed to monitor and validate certificate validity.

2. **Replay Attack**

   A replay attack involves an attacker capturing legitimate communication data and later resending it to deceive the recipient into repeating an action. In sensitive applications like financial payments, this can result in duplicate transactions. The TLS protocol defends against such attacks through multiple layers of mechanisms. At the record layer, each message carries an incrementing sequence number and undergoes integrity verification via a MAC (TLS 1.2) or AEAD tag (TLS 1.3). Since sequence numbers are considered invalid upon repetition, the receiver can identify and discard replayed messages, effectively preventing duplicate requests [4].

   Defensive Measures: The application layer should further ensure idempotency of operations, such as using unique transaction IDs in payment requests, to prevent attackers from exploiting the 0-RTT data replay vulnerability for fraudulent activities.

3. **Denial-of-Service Attack**

   Denial-of-service attacks aim to exhaust a target server's resources by flooding it with malicious requests, preventing it from handling legitimate user connections [5]. Within the TLS protocol, the computational overhead of the handshake phase is particularly vulnerable to attack. For instance, attackers may repeatedly initiate incomplete TLS handshake requests, consuming the server's session and computational resources; or exploit source IP address spoofing to launch large-scale "flood attacks." Additionally, TLS can be leveraged for amplification attacks, where attackers amplify request traffic using session recovery or the 0-RTT mechanism.

Defensive Measures: Typical countermeasures include rate limiting, connection queue management, and deploying anti-DDoS devices to cleanse and filter suspicious traffic. Some deployments utilize hardware acceleration cards or dedicated handshake proxies to offload encryption/decryption computational pressure, ensuring server resources prioritize legitimate users.

5.3.2 TLS Optimization for MIN-QUIC

The National Cryptographic Algorithm System (NCAS) is a cryptographic algorithm framework independently developed by China, encompassing symmetric encryption algorithm SM4, asymmetric encryption algorithm SM2, and hash algorithm SM3. Compared to international standard algorithms (such as AES and RSA), NCAS algorithms offer unique advantages in security and performance, finding extensive application particularly in China's critical information infrastructure sectors. The SM4 algorithm employs a 128-bit key length with a 128-bit block size, delivering high encryption efficiency and security. The SM2 algorithm, based on elliptic curve cryptography, uses a 256-bit key length. At equivalent security levels, its key length is shorter than RSA's, resulting in higher computational efficiency. The SM3 algorithm is China's hash standard, producing a 256-bit hash value with security equivalent to SHA-256.

QUIC utilizes the cryptographic components from TLS 1.3. Considering the characteristics of the MIN network, MIN-QUIC employs different cryptographic components than QUIC, specifically implementing encryption using the Guomi cryptographic standards.

Guomi refers to domestically developed commercial cryptographic algorithms certified by the State Cryptography Administration. The Guomi algorithms primarily include four types: SM1, SM2, SM3, and SM4. SM1 is a symmetric block cipher algorithm whose implementation principles are not publicly disclosed. SM2 is an elliptic curve-based asymmetric public-key cryptographic algorithm comprising three components: encryption, signing, and key exchange. SM3 is a hash function used for generating message digests or digital signatures. SM4 is a symmetric block cipher algorithm, also known as SMS4 or WAPI.

RFC8998 (Using the SM2 Algorithm Suite with TLS 1.3) defines how to utilize the Guomi SM2 algorithm suite within the TLS 1.3 protocol. RFC 8998 specifies two complete national cryptographic algorithm suites:

TLS_SM4_GCM_SM3: Uses the SM4 block cipher algorithm with GCM mode for encryption/decryption, and the SM3 hash function for message authentication and pseudorandom function operations.
RFC 8998 also defines how to use the SM2 signature algorithm and curve parameters during the ECDHE handshake. RFC 8998 removes the requirement for client certificates and temporarily relaxes the dual-certificate requirement.

MIN-QUIC implements the technical specifications of RFC 8998. The default cipher suite for MIN-QUIC is TLS_SM4_GCM_SM3 (ID: 0 × 00c6), the default signature scheme is sm2sig_sm3 (ID: 0 × 0708), and the default curve is curveSM2 (ID: 41) [6].

In MIN-QUIC, both communicating parties must possess a MIN identifier token containing public and private keys. The national cryptographic certificates required during MIN-QUIC communication are issued by MIS, whose public and private keys correspond to those within the identity token.

The similarities and differences between MIN-QUIC and QUIC in their cryptographic components are as follows:

At the handshake layer, both MIN-QUIC and QUIC employ the ECDHE protocol for key exchange and utilize TLS 1.3 as the security parameter negotiation mechanism. Their specific implementation differences are as follows:

MIN-QUIC employs the national cryptographic SM2 signature algorithm and curve parameters for identity authentication, adhering to the RFC 8998 specification. MIN-QUIC utilizes certificates issued and verified by MIS, carrying them within MIN packets.

QUIC employs RSA or ECDSA signature algorithms and curve parameters for identity authentication, adhering to the RFC 8446 specification.

At the record layer, both MIN-QUIC and QUIC use session keys to encrypt and decrypt application-layer data, adding authentication tags or message authentication codes (MACs) for integrity checks. The differences in their specific implementations are as follows:

MIN-QUIC employs the national cryptographic SM4 block cipher algorithm in GCM or CCM mode for encryption/decryption, and uses the national cryptographic SM3 hash function for message authentication and pseudorandom function operations. QUIC employs the AES block cipher algorithm with GCM or CCM modes for encryption/decryption, utilizing SHA-256 or SHA-384 hash functions for message authentication and pseudorandom function operations.

MIN-QUIC uses MIN packets as its record layer packet format, containing fields such as session ID, session stream ID, offset, length, and encrypted payload. QUIC employs UDP packets as its record layer format, containing fields such as connection ID, packet number, length, and encrypted payload.

MIN-QUIC utilizes session ID and session stream ID to identify a MIN-QUIC session and a session stream, respectively, and participates in the encryption and decryption process. QUIC uses connection ID and packet number to identify a QUIC connection and a packet, respectively, and participates in the encryption and decryption process.

MIN-QUIC supports SM2-based connection encryption. If a client requires an encrypted connection, it must declare connection encryption during the initial handshake by setting the encryption flag in the connection header to active. Subsequently, both parties enter the encrypted connection establishment process.

Figure 5.5 shows the MIN-QUIC encryption handshake. MIN-QUIC merges the connection establishment handshake and key negotiation handshake to achieve faster

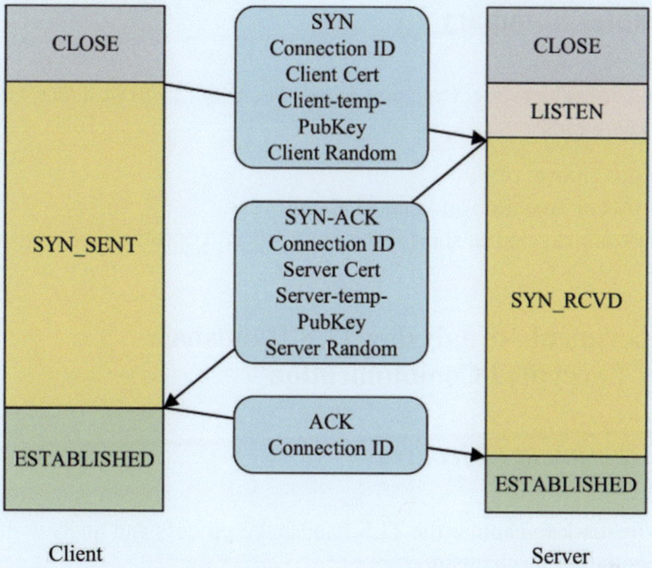

Fig. 5.5 MIN-QUIC encryption handshake

connection setup. Encrypted connection establishment is completed through a three-way handshake, with the following steps:

1. Client Synchronize (SYN) Packet Transmission: Client A sends a SYN packet to Server B, specifying a connection ID within the packet. Additionally, the client generates a temporary public–private key pair and a random number, attaching the temporary public key, random number, and its own certificate to the packet.
2. Server ACK-SYN Response: Upon receiving Client A's SYN packet, Server B responds with an ACK-SYN packet acknowledging the connection ID. The server also generates a temporary public–private key pair and a random number, attaching its temporary public key, the random number, and its own certificate to this packet.
3. Client Acknowledgment Response: Upon receiving Server B's SYN-ACK packet, Client A sends a corresponding ACK packet as a response, reconfirming the connection ID.

Through the three-way handshake, both parties possess an identity-based long-term public–private key pair, generate temporary private keys, and exchange temporary public keys.

Therefore, in the design of its encryption components, MIN-QUIC complies with national cryptographic standards and specifications, utilizing national cryptographic algorithms and certificates to achieve secure communication. Furthermore, it simplifies identity verification and data transmission between communicating parties through the use of MIN identity identifiers and MIN packets.

5.4 Chapter Summary

This chapter introduces the Transport Layer Security (TLS) protocol, covering the following key topics:

1. TLS protocol overview.
2. TLS protocol operation and handshake process.
3. Common attacks on transport layer protocols and optimization measures.

5.5 Experiment—Analyzing TLS Handshake and Encrypted Communication

5.5.1 Experiment Objectives

1. Use Wireshark to capture the TLS handshake process and analyze the TLS 1.3 key negotiation mechanism.
2. Understand how the TLS protocol ensures data confidentiality and integrity.
3. Compare packet differences before and after TLS encryption.

5.5.2 Tools and Environment

1. Tools: Wireshark, a browser supporting TLS 1.3 (Chrome 70+, Firefox 63+), and the openssl command.

5.5.3 Experiment Steps

1. Prepare TLS Communication Scenario
   (1) Launch Wireshark, set the filter to 'tls', and start capturing.
   (2) Open a browser and visit a website supporting TLS 1.3 (e.g., https://www.cloudflare.com).
   (3) After completing an HTTPS request (e.g., viewing the homepage content), close the page.
2. Analyze the TLS 1.3 Handshake Process
   (1) Locate key TLS handshake packets in Wireshark:
      (a) Client Hello: Client sends supported cipher suites, TLS version (TLS 1.3), random, etc (Fig. 5.6).

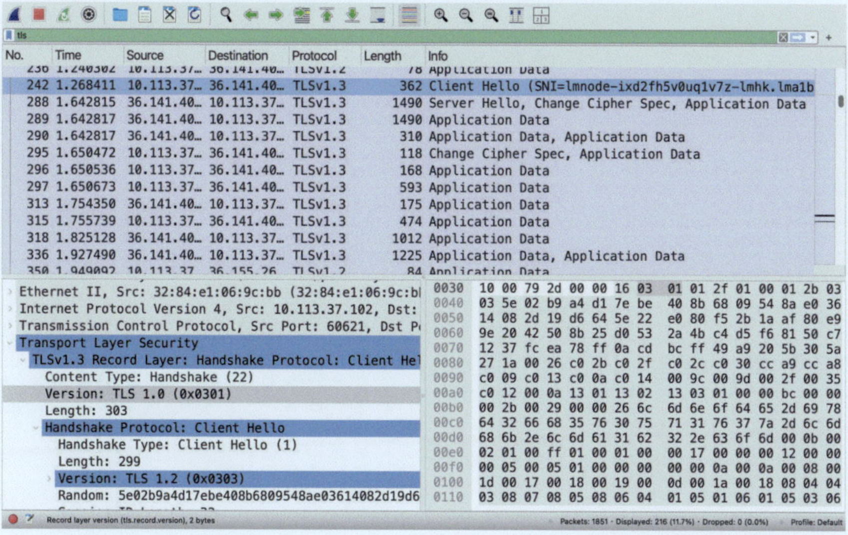

Fig. 5.6 TLS client hello packet format

(b) Server Hello: The server selects a cipher suite (e.g., TLS_AES_128_GCM_SHA256), sends a random, and transmits the server certificate (Fig. 5.7).

(c) Encrypted Extensions: The server sends extension information (e.g., ALPN protocol).

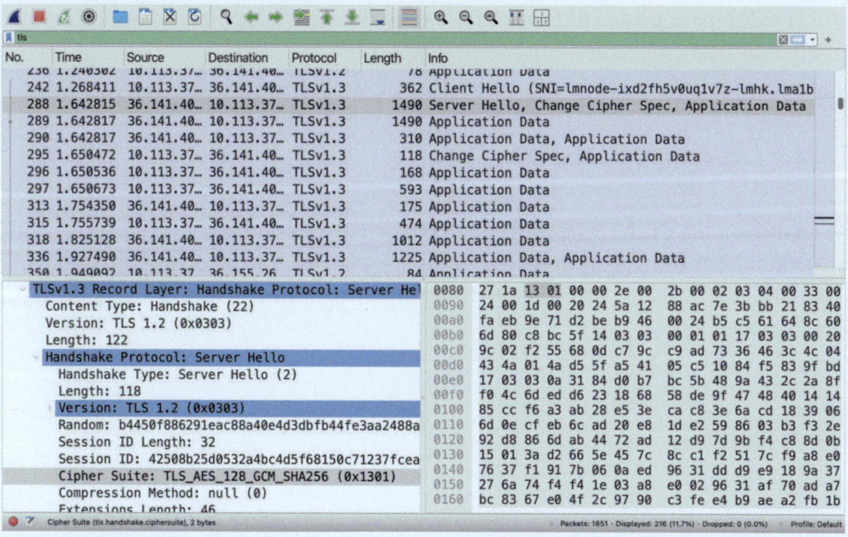

Fig. 5.7 TLS server hello packet format

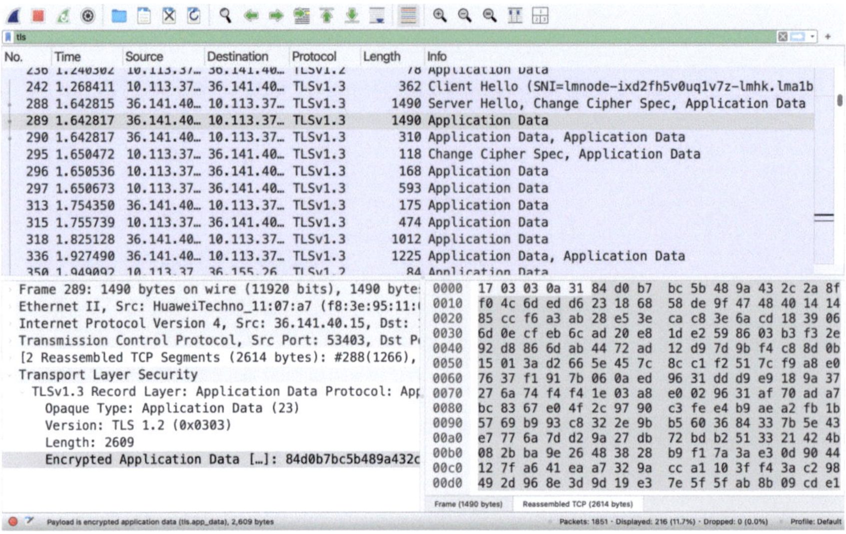

Fig. 5.8 TLS packet format

   (d) Certificate Verify: The server proves ownership of the private key.
   (e) Finished: The client and server confirm the handshake is complete.

3. Analyzing Encrypted Data Transmission

   (1) Locate the application data (Application Data) after the handshake completes and observe whether its content is encrypted gibberish (demonstrating confidentiality) (Fig. 5.8).
   (2) Compare packet differences between the TLS handshake phase (plaintext) and data transmission phase (ciphertext).

5.5.4 *Experiment Summary*

By analyzing the TLS 1.3 handshake and data transmission process, we understood key negotiation and encryption algorithms, verified TLS's protection of data confidentiality and integrity, and laid the foundation for further study of transport layer security protocols.

5.6 Exercises

1. Briefly describe the primary functions of the TLS protocol.
2. Briefly describe the main technologies of the TLS protocol.

References

1. Rescorla E. The transport layer security (TLS) protocol version 1.3. RFC 8446, IETF; 2018.
2. Rescorla E. The transport layer security (TLS) protocol version 1.2. RFC 5246, IETF; 2008.
3. Meyer C, Schwenk J. SoK: lessons learned from SSL/TLS attacks. In: International workshop on information security applications. Cham: Springer International Publishing, 2013. p. 189–209.
4. Durumeric A, Ma Z, Li F, et al. The matter of Heartbleed. In: Proceedings of the ACM internet measurement conference (IMC). ACM; 2014. p. 475–488.
5. Krawczyk H, Paterson KG, Wee H. On the security of the TLS protocol: a systematic analysis. In: Proceedings of the 36th annual international cryptology conference (CRYPTO 2016). Berlin: Springer; 2016. p. 429–448.
6. Xiao M, Bai H, Li H, et al. A secure and efficient transport protocol for multi-identifier network. In: 2023 9th international conference on computer and communications (ICCC). IEEE; 2023. p. 1653–1659.

Chapter 6
Frontier Exploration of Transport Layer Protocols

In the preceding chapters, we systematically reviewed the core mechanisms, optimization methods, and practical strengths and limitations of both traditional and modern transport-layer protocols, such as TCP, UDP, QUIC, and TLS. Building on this foundation, this chapter focuses on the evolution of the transport layer in future network environments, examining the challenges and innovation requirements it faces in emerging application scenarios.

With the explosive growth of new technologies such as 5G, large-scale AI models, and network coding, transport layer protocols face unprecedented challenges in scenario adaptation, driving numerous cutting-edge technological innovations.

For emerging scenarios demanding high concurrency, low latency, and high reliability—such as mobile networks, data centers, and high-performance computing—traditional protocols struggle to meet requirements, necessitating targeted protocol optimization and innovation. The network landscape is constantly evolving, with the transport layer transcending the constraints of traditional protocols to meet the high-performance demands of the 5G, data center, and AI eras.

This chapter explores the development and optimization of transport protocols in cutting-edge domains, delving into transport layer innovations under future network architectures like MIN. Finally, it guides students to explore and contemplate the future direction of next-generation transport protocols through a thought-provoking question and discussion centered on future-oriented network protocol design principles.

H. Li and Z. Bao, *Transport Layer for Computer Networks*,
https://doi.org/10.1007/978-981-95-7374-5_6

6.1 Evolution and Challenges of Transport Protocols

6.1.1 Evolution and Development of Transport Protocols

The evolution of transport layer protocols constitutes a vital chapter in the history of computer networking. It has been an enduring thread throughout the development of computer networks, profoundly influencing every facet of network communication. From the basic data transmission requirements of early networks to today's complex applications supporting diverse network scenarios, transmission protocols have evolved through multiple stages. Each phase aimed to address specific network challenges and drive innovation in communication technology.

The development trajectory of transport layer protocols traces back to the nascent stages of computer networking. In the early days of computer networks, transmission protocols primarily focused on enabling point-to-point communication capabilities. Early protocols could only meet basic data transmission requirements, featuring simple designs but limited functionality. Transmission protocols at this stage were primarily tailored for low-speed, resource-constrained network environments, lacking robust reliability and flow control mechanisms.

Over time, the 1970s witnessed the birth of the TCP/IP protocol, a landmark achievement in network communication that provided standardized transmission mechanisms. TCP ensures data reliability through its three-way handshake and acknowledgment mechanism, while implementing flow control via the sliding window algorithm. UDP, leveraging its low-latency and high-efficiency characteristics, demonstrates unique advantages in real-time communication domains. In scenarios such as online gaming and live video streaming, UDP delivers smoother, more immediate interactive experiences for users. The success of TCP/IP laid the foundation for the rapid development of the Internet, but it gradually revealed its limitations in mobile and low-latency scenarios [1].

The current Internet architecture, established in the 1960s and 1970s, was constrained by hardware performance and resources. At that time, computer networks primarily addressed the challenge of sharing scarce resources between hosts, making the end-to-end push-based interaction design well-suited to the demands of the era. Over the past decade, the explosive growth of network scale has fueled rapid development in emerging applications like e-commerce, digital media, and social networking, making content distribution the primary function of the Internet. Users now prioritize content itself over how or where to access it. Simultaneously, the mismatch between the current Internet architecture and evolving user demands has driven researchers to continuously explore new architectural designs for future networks.

Academic circles have proposed two technical approaches: the "incremental improvement" path, exemplified by IPv6, aims to resolve the urgent issue of IPv4 address exhaustion by expanding the address space, providing a viable solution for the Internet's continued development.

Conversely, the "revolutionary disruption" philosophy has spawned entirely new architectures such as the Information Center Network (ICN) and its prototypical example, the Naming Data Network (NDN). NDN boldly introduces receiver-driven pull communication semantics, attempting to overturn the sender-driven paradigm of traditional IP networks. However, its singular communication semantics and disruptive architectural design have led to challenges in compatibility with existing IP networks and scalability to meet future, unknown communication demands.

To address these challenges, the Multi-Identifier Network (MIN) framework emerged. Developed and maintained by the CoG-MIN team at Peking University's Shenzhen Key Laboratory of Information Theory and Future Networks, MIN inherits the strengths of both IP and NDN networks. It supports both push and pull communication semantics while enabling the resolution and routing of multiple network identifiers.

Concurrently, the diversification of internet applications and rapid bandwidth growth have spurred the emergence of next-generation transport protocols. The UDP-based QUIC protocol integrates connection migration, built-in encryption, and traffic/congestion control. It not only resolves TCP's shortcomings in connection establishment and head-of-line blocking but also serves as the foundational protocol for HTTP/3, significantly enhancing transmission efficiency and security [1]. In data center and high-performance computing scenarios, specialized transport protocols like RDMA (Remote Direct Memory Access) and RoCE (RDMA over Converged Ethernet) are gaining widespread adoption. By bypassing the operating system kernel, they enable low-latency data exchange and are extensively used in distributed databases, storage systems, and artificial intelligence training clusters.

6.1.2 Evolution of Requirements from Traditional Networks to Future Networks

The current Internet architecture was established in the 1960s and 1970s. Constrained by hardware performance and resources, computer networks at that time primarily addressed the challenge of sharing scarce resources between hosts. Consequently, the end-to-end push-based interaction design effectively met the demands of the era. Over the subsequent decades, rapid advancements in integrated circuits led to increasingly sophisticated network devices with growing computational power and decreasing costs. This hardware evolution fueled the rapid expansion of computer networks. In the past decade, the explosive growth of network scale has accelerated the development of emerging applications like digital media, short videos, and social networks, making content distribution the primary function of the Internet. Users now focus more on the content itself rather than how or where to access it. The current Internet architecture design is inconsistent with existing user demands, prompting researchers to continuously explore new architectural designs for future networks.

Academic circles have proposed two technical approaches to address the issues in the current Internet architecture: The first adopts an "incremental improvement" philosophy, revising and expanding existing network models to adapt to new network requirements. A typical example is using IPv6 to solve the IPv4 address exhaustion problem; the second adopts a "revolutionary disruption" approach, reconstructing the existing network architecture to redesign a content-first network framework. Representative architectures include Information-Centric Networking (ICN), such as Named Data Networking (NDN).

The traditional IP address system can no longer meet the future network's demand for multiple identifiers, such as user identifiers and content identifiers. Future networks must support multi-identifier systems to enhance reliability and efficiency.

In these emerging architectures, content identification and retrieval become central concerns. For instance, ICN centers on content: users request content by sending interest packets, and network nodes forward data packets based on these interest packets.

This requires transport layer protocols to efficiently handle content-based requests and transmissions, ensuring rapid and accurate content distribution. These network architectures adopt disruptive design approaches, reconstructing a network layer that is difficult to scale. Consequently, they fail to achieve good compatibility with existing IP networks and cannot address potential new communication demands in future.

Named Data Networks (NDN) was proposed in 2010, succeeding the Content-Centric Networking (CCN) approach. It replaces the sender-driven push communication semantics of IP networks with receiver-driven pull communication semantics. However, due to NDN's disruptive architecture design and reliance on a single communication semantics, it reconstructs a network layer that is difficult to scale. Consequently, it fails to achieve good compatibility with existing IP networks and cannot address new communication demands that may arise in future. Emerging communication demands may necessitate radical network architecture overhauls or even the introduction of entirely new network architectures.

Against this backdrop, the MIN network [2] demonstrates unique advantages in meeting future network requirements. Its compatibility enables seamless collaboration with existing IP and NDN networks, safeguarding substantial corporate and user investments in current network infrastructure and software ecosystems. Enterprises can progressively introduce MIN Network's advanced capabilities without large-scale replacement of existing network equipment and software, enabling smooth network upgrades. For instance, in organizations already deploying IP networks, MIN Network can serve as a complementary extension. It provides more efficient and secure network support for specific business scenarios without disrupting existing operations.

The MIN network employs a Multi-Identifier System (MIS) based on blockchain technology in the management plane to enable multi-party governance. In the forwarding plane, it utilizes Multi-Identifier Routers (MIRs) to resolve, route, and forward multiple network identifiers. The MIN network adheres to the following design principles:

1. MIN introduces a decentralized, blockchain-based co-governance model for hierarchical cyberspace management. Top-level identifiers are governed through

consortium blockchain voting, ensuring global coordination, while low-level identifiers are autonomously managed to preserve sovereignty and flexibility.
2. The MIN architecture provides inherent security at the network layer, supporting packet verification and identity authentication at the network level. This ensures only traffic generated by legitimate network users can traverse the MIN network.
3. MIN supports sustainable network evolution through an identifier extension mechanism based on identifier rollback. It uses identity as the anchor identifier, with the support of addressing and routing of various existing and potential network identifiers. In this way, the network architecture can adapt to the extension of a variety of identifier space, such as Internet of Things, Internet of Vehicles, Industrial Internet of Things, and Space-Air Ground Integrated Network.

6.1.3 Adaptation and Exploration for Emerging Scenarios

To meet the demands of diverse application scenarios, transmission protocols have undergone extensive exploration in adaptability and innovation. These scenarios encompass mobile networks, data centers, computing networks, and support for real-time multimedia and high-performance computing, driving the continuous optimization and evolution of transport layer protocols.

In mobile network scenarios, the widespread adoption of 5G and Wi-Fi 6 technologies presents new challenges and opportunities for transport protocols. The frequent handover of mobile devices and network instability demand rapid recovery and high adaptability from transport protocols.

The QUIC protocol significantly enhances transmission performance in mobile scenarios through its connection migration and fast recovery mechanisms. For instance, when devices transition between Wi-Fi hotspots or switch from Wi-Fi to cellular networks, QUIC swiftly detects network changes and restores transmission without requiring connection reestablishment—unlike traditional TCP. This minimizes transmission interruptions and enhances user experience. In practical scenarios like mobile video conferencing and live streaming, QUIC significantly outperforms traditional protocols by effectively preventing stuttering and disconnections.

Simultaneously, the introduction of network coding technology offers innovative solutions for enhancing the reliability and efficiency of mobile network transmission. Reliable transmission methods incorporating network coding reduce retransmission overhead caused by data loss by embedding redundant coding information within packets, proving particularly effective in high packet loss and low-bandwidth environments. For instance, in wireless transmission scenarios, network coding significantly improves data transmission success rates, supporting highly reliable communication within mobile networks.

Amidst the digital development wave, the efficient operation of data centers and computing networks imposes higher demands on transmission protocol performance. Data centers handle massive data processing tasks, requiring their transport layer protocols to meet high throughput, low latency, and high reliability needs. Data center networks feature a single control domain, homogeneous architecture, and high-bandwidth/low-latency characteristics.

However, they also face challenges such as diverse application demands, complex traffic patterns, congestion control issues, and TCP Incast problems. To address these challenges, researchers have proposed various protocols and mechanisms. In data center scenarios, the FASTFLOW algorithm achieves a 50% performance improvement over traditional methods by integrating dual congestion signals (ECN and RTT) during AI training traffic bursts [3].

The host-based congestion control algorithm DCTCP leverages switches' explicit congestion notification (ECN) capabilities for fine-grained congestion management, though it lacks differentiation between large and small flows. Switch priority scheduling ensures rapid forwarding of high-priority traffic, yet hardware limitations restrict the number of priority queues. Furthermore, traditional TCP protocols show inadequacies in data center networks, prompting the adoption of RDMA technology. RDMA enables direct access to remote host memory, reducing latency and CPU overhead. Primarily implemented through InfiniBand, RoCE, and iWARP, RDMA also faces challenges like congestion management in practical applications.

The rapid advancement of generative large models, such as ChatGPT and Sora, poses significant challenges to network infrastructure. Taking the training of trillion-parameter models as an example, it involves multiple parallel approaches including data parallelism, pipeline parallelism, and tensor parallelism. This requires cross-server communication across hundreds of thousands or even millions of GPUs, demanding ultra-large-scale networking capabilities to support communication among such a vast number of compute nodes.

Moreover, for trillion-parameter models, end-to-end communication latency can account for up to 50% of total training time. Traditional flow control and congestion control algorithms are prone to congestion propagation, increasing communication delays. RDMA technology enables applications to directly access remote node memory without kernel intervention, offering high throughput, low latency, and zero CPU overhead. This enhances model training efficiency and is better suited for large-scale model training scenarios. Figure 6.1 shows a schematic of RDMA mode transmission.

RDMA encompasses protocols such as InfiniBand, RoCE, and iWARP. InfiniBand is designed for high-performance computing, offering high bandwidth and low latency, but requires specialized hardware, resulting in high costs and poor compatibility; RoCE implements RDMA over Ethernet, leveraging its widespread adoption and compatibility for lower costs and easier deployment; iWARP operates on TCP/IP protocols, offering good scalability and compatibility but relatively lower performance. It maintains reliability in lossy network conditions, though extensive TCP connections consume memory resources and flow control mechanisms impact performance, limiting its current large-scale adoption.

Faced with the complex challenges and diverse demands of these emerging scenarios, existing network architectures and transport protocols struggle to fully meet requirements. MIN networks offer flexible solutions for these emerging

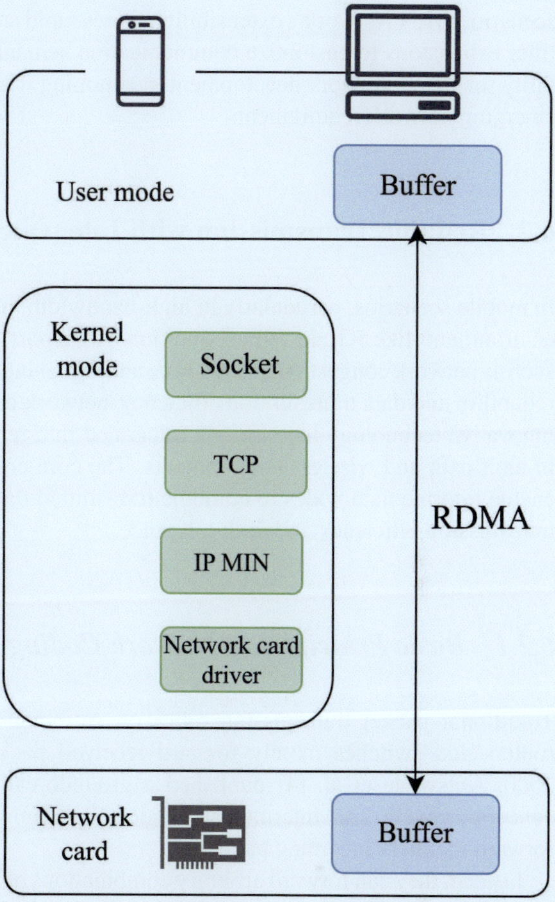

Fig. 6.1 RDMA mode transmission schematic

scenarios. Leveraging its integration of blockchain technology, MIN networks possess unique advantages in identity management and cybersecurity. Its decentralized identity management system supports multiple network identifiers, enabling precise location and recognition for diverse applications and data, thereby enhancing network addressing and data transmission efficiency.

Regarding security, the network layer's inherent security mechanisms and digital signature verification for network packets ensure data transmission integrity and traceability—features beyond the reach of many traditional network architectures. Simultaneously, MIN Network's compatible design philosophy enables seamless integration with existing network architectures, safeguarding current network investments while facilitating incremental upgrades. For emerging demands in new scenarios, MIN Network's extensibility allows rapid adaptation through simple identifier expansions to customize communication semantics. This provides vast scalability for future network development, positioning it as a key enabler for supporting emerging network requirements.

6.2 Reliable Transmission with Integrated Network Coding

In mobile scenarios, particularly in high-bandwidth, high-latency-variation network environments like 5G and WiFi 6, traditional transport layer protocols face challenges such as network congestion, packet loss, and signal interference. To enhance network reliability and data transmission efficiency, network coding (NC) has emerged as an innovative technology increasingly integrated into reliable transmission, especially in multipath and wireless environments. The core concept of network coding is to enable intermediate nodes to combine transmitted data packets, thereby improving transmission efficiency and fault tolerance.

6.2.1 Basic Principles of Network Coding

Traditional packet transmission relies on store-and-forward mechanisms, where routers and switches merely forward received packets without modification. In 2000, Ahlswede et al. [4] published a groundbreaking paper proposing a novel concept: routers and intermediate nodes in communication networks need not forward identical incoming packets.

Instead, they can forward arbitrary combinations of these packets by mixing them. Network coding breaks through this limitation by allowing intermediate nodes in the network to perform linear combinations on packets. For example, multiple packets can be encrypted, mixed, or even regenerated into new packets at network nodes, with these new packets containing the information from the original packets. The receiving end can recover the original data using appropriate decoding algorithms.

The core idea of network coding is to transmit data through linear combinations of packets, rather than simple "store-and-forward."

Suppose the source node needs to send n data packets, denoted as $x_1, x_2, \ldots, x_n$. These packets can be regarded as vectors of length m:

$$\begin{bmatrix} x_{i1} \\ x_{i2} \\ \vdots \\ x_{im} \end{bmatrix}, \quad i = 1, 2, \ldots, n. \tag{6.1}$$

At intermediate nodes within the network, upon receiving these data packets, new packets are generated through linear combination:

$$y_j = \sum_{i=1}^{n} c_{ji} \cdot x_i, \tag{6.2}$$

where: $\boldsymbol{y}_j$ is the jth new data packet generated by the intermediate node; c_{ji} is the coding coefficient; $\boldsymbol{x}_i$ is the original data packet transmitted by the source.

This implies that each new packet $\boldsymbol{y}_j$ is a linear combination of the original packet $\boldsymbol{x}_1, \boldsymbol{x}_2, \ldots, \boldsymbol{x}_n$.

At the receiving end, assuming k linearly combined packets $y_1, y_2, \ldots, y_k$ are received, these packets can be expressed as:

$$Y = \begin{bmatrix} y_1 \\ y_2 \\ \vdots \\ y_k \end{bmatrix} = C \cdot X, \tag{6.3}$$

where: Y is the matrix of received data packets. C is the matrix of encoding coefficients. X is the matrix of source data packets. The goal of decoding is to recover X from Y, which requires C to be a full-rank matrix, i.e., $\text{rank}(C) = n$. If this condition is satisfied, decoding can be performed using the inverse of the matrix:

$$X = C^{-1} \cdot Y. \tag{6.4}$$

This characteristic of network coding enables it to enhance bandwidth utilization in multipath transmission and effectively mitigate the impact of packet loss. Particularly in wireless network environments, where signal instability and path complexity prevail, network coding improves data reliability and transmission efficiency by combining packets from different paths.

The classic "Butterfly Network" serves as a quintessential example demonstrating the advantages of network coding. As illustrated, source node A aims to simultaneously multicast two data packets to destination nodes F and G. Assuming all links are error-free and each link can transmit only one packet per time slot. Under traditional forwarding, intermediate node D can only choose to forward either the packet from B or the packet from C. Even with alternating forwarding, the overall throughput reaches only 1.5 packets per time slot.

However, with network coding, node D can perform an XOR operation on the two packets to form a new coded packet:

$$y = p_1 \oplus p_2. \tag{6.5}$$

And transmits it to downstream nodes. At this point, receivers F and G combine the original data packet p_1 or p_2 they have already obtained to decode and reconstruct

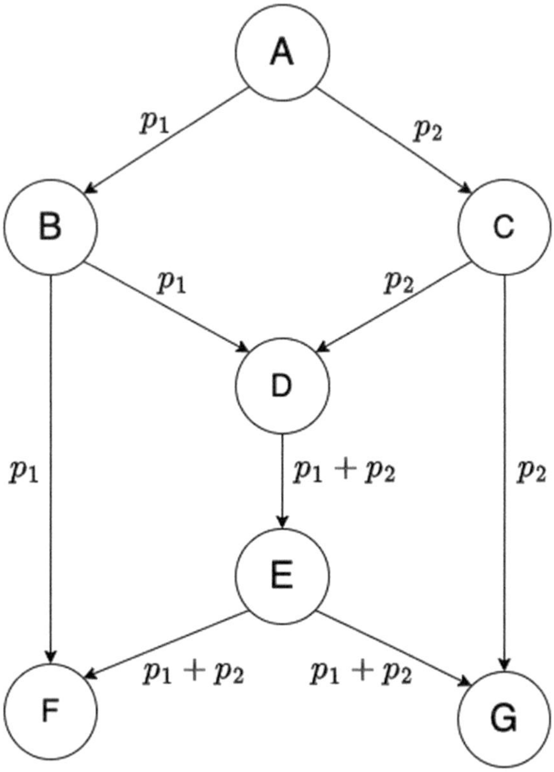

Fig. 6.2 Example diagram of a butterfly network [5]

another copy of the data. Thus, each time slot achieves throughput for two data packets, reaching the upper limit of the network's multicast capacity.

More generally, network coding extends beyond XOR operations to include linear combinations over finite fields, known as Linear Network Coding (LNC). Li et al. [5] demonstrated that in multicast scenarios, LNC alone suffices to achieve theoretically optimal throughput, thereby establishing network coding's pivotal role in both theory and practice. Figure 6.2 shows an example diagram of a butterfly network [5].

6.2.2 *Application and Development of Network Coding in Protocols*

Network coding in modern communication networks is implemented through specialized network protocols. Currently, a significant number of network coding protocols exist in both wired and wireless data transmission systems.

In 2006, the CodeCast protocol—a specialized multicast protocol based on network coding—was introduced to mobile ad hoc networks (MANETs) to reduce packet loss and traffic delay for services using multicast transmission [6]. The CodeCast protocol employs random network coding to provide partial recovery of lost packets and nearly redundancy-free transmission route separation. Simulations conducted by developers demonstrated that CodeCast can deliver nearly 100% packet delivery probability on MANET networks, regardless of the relative movement speeds of mobile network nodes or packet sizes. In contrast, when transmitting via the UDP protocol, the delivery probability drops to 94% as node speeds increase.

In 2007, a research team at MIT proposed the MAC-Independent Opportunistic Routing (MORE) protocol. Designed for IEEE 802.11-based wireless mesh networks, MORE pioneered the integration of network coding concepts into opportunistic routing, enabling flexible forwarding independent of the MAC layer. MORE employs random linear coding of data packets, enabling multiple relay nodes to simultaneously forward coded packets, thereby enhancing link utilization and end-to-end throughput [7].

In 2009, researchers from Purdue University and Northeastern University proposed the CCACK (Cumulative Coded Acknowledgments) protocol. This protocol employs a cumulative acknowledgment mechanism, allowing relay nodes to confirm received coded data streams to upstream nodes with minimal overhead. This avoids redundant overhead from per-packet acknowledgments and significantly reduces acknowledgment load in high-packet-loss environments [8].

That same year, a team of scientists from MIT, Harvard University, and the University of Porto introduced the TCP/NC protocol [9]. Its core innovation involves inserting a "network coding layer" between the transport layer and the IP layer. By modifying the ACK response mechanism, it achieves the integration of network coding techniques with the TCP protocol. This approach minimizes changes to the TCP protocol itself and utilizes standard TCP packets.

TCP/NC employs TCP Vegas and TCP Reno algorithms for congestion control [10]. In packet-loss-prone wireless networks, TCP/NC delivers significantly higher useful bandwidth than traditional TCP: at a 25% loss rate, available bandwidth can increase up to tenfold. However, encoding and decoding operations require additional computational overhead. TCP/NC adds its own header to transmitted packets, increasing redundancy. Consequently, on lossless networks, it provides approximately 10% lower useful transmission rates than TCP.

In recent years, domestic scholars have also been promoting the application of network coding in novel networks. Song et al. [11] proposed the SANC-TCP (Self-Adaptive Network Coding TCP) protocol in 2011, which builds upon TCP/NC. Its core idea introduces an adaptive redundancy factor (R). By carrying current network status information in TCP or ACK packet headers, the sender can dynamically adjust R based on packet loss feedback from the receiver. This work further advances the evolution of network coding within transport layer protocols, demonstrating that feedback-driven adaptive redundancy control can enhance support for lossy wireless networks without substantially modifying the TCP protocol stack.

Building upon this, Fan et al. [12] further proposed a scheme that dynamically adjusts the redundancy parameter in "Network Coding Meets TCP," introducing "time-cache" and "time-classification management algorithm" at the sender's network coding layer to determine the optimal redundancy parameter by analyzing the time difference in acknowledgements from the sink, thereby effectively masking TCP layer packet losses, particularly over lossy links.

6.2.3 Integration of Network Coding with Transport Layer Applications

Network coding has found extensive application, transitioning from mathematical theory to practical implementation. At the transport layer, it is primarily applied in the retransmission and acknowledgment processes during packet transmission.

In traditional TCP protocols, packet reliability is typically achieved through acknowledgment (ACK) and retransmission mechanisms. When the receiver detects packet loss, it requests the sender to retransmit the missing packets via timeouts or explicit negative acknowledgments (NACK). However, this mechanism suffers from two major issues:

- **Low Link Utilization**: Waiting for acknowledgments before retransmission increases idle time on the transmission link, especially in high-latency networks.
- **High Retransmission Overhead**: In networks with high packet loss rates, the volume of retransmitted data significantly increases transmission overhead.

The retransmission mechanism incorporating network coding effectively mitigates these issues. In this approach, the sender does not directly retransmit lost packets. Instead, it linearly encodes unacknowledged packets to generate new coded packets sent to the receiver. The receiver decodes the lost data by combining the received encoded packet with the original data packet, thereby reducing retransmission frequency and latency.

In TCP/NC, the sender performs network coding on all unacknowledged packets within the window, generating redundant packets that are appended to the header of TCP packets. The receiver recovers lost packets by solving a system of linear equations using the received data packet and the redundant packet. This mechanism offers the following advantages:

- **Enhanced Link Utilization**: During transmission, the sender can continuously send data packets and redundancy packets without waiting for acknowledgments from the receiver.
- **Reduced Retransmission Overhead**: Linear coding minimizes redundant retransmissions of individual packets, significantly improving reliability and efficiency.

Furthermore, when combined with congestion control algorithms (such as TCP Vegas and TCP Reno), TCP/NC performs exceptionally well in networks with high packet loss rates. Research indicates that in networks with a 25% packet loss rate, TCP/NC can deliver effective bandwidth up to 10 times that of traditional TCP.

QUIC, a UDP-based transport protocol developed by Google and detailed in Chap. 4 of this book, features low latency, multiplexing, and rapid handshaking. However, in high-packet-loss and high-latency networks, QUIC also faces challenges from packet loss impacting transmission efficiency.

To address this issue, Google incorporated a Forward Error Correction (FEC) mechanism during QUIC's initial development. Combined with network coding techniques, this further enhances data transmission reliability and efficiency. Notably, the IETF standard version of QUIC does not include FEC. Below are the specific implementation and optimization methods for QUIC's Forward Error Correction:

Within a given time window, the sender needs to transmit n original packets, denoted as $P_1, P_2, \ldots, P_n$. The sender can generate m redundant packets (typically) using an encoding algorithm, denoted as $R_1, R_2, \ldots, R_m$. The process for generating redundant packets is as follows:

$$R_i = \sum_{j=1}^{n} g_{ij} \cdot P_j. \tag{6.6}$$

Among these, g_{ij} is the encoding coefficient, typically generated through Galois field operations. The sender transmits these redundancy packets alongside the original data packets to the receiver.

Upon receiving partial original data packets and redundancy packets, the receiver can recover the lost original data packets using a decoding algorithm. The core of decoding involves solving the following system of linear equations:

$$R = C \cdot P, \tag{6.7}$$

where: R is the matrix of received incomplete packets. C is the matrix of encoding coefficients. P is the matrix of original data packets.

As long as C is a full-rank matrix (i.e., its determinant is non-zero), the receiver can recover lost packets by performing matrix inversion.

Unlike TCP, which can only retransmit packets after they are lost—resulting in more retransmissions and degraded performance as packet loss increases—QUIC's FEC recovers data using redundant packets when some packets are lost. This reduces retransmission frequency and enhances resilience against packet loss. Especially in high-loss networks (such as mobile networks and Wi-Fi), QUIC demonstrates significantly superior reliability compared to TCP.

In practical applications, such as live video streaming over 5G networks, packet loss is highly likely due to rapidly changing channel conditions and increased mobility. Relying solely on traditional retransmission-based mechanisms often requires one or more round-trip delays for packet recovery, resulting in video playback stuttering. In contrast, the Forward Error Correction (FEC) mechanism within the QUIC protocol enables the sender to generate redundant information in real-time and transmit it alongside the video data. When the receiver detects packet loss, it can immediately utilize this redundancy for recovery without waiting for retransmission, significantly enhancing video stream continuity and user experience. This mechanism demonstrates clear advantages in applications demanding high real-time performance, such as live video streaming, cloud gaming, and remote interactions.

Beyond transport layer optimization, network coding finds extensive applications in other domains:

Distributed Storage Systems: Network coding enhances data redundancy and reliability. Typical implementations include Hadoop HDFS-RAID, Microsoft Azure's Locally Repairable Codes (LRC), and network coding-based distributed file systems. These systems leverage coding techniques to reduce storage overhead while accelerating data repair processes, thereby improving fault tolerance in storage clusters.

Multimedia Streaming: In video-on-demand and live streaming, Application-Layer Network Coding (ALNC) mitigates stuttering and latency caused by packet loss. Particularly in wireless networks or P2P streaming scenarios, network coding enhances transmission robustness and bandwidth utilization by combining multiple source data streams, thereby improving user experience.

In summary, reliable transmission through integrated network coding offers novel approaches for mobile transmission protocols, demonstrating significant advantages in the high-bandwidth, high-latency-variation environments of 5G and Wi-Fi 6. The next subsection will provide detailed insights. Future breakthroughs in practical scenarios are anticipated through further optimization of the integration between network coding algorithms and transmission protocols.

6.3 Low-Latency, High-Reliability Transmission in Mobile Scenarios

6.3.1 Transmission Challenges in Mobile Scenarios

Achieving ultra-low latency and high reliability is a core objective in the development of 5G networks for mobile scenarios. Realizing this goal relies not only on advancements in communication technology itself but also on continuous optimization of transmission protocols. With the evolution of 4G/5G technology, network bandwidth and the scale of connected devices have significantly increased. However, this progress also brings challenges such as network dynamism, channel instability, and latency sensitivity. Therefore, designing efficient transmission protocols capable of adapting to mobile scenario demands is particularly crucial.

With the continuous emergence of real-time applications in 5G networks—such as autonomous driving, remote medical surgeries, and real-time industrial control—demands for data transmission latency have become extremely stringent. In autonomous driving scenarios, vehicles must receive information in real time from sensors, other vehicles, and traffic infrastructure to make accurate driving decisions.

According to relevant safety standards, the end-to-end latency of autonomous driving systems must be controlled within 10 ms; otherwise, it could lead to serious accidents such as collisions. In remote surgical procedures, doctors must control surgical instruments in real time over the network to operate on patients. Any delay could compromise surgical precision and safety, making latency requirements equally stringent. The widespread adoption of these real-time applications makes reducing latency and enhancing reliability critical tasks for mobile transmission scenarios, directly impacting user experience and service quality.

6.3.2 Evolution of Transmission Protocols in Mobile Scenarios

During 5G network deployment, researchers typically integrate TCP, UDP, and their variants with specific networks to reduce latency and enhance reliability.

To improve communication, the primary approach involves enhancing the communication protocols themselves. New communication protocols primarily fall into three categories.

1. **Single-Path Protocols**

   Each scenario requires appropriate communication protocols to fully leverage the network's capabilities [13]. In traditional single-path transmission protocols like TCP, UDP, and their variants, performance optimization hinges on improving congestion control, traffic management, and error recovery mechanisms. For instance, the QUIC protocol significantly reduces latency and enhances transmission reliability in packet-loss scenarios by integrating forward error correction (FEC) technology alongside multiplexing and 0-RTT handshake.

2. **Multipath Transmission Protocol Optimization**

   As network environments diversify, multipath transmission protocols (e.g., MPTCP and MPQUIC) have emerged as research focal points. By leveraging multi-host capabilities and path diversity, multipath transmission distributes traffic across multiple paths, thereby enhancing transmission reliability and resource utilization. Figure 6.3 shows a schematic of MPTCP.

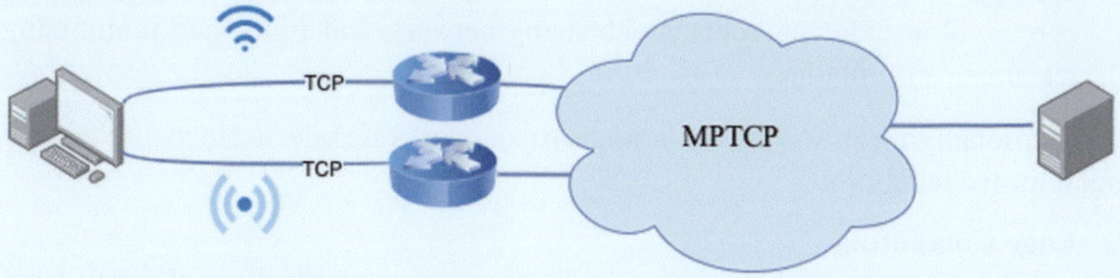

Fig. 6.3 MPTCP schematic

MPTCP (Multi-Path TCP) enables establishing multiple TCP connections across network interfaces, segmenting data streams for distribution across these connections. When a path fails or becomes congested, MPTCP automatically redirects traffic to other available paths, effectively mitigating the impact of single-path failures on overall transmission performance. In data center networks, MPTCP distributes data traffic across multiple links, achieving load balancing and enhancing overall network throughput and reliability.

As a multi-path extension of the QUIC protocol, MPQUIC inherits QUIC's advantages—such as UDP-based rapid transmission, multiplexing, and forward error correction—while adding multi-path transmission capabilities. In complex mobile network environments, MPQUIC dynamically adjusts data distribution based on real-time path conditions. For instance, when congestion or signal degradation occurs on one path, MPQUIC swiftly redirects traffic to alternative available paths, ensuring continuous and stable data transmission. This significantly enhances reliability and efficiency in mobile scenarios. In vehicle-to-everything (V2X) scenarios, where vehicles simultaneously connect to multiple roadside base stations, MPQUIC intelligently allocates transmission paths for diverse data types—such as vehicle sensor data and navigation information—based on each base station's signal strength and bandwidth. This ensures stable transmission of all data during vehicle operation.

3. **Multicast Protocol**

A multicast protocol refers to a protocol that sends the same information to multiple recipients at a given time. Poularakis et al. [14] and Araniti et al. [15] have reflected on the growth of mobile multicast applications, identifying multicast as a key opportunity for future 5G networks. Sending the same information to multiple recipients simultaneously offers lower latency, higher scalability, and network offloading. By transmitting data to multiple recipients at once, multicast technology holds significant application value in scenarios like intelligent transportation and assisted driving.

In intelligent transportation systems, traffic management centers can use multicast protocols to broadcast real-time traffic information—such as road conditions and accident alerts—to all vehicles within a region. Vehicles can promptly receive these updates to adjust routes, thereby enhancing traffic flow and safety. In assisted driving scenarios, multicast protocols facilitate information sharing between vehicles (e.g., speed and direction) to improve driving decision-making and safety. Research indicates that mobile multicast protocols excel in reducing latency, enhancing network scalability, and minimizing resource consumption.

Additionally, the following technologies or networks are selected to reduce latency and improve reliability:

1. **Edge Computing**

Edge computing involves moving cloud and network functions closer to users to deliver services locally, thereby improving performance, such as reducing latency. In traditional cloud computing models, data must travel long distances to remote data centers for processing before results are returned to users, introducing significant latency. Edge computing deploys computational and storage resources at the network edge, enabling rapid local data processing and drastically reducing processing time. In ITS, vehicle sensors continuously collect vast amounts of real-time data—including speed, direction, and environmental conditions. If all this data were transmitted to the cloud for processing, factors like long transmission distances and network congestion could cause processing delays, failing to meet the real-time requirements of autonomous driving. By leveraging edge computing, this data can be processed in real-time on edge computing devices near the vehicle, enabling rapid driving decisions—such as acceleration, deceleration, or turning—to ensure safe and smooth vehicle operation.

2. **Future Networks**

Innovative future network technologies like Information-Centric Networking (ICN) and Multi-identifier Networking (MIN) aim to redesign the current internet infrastructure. They move beyond traditional peer-to-peer communication paradigms toward data-centric communication models. Future networks treat content itself as the core of network communication, routing and distributing data based on unique content identifiers (e.g., content names) rather than relying on traditional IP addresses. Under this model, network nodes can cache and replicate content. When users request the same content, it can be retrieved from the nearest caching node instead of the original source, significantly reducing the number of hops and latency in data transmission.

When a user requests popular video content on a mobile device, nodes in future network will cache that video at edge nodes near the user based on its popularity and request frequency. Subsequent users requesting the same video can retrieve it directly from these edge nodes, bypassing complex network paths to the video server. This approach substantially reduces latency, enhances content delivery efficiency, and improves user experience.

ICN represents a reimagining of current internet infrastructure, moving beyond the peer-to-peer paradigm to embrace data replication, content distribution, naming schemes, and capture. While not a single technology but rather a combination of techniques for evolving the internet architecture, ICN functions similarly to EDGE, SDN, or NFV—providing network assistance and evolution to enhance KPIs like latency in content delivery applications. Therefore, we deem it appropriate to introduce this paradigm in this section. In mobile scenarios, when users request popular content, ICN leverages its distributed caching and content routing mechanisms to retrieve content from the cache node closest to the user, reducing the number of hops and latency in data transmission.

Simultaneously, ICN's content replication capability enables storing identical content across multiple nodes, improving content availability and transmission reliability. For instance, in mobile video platforms, popular video content is cached at multiple edge nodes near users. When numerous users simultaneously request the same video, ICN can rapidly retrieve video data from the nearest cache node for delivery, reducing latency while alleviating core network load.

3. **Software-Defined Networking (SDN)**

   SDN represents an innovative approach involving the creation of a decoupled architecture that separates the control plane from the data plane. SDN enables intelligent routing, flexibility, programmability, and facilitates virtualization [16]. In traditional network architectures, the control plane and data plane are tightly coupled within network devices (such as routers and switches). Each device must independently run routing protocols and make forwarding decisions, complicating network management and configuration while hindering flexibility in responding to changing network demands. SDN centralizes control functions onto one or more controllers, enabling centralized network management and control. Controllers dynamically generate and distribute forwarding rules (flow tables) to data plane devices via software-defined methods, based on real-time network status and user requirements. This facilitates flexible scheduling and management of network traffic. Figure 6.4 shows the architecture of software-defined networking.

Below are common solutions for achieving low latency and high reliability in mobile network scenarios:

One of the most direct approaches to addressing latency and reliability for end-to-end protocols (such as TCP, UDP, or SCTP) in mobile networks is modifying the fundamental mechanisms these protocols use to manage data flows. This includes enhancing congestion control algorithms, improving retransmission mechanisms (e.g., Fast Retransmission), and leveraging future network caching. By storing frequently accessed data and routing popular requests, caching significantly reduces end-to-end transmission and lookup delays. Regarding congestion control algorithm

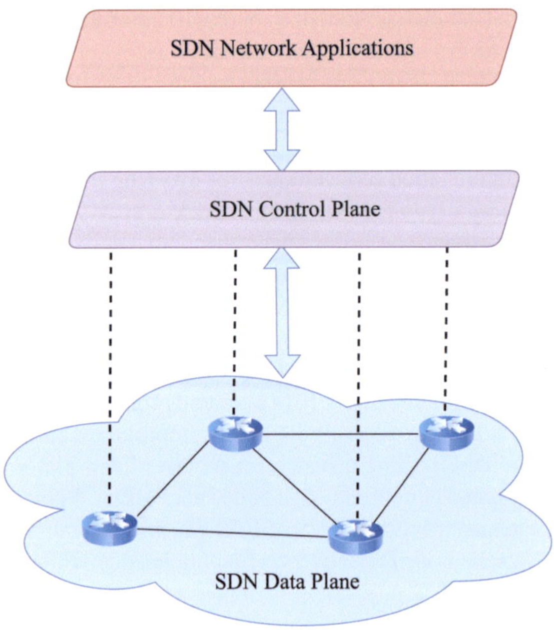

Fig. 6.4 Software-defined networking architecture diagram

enhancements, novel approaches can more accurately detect network congestion states.

For instance, machine learning-based congestion control algorithms can predict congestion occurrences by analyzing vast amounts of network data, proactively adjusting transmission rates to prevent packet loss and increased delays caused by congestion. Regarding retransmission algorithm enhancements, fast retransmission mechanisms enable swift notification to the sender upon packet loss detection at the receiver, eliminating the need to wait for timeout retransmission timers to expire. This significantly shortens retransmission intervals, improving data transmission reliability and efficiency.

In data transmission, encoding refers to modifying information to enhance communication. In most cases, this encoding incorporates redundancy, enabling data to be received in different forms and decoded at the destination. The two primary encoding forms considered in this study are forward error correction (FEC) and network coding. FEC is an end-to-end technique for detecting and correcting a finite number of errors over noisy communication channels without requiring retransmissions. This coding is utilized in the QUIC transport protocol introduced earlier. Proper application of this method can enhance reliability, throughput, or latency levels [17].

Furthermore, network coding enables intermediate nodes (such as routers) to transmit data encoded across multiple packets. In most variants, the original message can be decoded as long as a sufficient number of packets reach the destination. In multi-path transmission scenarios, network coding can combine packets from different paths. Upon receiving a sufficient number of coded packets, the receiver can reconstruct the original data. This not only enhances transmission reliability but also improves bandwidth utilization to some extent, reduces transmission delays, and adapts to the highly dynamic and unstable channel characteristics of mobile networks.

In summary, low-latency, high-reliability transmission in mobile scenarios represents a complex and critical research domain, encompassing communication protocols, network technologies, data coding, and the integration of emerging technologies. Regarding transmission protocols, the integration of TCP, UDP, and their variants with other networks, alongside innovations in new single-path protocols like QUIC, multi-path transmission protocols (MPTCP, MPQUIC), and multicast protocols, has effectively enhanced data transmission efficiency, reliability, and resource utilization. This meets the diverse data transmission demands of various application scenarios.

With ongoing technological advancement and innovation, the future holds promise for achieving more efficient, reliable, and low-latency mobile data transmission. This will lay a solid foundation for mobile scenarios and the widespread application of future network communications.

6.4 Transmission Protocols in Data Center Scenarios

Data centers serve as resource pools providing extensive computing and storage capabilities to support modern internet services. Transmission protocols, which define the rules and standards for data transfer in computer networks, have existed since the inception of computer networking and continue to evolve and improve. However, their application in Data Center Networks (DCNs) emerged relatively late. Only in the past decade or so, with the rapid growth of data centers, have transmission protocols gained significant attention and widespread adoption within DCN environments.

In early DCNs, transmission protocol design primarily focused on three areas: host-based congestion control, network arbitration mechanisms, and switch priority scheduling. In recent years, however, as data center operations have grown increasingly complex and demands for network performance have intensified, receiver-driven active congestion control and RDMA transmission protocols have emerged as key research areas and development trends within DCN transmission protocols.

As the core infrastructure of modern information technology, data centers shoulder the tasks of storing, processing, and transmitting massive amounts of data. Their transport layer protocols are crucial for ensuring efficient data center operations and meeting stringent network performance requirements such as high throughput, low latency, and high reliability.

For instance, in applications demanding extreme real-time responsiveness—such as financial transactions, online gaming, and live video streaming—data centers must process and transmit massive data volumes within minimal timeframes. Any delay or data loss could trigger severe consequences. The explosive growth of network applications has driven revolutionary changes in data center network architecture and scale. They have evolved from traditional small-scale facilities to large-scale, distributed centers. Network topologies have grown increasingly complex, server and network device counts have surged dramatically, and data traffic exhibits explosive growth and heightened diversity. These changes pose unprecedented challenges and demands on data center transport layer protocols, driving researchers to continually explore and optimize transmission protocols to meet evolving data center requirements.

As the core infrastructure of modern information technology, data centers rely critically on transport layer protocols to meet demands for high throughput, low latency, and high reliability. The rapid advancement of network applications has driven significant architectural and scale transformations in data center networks, presenting new challenges and requirements for transport layer protocols. Therefore, in-depth research and optimization of transport layer protocols in data center scenarios are crucial for enhancing overall network performance and fulfilling diverse application needs.

6.4.1 *Characteristics and Challenges of Data Center Networks*

Compared to traditional wide-area internet, data center networks (DCN) exhibit several distinct features.

First, data centers typically operate under a single control domain, enabling centralized optimization of network device configurations and transport protocols under unified management policies. This allows for highly customized network configuration and operations tailored to specific business requirements and performance objectives. For instance, operators can flexibly adjust forwarding policies and routing rules through a unified Software-Defined Networking (SDN) platform to more efficiently meet the dynamic demands of application services.

Second, data center network topologies adopt homogeneous and highly standardized designs. To ensure scalability and fault tolerance, large-scale data centers commonly deploy multi-level interconnection structures like Clos and Fat-tree. These topologies create equivalent multipath network environments through cascaded hierarchical switches, providing ample ports and bandwidth while enabling rapid redundancy switching during link or node failures. For instance, the Fat-tree topology employs symmetrical switching and aggregation layers, enabling multiple communication paths between any two servers. This fully unleashes the data center's parallel transmission capabilities.

Third, data center network design places exceptional emphasis on high bandwidth and low latency. To simultaneously support massive concurrent requests and large-scale data processing tasks—such as video-on-demand, distributed storage, and big data computing—links must possess sufficient throughput to sustain high-speed communication between servers. To achieve this, data centers extensively adopt efficient transmission technologies like 10 Gigabit Ethernet, fiber interconnects, and RDMA (Remote Direct Memory Access), while optimizing routing and queue scheduling to minimize end-to-end latency.

(a) However, these advantages also introduce new challenges:

- Diverse Application Demands: Data centers host a wide array of applications, each with vastly different network performance requirements. For instance, online search and financial transactions demand ultra-low latency to ensure users receive search results and transaction confirmations promptly. Conversely, applications like data backup and large-scale data synchronization prioritize high throughput to maximize data transfer efficiency. Addressing these varied demands is the foremost challenge for data center transport layer protocols.
- Complex Traffic Patterns: Traffic patterns within data centers exhibit high complexity, encompassing both short, burst-like traffic (e.g., web requests, database queries) and sustained, high-volume traffic (e.g., video streaming, big data transfers). The uneven temporal and spatial distribution of these diverse traffic types poses significant challenges for traffic management in

transport layer protocols. Traditional flow control and scheduling algorithms often struggle to effectively handle such complex patterns, frequently leading to network congestion and performance degradation.

- Congestion Control: Due to the high connection density between servers and switches within data centers, network congestion frequently occurs. Traditional congestion control mechanisms may exhibit limitations in data center environments, such as sluggish response times and excessive transmission rate reductions, rendering them ineffective against the rapid congestion changes inherent in data center networks. Therefore, research and design of more efficient and flexible congestion control mechanisms tailored to data center characteristics are needed to ensure high throughput and low latency performance
- TCP Incast Problem: TCP Incast is one of the critical performance issues in data center networks. It refers to the catastrophic throughput collapse that occurs when numerous servers simultaneously send data to a single receiver under high-bandwidth, low-round-trip-time conditions.

6.4.2 Evolution of Data Center Transport Layer Protocols

To address these challenges, researchers have proposed various transport layer protocols and mechanisms to optimize data center network performance.

1. **Host-Based Congestion Control**

   DCTCP (Datacenter TCP), introduced by researchers from Stanford University and Microsoft in 2010, is an innovative host-based congestion control algorithm. Its core principle is to fully leverage switches' Explicit Congestion Notification (ECN) functionality. When network congestion occurs, switches send congestion signals to end hosts by setting specific flag bits in packets. Upon receiving these signals, end hosts can precisely adjust their send window size based on congestion severity, enabling fine-grained control over network congestion.

   Compared to traditional TCP congestion control algorithms, DCTCP avoids excessive transmission rate reductions during light congestion, effectively improving network throughput and latency performance. This makes it particularly suitable for high-bandwidth, low-latency applications in data center networks. The endpoint-based congestion control mechanism requires only modifications to the endpoint's software protocol stack and simple ECN marking configuration on switches, offering the advantages of straightforward configuration and ease of deployment. However, host-based congestion control mechanisms typically fall short of theoretical optimal performance due to insufficient integration with additional switch support. For instance, DCTCP fails to distinguish between small and large flows, causing both to coexist within a single queue. Consequently, the completion time for small flows becomes significantly prolonged due to queuing delays imposed by large flows.

2. **Limitations of the TCP Protocol in Data Center Networks**
   As data center networks evolve, traditional TCP transport layer protocols and their variants increasingly struggle to deliver expected network performance. On one hand, TCP's reactive congestion control algorithms fail to handle the burstier traffic patterns of high-speed networks. On the other hand, the TCP stack's reliance on kernel-level software causes high CPU consumption and network protocol stack latency, as each packet must traverse the kernel network stack after being received by the network interface card.
3. **Switch-Based Priority Scheduling**
   Another optimization approach involves moving congestion management to the switch layer. A prime example is the pFabric protocol, whose core concept involves prioritizing traffic at the switch based on the remaining transmission size of each flow. Low-bandwidth traffic is assigned to high-priority queues, enabling rapid forwarding during contention and significantly reducing average completion time. This "minimalist scheduling" approach theoretically approaches optimal scheduling performance. However, constrained by the limited number of queues in switch hardware, practical deployments struggle to guarantee ideal priority allocation for all traffic, introducing risks of suboptimal scheduling.
4. **Application of Remote Direct Memory Access (RDMA) Technology**
   To address performance bottlenecks in data center networks during high-speed and low-latency development—particularly the processing overhead introduced by traditional TCP kernel protocol stacks—Remote Direct Memory Access (RDMA) technology is increasingly being integrated into data center networks. The core concept of RDMA is to enable servers to transfer data directly from the local host's memory to the remote host's memory without involving the kernel protocol stacks of either operating system, thereby achieving kernel bypass. This mechanism not only avoids multiple data copies between user mode and kernel mode but also reduces additional delays caused by interrupt handling and context switching. It significantly lowers CPU utilization, demonstrating immense potential for RDMA in High-Performance Computing (HPC) and next-generation data centers [18]. Figure 6.5 shows the RDMA protocol execution process.

   While RDMA technology has gained widespread adoption in HPC, large-scale deployment in data centers still faces numerous challenges. A critical issue is how to deeply integrate this efficient transmission mechanism with hardware devices (including smart network interface cards and switches) to maintain low cost and compatibility while ensuring performance.

   In data centers, RDMA technology is primarily implemented through the following methods:

   - InfiniBand (IB): InfiniBand is a high-speed networking technology specifically designed for high-performance computing and data centers. It delivers extremely high bandwidth and ultra-low latency, meeting the high-performance networking demands of data centers. However, InfiniBand requires dedicated hardware devices such as InfiniBand NICs and switches, increasing data center construction costs and complexity [19].

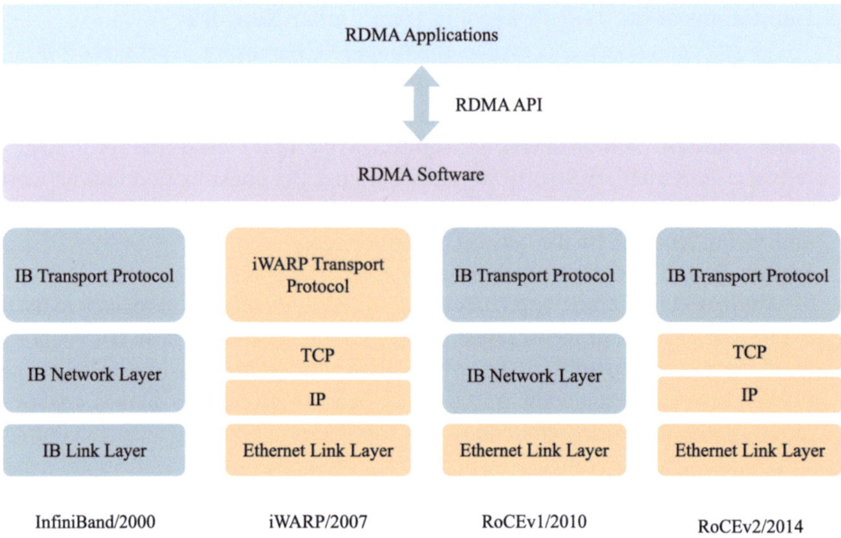

Fig. 6.5 RDMA protocol execution process

- RoCE (RDMA over Converged Ethernet): RoCE is a technology that implements RDMA over Ethernet. It leverages Ethernet's widespread adoption and compatibility, enabling data centers to achieve RDMA functionality on existing Ethernet infrastructure. Through appropriate configuration and optimization of Ethernet, RoCE can deliver performance comparable to InfiniBand. Compared to InfiniBand, RoCE offers lower costs and easier deployment and management, leading to its growing adoption in data centers.
- iWARP: iWARP is a technology that implements RDMA over the TCP/IP protocol. It offers excellent scalability and compatibility, enabling seamless integration with existing network devices and operating systems. By adding RDMA-related functional modules within the TCP/IP protocol stack, iWARP enables remote memory access capabilities. Although iWARP exhibits relatively lower performance, its foundation on the mature TCP/IP protocol still provides significant value in application scenarios where performance demands are not particularly stringent [20].

In summary, RDMA technology demonstrates significant potential for enhancing data center network performance. However, challenges remain in congestion management, traffic isolation, and scalability during large-scale deployment. Further optimization requires integration with SmartNICs, programmable switches, and next-generation congestion control algorithms [21].

6.5 Transmission Protocols for High-Performance Computing Scenarios

In today's digital era, the rapid advancement of generative large models (such as ChatGPT and Sora) poses unprecedented challenges to network infrastructure. Training these models involves processing massive datasets and leveraging tens of thousands of GPUs for parallel computing, demanding higher standards for network scale, bandwidth, latency, and reliability. Traditional data center network architectures struggle to meet these demands, necessitating in-depth research and optimization of transmission protocols tailored for computing-intensive network scenarios.

6.5.1 Challenges to Network Infrastructure from Generative Large Models

As model parameter scales rapidly expand from tens of millions to trillions, training processes typically combine multiple approaches, including data parallelism, pipeline parallelism, and tensor parallelism. The resulting network requirements primarily include:

First, ultra-large-scale networking. Training involves full interconnect communication across servers, potentially involving hundreds of thousands or even millions of GPUs, demanding networks capable of supporting extremely high access density and capacity.

Second, ultra-high bandwidth. Massive collective communications between GPUs (e.g., AllReduce operations) can transfer hundreds of gigabytes per communication, placing extreme demands on single-port bandwidth, link count, and overall throughput.

Third, ultra-low latency. In training trillion-parameter models, communication latency can account for over 50% of total training time. Traditional congestion control algorithms are prone to congestion propagation in high-concurrency environments, further increasing delays.

6.5.2 Evolution of Transmission Protocols in Large Model Contexts

Generative large model training requires frequent, massive data transfers and exchanges between servers. Traditional Transmission Control Protocol/Internet Protocol (TCP/IP) requires multiple data copies between the user space and kernel space during transmission, reducing efficiency. In contrast, Remote Direct Memory Access (RDMA) enables applications to directly access remote node memory without kernel intervention. Its advantages—high throughput, low latency, and zero CPU overhead—enhance training efficiency, making it more suitable for generative large model training.

Since its inception in 1999, RDMA has evolved over two decades, expanding its application scope from initial high-end high-performance computing (HPC) domains to broader general-purpose data centers. Today, it is widely adopted in scenarios such as large model training and high-performance computing. RDMA primarily encompasses three protocol types: InfiniBand (IB), Ethernet-based RDMA (RoCE), and TCP/IP-based RDMA (iWARP). All three protocols adhere to RDMA standards and utilize the same upper-layer interface.

The IB protocol establishes a novel hierarchical architecture from the link layer to the transport layer, specifically engineered for high-performance computing. However, deploying IB requires dedicated hardware such as IB switches, IB NICs, and IB cables, rendering it incompatible with existing Ethernet equipment and limiting its application scope.

Considering the extensive deployment of Ethernet-based products in current networks, the InfiniBand Technology Alliance (IBTA) developed the Ethernet-based RoCE (Real-time Communication over Ethernet) standard to broaden RDMA's applicability. RoCE enables RDMA operations on standard Ethernet devices by extending the Ethernet protocol stack, combining high-performance remote memory access with Ethernet's ease of use and widespread deployment.

iWARP is a TCP-based RDMA protocol proposed by the Internet Engineering Task Force (IETF). As TCP is a connection-oriented, reliable protocol, iWARP offers superior reliability compared to RoCEv2 and IB in lossy network scenarios. However, the large number of TCP connections consumes significant memory resources, and TCP's complex flow control mechanisms can cause performance issues, limiting its application scope. Consequently, it is not yet widely adopted.

6.5.3 *Emerging Transport Protocols in the Large-Model Context*

In 2023, the Ultra Ethernet Consortium (UEC)—co-founded by cloud computing and networking vendors—proposed Ultra Ethernet Transport (UET) to address the closed ecosystem of IB and the limitations of RoCE. UET is designed around IP and Ethernet, offering multiple configuration options to meet diverse scenario requirements. UET also incorporates two congestion control mechanisms: First, a sender-based dynamic adjustment mechanism that controls the transmission window size based on RTT, ECN flags, and packet loss conditions; Second, a receiver-side credit-based control mechanism that limits transmission rates based on feedback of available windows from the receiver, mitigating transient congestion.

That same year at the OCP Global Summit, Google introduced the Falcon protocol, integrating its innovations in transmission technology with new hardware. Falcon employs a layered architecture comprising a transaction layer and a data transport layer.

Transaction Layer: Handles operation mapping for upper-layer protocols (e.g., RDMA send/read requests), supporting two transaction types: Push (send/write operations) and Pull (read/atomic operations). Each transaction tracks state via a request sequence number (RSN), ensuring ordered or unordered transmission.

Packet Transport Layer: Implements reliable transmission and congestion control. It prevents protocol deadlocks through two sliding windows (request window and data window) and supports multipath transmission and connection encryption.

Figure 6.6 shows the layered architecture of Falcon. Falcon also incorporates congestion control, Swift, and protective load balancing, designed to meet the stringent data transmission demands of scenarios like artificial intelligence and high-performance computing. It features low latency, high performance, and high reliability. It drives Ethernet modernization to meet the high-reliability, high-performance, and low-latency requirements of next-generation large-scale AI cluster networks.

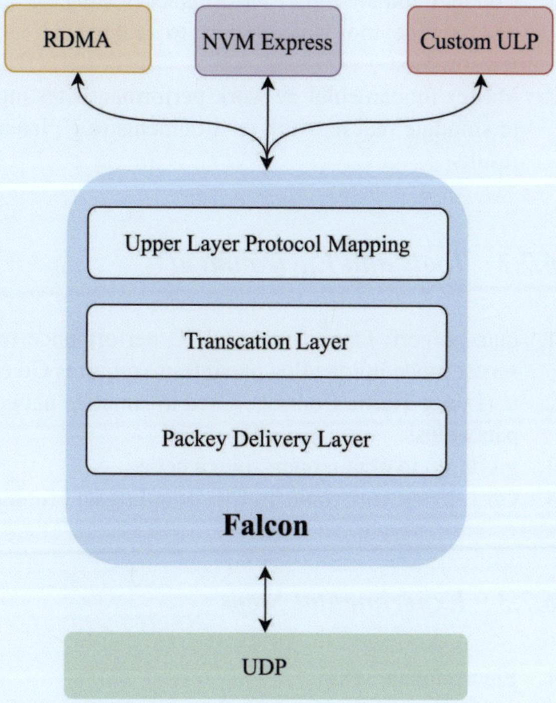

Fig. 6.6 Falcon layered architecture diagram

6.6 Chapter Summary

This chapter introduces the application of transport layer protocols, covering the following key points:

1. The evolution and challenges of transport layer protocols.
2. Transport requirements in future networks.
3. Transport layer protocols in emerging scenarios.

6.7 Experiment—Transmission Protocol Performance Testing

6.7.1 Experiment Objectives

1. Conduct foundational performance testing of the QUIC protocol using the open-source tool quic-go/perf to understand its core characteristics in data transmission.
2. Master fundamental network performance testing methods, learn to use tools to simulate real network environments (e.g., latency, packet loss), and analyze results.

6.7.2 Tools and Environment

1. quic-go/perf: Open-source QUIC performance testing tool supporting client–server mode upload/download tests (requires Go environment) [22].
2. tc (Linux Traffic Control): Used to simulate network scenarios like latency and packet loss.
3. git: Used to obtain open-source code.
4. Go 1.23 + : Environment for compiling and running quic-go/perf.

6.7.3 Experimental Steps

1. Environment Setup

    (1) Install project and dependencies:

```
# Clone the quic-go/perf repository
git clone https://github.com/quic-go/perf.git
cd perf
# Download project dependencies
go mod tidy
```

```
zhemingbao@MacBook-Pro-6 perf % go run cmd/main.go --run-server --server-address
=0.0.0.0:6060
2025/08/31 14:43:56 Listening on [::]:6060
```

Fig. 6.7 Example of launching the test server

```
zhemingbao@MacBook-Pro-6 perf % go run cmd/main.go --server-address=127.0.0.1:6060 --upload-bytes=10
0M --download-bytes=200M
{"type":"intermediary","timeSeconds":1.000220875,"uploadBytes":84017152,"downloadBytes":0}
{"type":"intermediary","timeSeconds":1.000853135,"uploadBytes":0,"downloadBytes":51061026}
{"type":"intermediary","timeSeconds":1.000418922,"uploadBytes":0,"downloadBytes":39833766}
{"type":"intermediary","timeSeconds":1.000031779,"uploadBytes":0,"downloadBytes":46224320}
{"type":"intermediary","timeSeconds":1.000048627,"uploadBytes":0,"downloadBytes":50224040}
2025/08/31 14:44:08 uploaded 100.0 MiB: 1.25s (80.1 MiB/s)
2025/08/31 14:44:08 downloaded 200.0 MiB: 4.44s (45.0 MiB/s)
{"type":"final","timeSeconds":5.705057835,"uploadBytes":104857600,"downloadBytes":209715200}
```

Fig. 6.8 Example of launching the test client and conducting tests

2. Launch client and server for basic testing

   (1) Open a new terminal and run the following command to start the server (Fig. 6.7):

   ```
   go run cmd/main.go --run-server=true --server-address=0.0.0.0:6060
   ```

   (2) Open another terminal and run the following command to start the client and test upload/download speeds (Fig. 6.8):

   (a) Test 100 MB upload and 200 MB download

   ```
   go run cmd/main.go --server-address=127.0.0.1:6060 --upload-bytes=100M --download-bytes=200M
   ```

   (b) Test 500 MB upload and 1 GB download (optional, for large file scenarios) (Fig. 6.9)

   ```
   go run cmd/main.go --server-address=127.0.0.1:6060 --upload-bytes=500M --download-bytes=1G
   ```

   (3) Record key metrics from client output: upload rate (MiB/s), download rate (MiB/s), total duration (seconds).

3. Weak network environment simulation testing

   (1) Simulate network latency and packet loss: Use the tc tool on the client to add network rules (using eth0 as an example; replace with actual network interface name):

   Simulate 100 ms delay and 5% packet loss rate.

   ```
   sudo tc qdisc add dev eth0 root netem delay 100ms loss 5%
   ```

   (2) Repeat the above test

```
{"type":"intermediary","timeSeconds":1.000004725,"uploadBytes":0,"downloadBytes":35700736}
{"type":"intermediary","timeSeconds":1.000101368,"uploadBytes":0,"downloadBytes":40370165}
{"type":"intermediary","timeSeconds":1.00002692,"uploadBytes":0,"downloadBytes":36137451}
{"type":"intermediary","timeSeconds":1.000026138,"uploadBytes":0,"downloadBytes":37613416}
{"type":"intermediary","timeSeconds":1.000041255,"uploadBytes":0,"downloadBytes":43417600}
{"type":"intermediary","timeSeconds":1.00001751,"uploadBytes":0,"downloadBytes":40088816}
{"type":"intermediary","timeSeconds":1.00002682,"uploadBytes":0,"downloadBytes":41348160}
{"type":"intermediary","timeSeconds":1.000039946,"uploadBytes":0,"downloadBytes":35373045}
{"type":"intermediary","timeSeconds":1.000031896,"uploadBytes":0,"downloadBytes":38469643}
{"type":"intermediary","timeSeconds":1.047041676,"uploadBytes":0,"downloadBytes":40076680}
{"type":"intermediary","timeSeconds":1.000000319,"uploadBytes":0,"downloadBytes":43099224}
{"type":"intermediary","timeSeconds":1.000002562,"uploadBytes":0,"downloadBytes":43976072}
{"type":"intermediary","timeSeconds":1.00006063,"uploadBytes":0,"downloadBytes":43082840}
{"type":"intermediary","timeSeconds":1.00007149,"uploadBytes":0,"downloadBytes":44164792}
{"type":"intermediary","timeSeconds":1.000098912,"uploadBytes":0,"downloadBytes":39490496}
{"type":"intermediary","timeSeconds":1.000123061,"uploadBytes":0,"downloadBytes":32487248}
{"type":"intermediary","timeSeconds":1.000011027,"uploadBytes":0,"downloadBytes":38812280}
{"type":"intermediary","timeSeconds":1.000194384,"uploadBytes":0,"downloadBytes":34384341}
{"type":"intermediary","timeSeconds":1.000069005,"uploadBytes":0,"downloadBytes":37239427}
{"type":"intermediary","timeSeconds":1.00000345,"uploadBytes":0,"downloadBytes":36911736}
{"type":"intermediary","timeSeconds":1.000057941,"uploadBytes":0,"downloadBytes":37799304}
{"type":"intermediary","timeSeconds":1.00001831,"uploadBytes":0,"downloadBytes":31495712}
{"type":"intermediary","timeSeconds":1.000082385,"uploadBytes":0,"downloadBytes":32467413}
2025/08/31 14:49:28 uploaded 500.0 MiB: 6.81s (73.4 MiB/s)
2025/08/31 14:49:28 downloaded 1.0 GiB: 29.69s (34.5 MiB/s)
{"type":"final","timeSeconds":36.501791263,"uploadBytes":524288000,"downloadBytes":1073741824}
```

Fig. 6.9 Launching the test client and testing large file upload/download example

6.7.4 Experiment Summary

Master fundamental network performance testing methods through open-source tools, learn to simulate real-world network conditions (e.g., latency, packet loss), and analyze results.

6.8 Exercises

1. Briefly describe the changes in demand under future networks.
2. Briefly describe the emerging scenarios for transport layer protocols.

References

1. Polese M, Chiariotti F, Bonetto E, et al. A survey on recent advances in transport layer protocols. IEEE Commun Surv Tutor. 2019;21(4):3584–608.
2. Li H, Bai H. Principle of architecture, protocol, and algorithms for CoG-MIN: a sustainably ecological and evolutionary solution for packet network system. Springer; 2025. https://doi.org/10.1007/978-981-96-3596-2.
3. Le HD, Trinh PV, Pham TV, et al. Throughput analysis for TCP over the FSO-based satellite-assisted internet of vehicles. IEEE Trans Veh Technol. 2021;71(2):1875–90.

4. Ahlswede R, Cai N, Li SYR, et al. Network information flow. IEEE Trans Inf Theory. 2000;46(4):1204–16.
5. Li SYR, Yeung RW, Cai N. Linear network coding. IEEE Trans Inf Theory. 2003;49(2):371–81.
6. Park JS, Gerla M, Lun DS, et al. Codecast: a network-coding-based ad hoc multicast protocol. IEEE Wirel Commun. 2006;13(5):76–81.
7. Chachulski S, Jennings M, Katti S, et al. Trading structure for randomness in wireless opportunistic routing. ACM SIGCOMM Comput Commun Rev. 2007;37(4):169–80.
8. Koutsonikolas D, Wang CC, Hu YC. Efficient network-coding-based opportunistic routing through cumulative coded acknowledgments. IEEE/ACM Trans Netw. 2011;19(5):1368–81.
9. Sundararajan JK, Jakubczak S, Médard M, et al. Interfacing network coding with TCP: an implementation. arXiv preprint arXiv:0908.1564; 2009.
10. Sundararajan JK, Shah D, Médard M, et al. Network coding meets TCP: theory and implementation. Proc IEEE. 2011;99(3):490–512.
11. Song S, Li H, Pan K, Liu J, Li SYR. Self-adaptive TCP protocol combined with net-work coding scheme. In: International conference on systems and networks communications (ICSNC). 2011. p. 20–25.
12. Fan X, Li H, Pan K. A dynamic self-adapting algorithm of redundancy parameter in TCP-NC. In: 2012 IEEE 14th international conference on communication technology. IEEE, 2012. p. 1276–1280.
13. Handley M. Why the Internet only just works. BT Technol J. 2006;24(3):119–29.
14. Poularakis K, Iosifidis G, Sourlas V, et al. Exploiting caching and multicast for 5G wire-less networks. IEEE Trans Wirel Commun. 2016;15(4):2995–3007.
15. Araniti G, Condoluci M, Scopelliti P, et al. Multicasting over emerging 5G networks: challenges and perspectives. IEEE Netw. 2017;31(2):80–9.
16. Awobuluyi O, Nightingale J, Wang Q, et al. Video quality in 5G networks: context-aware QoE management in the SDN control plane. In: 2015 IEEE international conference on computer and information technology; ubiquitous computing and communications; dependable, autonomic and secure computing; pervasive intelligence and computing. IEEE, 2015. p. 1657–1662.
17. Bensky A. Wireless personal area networks. Short-range wireless communication. Newnes; 2019. p. 317–360.
18. Liu J, Wu J, Kini SP, et al. High performance RDMA-based MPI implementation over InfiniBand. In: Proceedings of the 17th annual international conference on supercomputing. 2003. p. 295–304.
19. InfiniBand Trade Association. InfiniBand architecture specification: release 1.3. InfiniBand Trade Association; 2015.
20. Recio R, Metzler B, Culley P, et al. A remote direct memory access protocol specification. RFC 5040, IETF; 2007.
21. Firestone D, Putnam A, Mundkur S, et al. Azure accelerated networking: SmartNICs in the public cloud. In: 15th USENIX symposium on networked systems design and implementation (NSDI). USENIX Association; 2018. p. 51–66.
22. quic-go contributors. perf [EB/OL]; 2025. https://github.com/quic-go/perf. Accessed 05 Oct 2025.

Chapter 7
Applications of Transport Layer Protocols

In the preceding chapters, we systematically introduced the core mechanisms of transport-layer protocols and examined their development and optimization in emerging application scenarios. Transport layer protocols serve as the critical link between theory and practical application. Understanding protocol design is only half the story; observing how it performs under real-world stress reveals its true value.

This chapter focuses on the practical implementation of transport layer protocols, analyzing differentiated performance requirements across scenarios such as cloud gaming (low latency), microservices (high connection efficiency), data centers, and high-performance computing. This chapter delves into optimization strategies tailored for different scenarios and introduces the MIN-QUIC-based MIN-HTTP/3 optimization within web protocols. Its core content features case studies from major tech companies like Meta, ByteDance, and others, demonstrating how they deploy QUIC at scale. Finally, a hands-on experiment enabling HTTP/3 in browsers helps students grasp how to select and optimize transport protocols based on application contexts, enhancing their engineering practice skills.

7.1 Application Scenarios for Transport Layer Protocols

Transport layer protocols serve as the core hub in the network communication architecture, with their design characteristics directly determining the performance boundaries and quality of service for upper-layer applications. With the continuous evolution of cloud computing, edge computing, and artificial intelligence, traditional TCP and UDP protocols are increasingly revealing limitations in certain complex environments. Particularly in scenarios involving high packet loss, long latency, and high concurrency, they struggle to meet the demands of diverse applications. Consequently, novel transport protocols (such as QUIC) and customized solutions tailored for specific scenarios (like RDMA and SCTP) are emerging as

H. Li and Z. Bao, *Transport Layer for Computer Networks*,
https://doi.org/10.1007/978-981-95-7374-5_7

critical enabling technologies. This section focuses on exploring the practical applications and challenges of transport layer protocols in typical scenarios such as cloud gaming, microservices architectures, data centers, high-performance computing, and web/video transmission.

7.1.1 *Cloud Gaming: The Balancing Act of Low Latency and High Throughput*

By migrating computational tasks to cloud servers, cloud gaming demands stable transmission of 4 K/120fps video streams with end-to-end latency under 100 ms. Traditional TCP congestion control mechanisms (e.g., Cubic) are prone to latency fluctuations in high-packet-loss scenarios. In contrast, the QUIC protocol has emerged as the mainstream choice due to its 0-RTT connection establishment and independent multi-stream transmission capabilities. For instance, NVIDIA GeForce NOW employs QUIC to achieve dynamic bitrate adaptation. Through Forward Error Correction (FEC) and adaptive retransmission strategies, it maintains smooth gameplay even at a 15% packet loss rate [1].

Beyond video streams, user input (e.g., controller events) also demands low-latency transmission. When input and video share the same link, traffic prioritization becomes critical. Google Stadia leverages QUIC's stream priority tagging mechanism to assign the highest priority to control command streams, ensuring operational response latency remains below 30 ms. Furthermore, Microsoft xCloud builds upon WebRTC by introducing a proprietary UDP congestion control algorithm. Combined with machine learning methods to predict bandwidth fluctuations, this enables more stable dynamic throughput allocation.

7.1.2 *Microservices Architecture: Connectivity Explosion and Efficiency Optimization*

In microservices scenarios, a single request may trigger dozens of inter-service calls. The overhead of traditional TCP's three-way handshake and the management costs of persistent connections become performance bottlenecks. Netflix employs gRPC (based on HTTP/2) for multiplexing, supporting thousands of concurrent streams per connection and reducing service latency by 40%. Within service meshes, Istio replaces TCP + TLS with mTLS over QUIC, cutting connection establishment time by 50%.

For high-frequency short-connection scenarios (e.g., e-commerce promotions), Alibaba's proprietary RSocket protocol leverages connectionless semantics and reactive backpressure control to support millions of RPC calls per second during Double 11, reducing CPU utilization by 30% compared to gRPC. The financial sector, however, favors SCTP protocols, whose multi-homing capability automatically switches to redundant links, ensuring high availability for trading systems.

7.1.3 Data Centers: Pushing Throughput Limits

Modern data centers exhibit east–west traffic dominance, where traditional TCP fairness algorithms can trigger Incast issues (sudden throughput drops in many-to-one communication). Facebook deployed DCQCN (Data Center Quantized Congestion Notification) over RoCEv2 (RDMA over Converged Ethernet), achieving microsecond-level latency and 90% link utilization [2].

In hyperscale clusters, Google optimized TCP throughput with the BBR v2 algorithm. Combined with explicit congestion feedback (e.g., INT, In-band Network Telemetry) from programmable switches, this tripled the cross-zone transaction processing capability of the Spanner database. Tencent Cloud dynamically adjusts transmission rates via HPCC (High-Precision Congestion Control), achieving 95% bandwidth utilization on 100Gbps networks while avoiding global pauses caused by PFC (Priority Flow Control).

7.1.4 High-Performance Computing: The Transmission Revolution for Large-Scale Computing Models

Training large models with hundreds of billions of parameters requires terabyte-scale gradient synchronization. Transmission layer protocols must address high-concurrency small-packet issues in high-speed networks like RoCE and InfiniBand. Meta's PyTorch clusters utilize the Libfabric API to directly operate RDMA queues, reducing kernel-mode copy overhead and lowering AllReduce operation latency to 2 μs. For cross-region training, Huawei's Hetero-CC algorithm dynamically switches between TCP and QUIC protocols, boosting bandwidth by 70% in long-fat pipeline scenarios [3].

In scientific computing, CERN's LHC experiment employs UDT (a UDP-based data transport protocol) to transmit petabyte-scale particle data. By aggregating multiple 10Gbps links through bandwidth bonding technology, it achieves a stable 80Gbps transmission across continents. NASA's Deep Space Network (DTN) employs LTP (Licklider Transmission Protocol), leveraging resume-from-breakpoint and delay-tolerant mechanisms to ensure reliable transmission between Mars probes and Earth under a maximum 22-min latency.

7.1.5 Web and Video Transmission: From Efficiency to Experience

In web scenarios, HTTP/3 adoption has enabled QUIC to cover over 35% of traffic across Chrome and Cloudflare's global networks. TikTok reduces video first-packet-received time to 200 ms through multi-CDN + QUIC. In streaming media, Netflix's Dynamic Optimizer dynamically adjusts bitrates based on TCP throughput predictions, reducing buffer interrupt rates by 76%.

7.2 Transport Layer Protocols and Web Applications

7.2.1 TCP-Based HTTP/1 and HTTP/2

HTTP (Hypertext Transfer Protocol) is the most widely used protocol in web applications, and TCP, as its underlying transport layer protocol, significantly impacts HTTP's performance. HTTP/1 and HTTP/2, as two major milestones in web technology development, fully demonstrate the evolutionary role of transport layer protocols in web applications.

HTTP/1 was designed to address the data transmission needs of early Web environments, employing a simple request-response model. Each request is sent over a separate TCP connection, and each connection requires a three-way handshake, leading to significant latency and resource waste. For instance, when loading a webpage containing multiple images, scripts, and style sheets, the browser must establish a separate TCP connection for each resource. This necessitates multiple three-way handshakes, substantially increasing page load times. Furthermore, TCP's slow-start mechanism limits initial data transmission rates per connection, further degrading efficiency.

To enhance performance, HTTP/1.1 introduced persistent connections and pipelining. Persistent connections allow multiple requests to reuse the same connection, reducing handshake overhead. Pipelining attempts to boost transmission efficiency by sending multiple requests simultaneously. However, due to TCP's flow control characteristics, pipelining is susceptible to head-of-line blocking. When a response for one request is delayed, subsequent requests—even if ready to send—get blocked in the queue and cannot be processed promptly, limiting its effectiveness. For example, in an unstable network environment, if a large image file transfer experiences delays, subsequent requests for resources like scripts and style sheets will also be blocked. This slows down the entire webpage loading process, resulting in a poor user experience.

HTTP/2 comprehensively optimizes HTTP/1, addressing performance bottlenecks caused by multiple connections. Its core improvements include:

Multiplexing: By transmitting multiple streams concurrently over a single TCP connection, HTTP/2 eliminates head-of-line blocking and enhances connection utilization. When loading a complex webpage, the browser can send multiple resource requests simultaneously. These requests are processed in parallel on the server side, with response data returned to the browser over the same TCP connection, significantly accelerating page loading. For instance, on a webpage containing multiple images, videos, and text content, HTTP/2 can handle requests and responses for these resources concurrently. This prevents transmission issues with one resource from blocking others, enabling faster page rendering for users.

Binary Framing: HTTP/2 employs binary framing for messages, enhancing data transmission efficiency while reducing parsing overhead. Compared to HTTP/1's text-based format, binary-framed packets are more compact, enabling higher transmission efficiency and faster, more accurate parsing at the receiving end. This significantly improves network performance and reduces resource consumption.

Priority and Flow Control: The introduction of a stream priority mechanism allows clients to dynamically adjust resource allocation based on application needs, thereby improving overall performance. For instance, critical content within a webpage—such as textual information and important images—can be assigned higher priority to ensure rapid delivery. Conversely, non-essential elements like advertising images or script files can be assigned lower priority, allowing their transmission to be delayed when network resources are constrained. This ensures users receive vital information promptly, enhancing the user experience.

Header Compression: Utilizes the HPACK algorithm to compress HTTP headers, significantly reducing transmitted data volume. HTTP requests and responses often contain repetitive header fields, such as browser identifiers and user preferences. HPACK compresses these headers, eliminating redundant data, decreasing network transmission volume, and improving transfer efficiency.

Although HTTP/2 significantly improves performance through these enhancements, it remains dependent on TCP's transmission mechanism. In network environments with high packet loss or latency, TCP's congestion control characteristics can limit HTTP/2's performance. When packet loss occurs, TCP automatically reduces the transmission rate to prevent further network congestion. However, in certain scenarios, this congestion control mechanism may become overly conservative, leading to a significant decrease in HTTP/2's transmission speed. For instance, in certain wireless network environments, unstable signals may increase packet loss rates. Under such conditions, HTTP/2 performance may be substantially impacted, preventing it from fully leveraging its multiplexing and other optimization mechanisms.

7.2.2 *MIN-HTTP/3 Based on MIN-QUIC*

As mentioned in previous sections, QUIC offers numerous advantages—such as resolving head-of-line blocking, faster connection establishment, and pluggable congestion control—making it significantly faster and more efficient than TCP. The

MIN network [4] builds the MIN-QUIC [5] transport control protocol at the transport layer, based on push semantics. This protocol combines the strengths of both the MIN network and QUIC, delivering a more efficient, secure, and flexible transmission experience for web applications.

MIN-QUIC first inherits QUIC's rapid connection establishment mechanism. Traditional TCP connections require a three-way handshake, which inherently increases connection setup latency. By leveraging UDP as its underlying transport protocol and incorporating encryption, QUIC enables the swift establishment of secure connection channels during the initial connection attempt. MIN-QUIC further optimizes this process. In web applications, when a user requests a webpage, it enables faster connection establishment with the server, reducing wait times and accelerating information retrieval. For example, when a user opens a webpage, MIN-QUIC can rapidly complete connection setup, allowing the page loading process to initiate sooner and enhancing the user experience.

Its ability to resolve head-of-line blocking also delivers significant advantages for web applications. While HTTP/2 employs multiplexing, its reliance on TCP means packet loss or delays in one stream can still block transmission in others. MIN-QUIC, built on UDP, avoids head-of-line blocking by implementing separate acknowledgment and retransmission mechanisms for each individual stream. During the loading of a webpage containing multiple resource requests, even if a packet for an image or script encounters issues, it won't affect the transmission of other resources. This ensures continuous and smooth webpage loading, improving both loading speed and stability.

MIN-QUIC's pluggable congestion control mechanism allows it to adapt flexibly to different network environments. Under favorable network conditions, it employs more aggressive congestion control strategies to maximize data transfer rates and fully utilize available bandwidth. Conversely, during network congestion or instability, it promptly adjusts its strategy by reducing transmission rates to prevent further network degradation. For instance, in a home broadband environment, MIN-QUIC rapidly transfers high-resolution images, videos, and other resources when the network is idle. When congestion occurs—such as when multiple devices simultaneously consume bandwidth—it automatically adjusts its congestion control algorithm to prioritize critical resources. This ensures basic webpage functionality remains operational, preventing prolonged lag or loading failures.

Furthermore, MIN-QUIC's integration with the MIN network's multi-identifier system provides web applications with more precise resource management and data transmission capabilities.

7.3 Enterprise-Level Transport Protocol Applications and Practices

7.3.1 Meta (Facebook)'s QUIC Implementation: From Protocol Development to Global Deployment

In the global social networking sphere, Facebook (now Meta)'s product portfolio—including Facebook, Instagram, WhatsApp, and others—processes billions of user interaction requests daily, encompassing diverse content types such as text, images, and videos. These requests demand exceptional stability and low latency for network transmission, while the performance bottlenecks of traditional TCP protocols in complex network environments have become increasingly apparent. As a key contributor to the IETF QUIC Working Group, Facebook has invested in QUIC protocol development and deployment since 2017, ultimately achieving large-scale adoption where over 75% of traffic is transmitted via QUIC and HTTP/3 [6]. This section details Facebook's technical approach, core challenges, and practical experience in migrating to QUIC.

Facebook has built a comprehensive open-source technology stack covering the entire client-to-server chain:

- **Proxygen**: A C++ HTTP framework supporting HTTP/1.1, HTTP/2, and HTTP/3. It maps application-layer GraphQL requests (Facebook/Instagram's core data interaction protocol) and static resource requests (images, videos) to QUIC streams.
- **Fizz**: An open-source TLS 1.3 implementation providing encryption for QUIC. It deeply integrates with the QUIC handshake process, eliminating the redundancy of traditional TLS and TCP handshakes.
- **mvfst**: Facebook's in-house QUIC transport protocol implementation, handling core logic like congestion control, packet loss recovery, and stream management. Supports both client-side and server-side deployment, enabling "end-to-end code sharing."
- **Katran**: A Layer 4 load balancer based on XDP and eBPF, supporting unified scheduling of TCP and QUIC connections to ensure stable distribution of inbound data center traffic.

The core advantage of this architecture lies in "end-to-end controllability": from client applications (e.g., Instagram's Android/iOS apps) to servers (data center web servers, load balancers), all protocol logic is implemented by the same codebase. Engineers can rapidly synchronize optimization strategies, avoiding compatibility issues caused by differences between client and server implementations.

Facebook's QUIC migration was not achieved overnight. From its inception in early 2017 to its large-scale deployment in 2020, the team spent over three years resolving a series of technical and operational challenges.

1. **Addressing UDP Blocking: Dual-Connection Race Mechanism**

   Although QUIC operates over UDP, approximately 1% of global network environments (such as certain corporate intranets and legacy routers) still block UDP port 443. To safeguard user experience in these scenarios, Facebook designed a "QUIC vs. TCP race" mechanism: When establishing a connection, clients simultaneously initiate both QUIC (UDP) and TCP connections. If QUIC fails to complete the handshake within 200 ms, it automatically switches to the TCP connection.

   This mechanism appears simple but resulted from extensive experimentation. The team tested various thresholds like 100 ms and 300 ms, finding 200 ms to be the optimal balance between user experience and resource consumption—avoiding delays from slow QUIC handshakes while preventing resource waste from premature TCP initiation. Additionally, the client records the outcome of the previous QUIC connection: if the last QUIC attempt failed, it delays the next TCP initiation to reduce futile contention.

   Early in the migration, the Instagram team encountered a counterintuitive issue: switching to QUIC actually slowed down image loading during app startup. Deep analysis revealed the root cause lay in the differing concurrency models of TCP and QUIC.

   Instagram's original architecture relied on 6 parallel TCP connections to load resources. Each TCP connection had an initial congestion window (i.e., the maximum packet size that could be sent initially) of 10 packets, allowing 60 packets to be sent simultaneously across all 6 connections. QUIC, however, achieves multiplexing through a single connection. Its initial congestion window also starts at 10 packets, resulting in only one-sixth of the original packet volume during the first transmission. This directly impacted resource loading efficiency during the startup phase.

   The solution was to "targeting expand the initial window of QUIC": the team adjusted QUIC's initial congestion window to 30 packets—a value higher than the 10 packets of a single TCP connection yet lower than the 60 packets of 6 TCP connections. This approach prevents network congestion while compensating for the initial packet volume. After this adjustment, Instagram's media loading time during startup not only returned to TCP-level performance but also decreased by an additional 15% due to QUIC's head-of-line blocking elimination.

2. **Exploring Flow Control Limits**

   Flow control is a mechanism that limits the size of the receiver's buffer to prevent memory overflow caused by the sender transmitting data too rapidly. In Facebook's HTTP/2 deployment, the application-layer flow control was statically set to 165 KB—a value optimized over time in TCP environments to balance buffering efficiency and memory consumption.

   However, this static value became a bottleneck in the QUIC environment. According to the Bandwidth-Delay Product (BDP) formula: Ideal congestion window = Link bandwidth $\times$ Round-trip time (RTT). For example, on a 10Mbps link with 100 ms RTT, the ideal window is approximately 122KB (10Mbps $\times$ 0.1s $\approx$ 125KB), where the 165KB flow control limit suffices. Yet in higher-bandwidth environments (e.g., 50Mbps), the ideal window increases to 625KB.

And a 165KB flow control limit would force transmission throttling, resulting in link utilization below 50%.

The team's solution is "dynamic adjustment of flow control limits": raising QUIC's flow control limit to 2 MB to prevent it from becoming a bottleneck in high-bandwidth scenarios. Simultaneously, dynamically shrinking the window based on real-time network conditions (like RTT and bandwidth) avoids buffer wastage in low-bandwidth scenarios. Post-optimization, average video transmission throughput increased by 30%, with particularly notable improvements in 4G/5G high-bandwidth environments.

After over three years of iteration, Facebook's QUIC deployment achieved significant performance gains, especially in core scenarios like video transmission:

Video Stability: Mean Time Between Runs (MTBR) decreased by 22%, stutter rate dropped by 20%, and network errors reduced by 8%. This means users watching Instagram Reels or Facebook Live experience virtually no interruptions due to transmission issues.

Interaction Responsiveness: GraphQL request error rate decreased by 6%, tail latency (P99 latency) reduced by 20%, and feedback speed for user actions like liking and commenting significantly improved.

Resource Loading: Static resource (images, short videos) loading completion time shortened by 15%. Particularly in weak network environments, QUIC's packet loss resilience increased loading success rates by 10%.

7.3.2 TikTok Group's QUIC Application Practice at 10 Million QPS

With the rapid development of mobile internet, users increasingly demand faster network transmission speeds and real-time responsiveness. Faced with frequent transfers of large-volume data such as images, videos, and audio, the traditional Transmission Control Protocol (TCP) has gradually revealed its limitations, manifesting in issues like slow page loading and video playback stuttering. This primarily stems from TCP's inefficiencies in connection establishment, head-of-line blocking, and packet loss recovery.

To address these challenges, Douyin Group launched its QUIC project in 2018 and has progressively deployed it across multiple core business scenarios [7]. Initially, QUIC was introduced into internal API services, achieving performance optimization for low-latency calls. Subsequently, protocol support expanded to critical services like file transfer, image distribution, and video-on-demand. By 2020, QPS (Queries Per Second) in file transfer scenarios exceeded 3 million; by 2021, image services surpassed 20 million QPS; and by 2023, video-on-demand scenarios achieved over 30 million QPS. Throughout this iterative process, the Group not only completed the standardization implementation of IETF QUIC but also introduced the Multi-Path

QUIC (MPQUIC) protocol in certain scenarios to further enhance throughput and stability in multi-link environments.

The advantages of the QUIC protocol are primarily reflected in several key features. First, the 0-RTT handshake significantly reduces connection establishment latency, enabling users to initiate data transmission rapidly. Second, QUIC implements its protocol stack in user mode, circumventing the slow updates inherent in traditional kernel-mode protocols and facilitating rapid iteration and customized optimization. Third, QUIC supports connection migration, allowing mobile terminals to maintain uninterrupted sessions during network handoffs (e.g., between Wi-Fi and cellular networks). Finally, its multiplexing mechanism effectively prevents TCP head-of-line blocking, significantly improving link utilization and application-layer experience.

In engineering implementation, Douyin Group embedded QUIC capabilities across the entire chain through its "end-to-edge-to-cloud integrated" architecture, enhancing development and operations synergy. Simultaneously, leveraging eBPF technology to build connection scheduling modules achieves high reliability and observability under massive business traffic. Furthermore, to address differentiated requirements across various services, the group customized multiple protocol optimization algorithms and introduced advanced features like Forward Error Correction (FEC) and multipath transmission to further enhance packet loss resilience and overall transmission performance. This series of explorations demonstrates that QUIC and its evolved variants are increasingly becoming a crucial foundation for next-generation internet transport protocols.

1. **Volcano Engine QUIC Architecture Design**

   End-Edge-Cloud Integration: Volcano Engine QUIC fully leverages the advantages of an integrated edge-cloud-end architecture. Building upon the existing client, edge node, and central data center access framework, it embeds QUIC capabilities across the entire end-edge-cloud chain with minimal overhead. Simultaneously, a unified QUIC network library is shared across client, edge, and cloud, eliminating redundant implementation of identical functionality across different libraries and significantly boosting development and operational efficiency. Figure 7.1 shows the QUIC architecture of the Volcano Engine.

   High Reliability: During Nginx upgrades, TCP achieves lossless upgrades by closing the Listen FD. Volcano Engine QUIC employs an EBPF-based connection scheduling module that routes new and existing connections to new and legacy workers, respectively, during upgrades, ensuring seamless transition. Furthermore, as a new protocol, QUIC lacks mature monitoring and observability tools. To address this, Volcano Engine implements protocol information reporting capabilities on both ends, enabling real-time monitoring.

   High Performance: For transmission optimization, Volcano Engine tailors protocol optimization algorithms to specific business network characteristics. For CPU optimization, it employs diverse strategies to enhance QUIC CPU performance, resolving the high CPU consumption challenge. For advanced scenarios demanding exceptional network performance, Volcano Engine offers

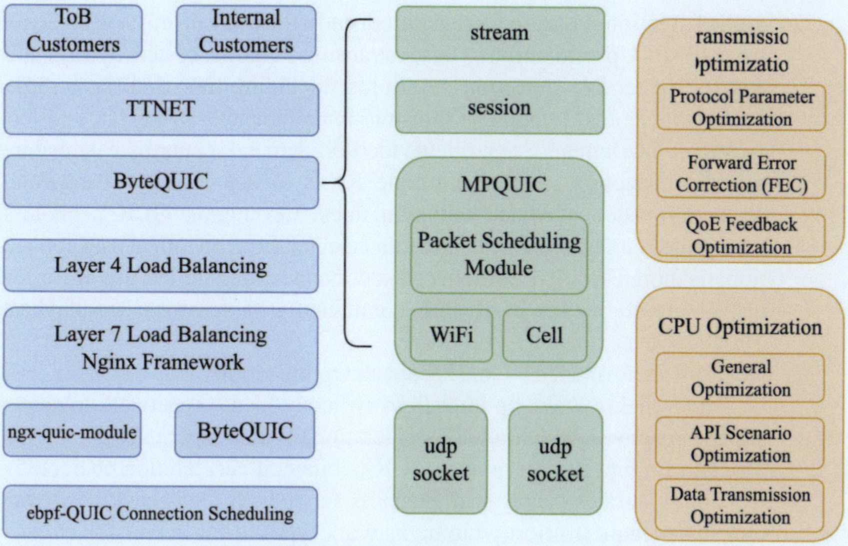

Fig. 7.1 Volcano engine QUIC architecture diagram

features like MPQUIC and FEC to further enhance QUIC capabilities. These fully leverage client multi-network card capabilities and strengthen resilience against weak network conditions.

2. **Volcano Engine QUIC—Network Performance Optimization**

As a new end-to-end encrypted transport protocol, QUIC lacks corresponding analysis systems. However, performance issues inevitably arise during deployment, making a comprehensive end-to-end analysis system crucial. Taking video-on-demand scenarios as an example, Volcano Engine uses a global TraceId to track each request through critical modules like Nginx, dual-end QUIC network libraries, and players, enabling full request traceability. This data forms a performance monitoring dashboard.

(1) Network Performance—Scenario-Specific Optimization

Using three typical scenarios—dynamic API requests, video uploads, and video-on-demand playback—engineers can perform targeted optimizations for various online scenarios based on the end-to-end analysis system.

Dynamic API Requests: During Feishu's QUIC trials, users within corporate networks encountered UDP block issues, causing QUIC request failures. Volcano Engine leveraged TCP's universality and QUIC's performance advantages by introducing a TCP/QUIC race mechanism during new connections. Remote cloud control race strategies enabled TCP and QUIC to complement each other, enhancing stability and network performance.

Video Upload Scenario: In video uploads, high RTT jitter on wireless networks triggers excessive false retransmissions from packet loss detection algorithms. This reduces effective bandwidth utilization and increases upload duration. Volcano Engine introduced a false retransmission detection mechanism. Upon identifying false retransmissions, the system dynamically adjusts packet loss detection thresholds (including time and out-of-order packet thresholds) to improve transmission efficiency.

Video-on-Demand Scenario: In video-on-demand scenarios, establishing a new connection requires multiple RTTs to detect stable bandwidth, impacting video playback initiation rates. Leveraging QUIC's bilateral protocol advantages, stable bandwidth detected from historical user connections is stored locally. Subsequent new connections utilize this historical data to rapidly restore bandwidth, significantly improving video playback initiation rates.

(2) Network Performance—QoE Feedback Optimization

Traditional protocol optimizations typically focus on network transmission perspectives, with limited consideration for user experience perception. Volcano Engine fully leverages QUIC's bilateral acceleration characteristics and integrates deeply with business services. It feeds back client-side QoE data (request priority/bitrate/network type) to the server for targeted optimization, effectively reducing user stuttering rates and retransmission rates to achieve cost reduction and efficiency gains.

(3) Network Performance—MPQUIC Optimization

Implementing MPQUIC requires engineering modifications to intermediate links, including Layer 4 load balancers and QUIC connection scheduling modules. Volcano Engine redefines QUIC CIDs, using distinct fields to represent QUIC connections, backend RS, and path information.

By simultaneously transmitting data over both Wi-Fi and cellular channels on mobile devices, we enhance speed, improve resilience in weak network conditions, and further leverage the advantages of QUIC's dual-end user-space protocol to elevate user experience. In terms of effectiveness, AB testing results in the online feed recommendation stream scenario demonstrate that MPQUIC significantly improves single-path QUIC network performance, reducing P99 network latency by approximately 40% and lowering the average and P90 values by over 20%.

7.3.3 Tencent TQUIC Deployment Across Multiple Core Internal Services

The Tencent Application Framework team developed TQUIC [8], a high-performance, lightweight, cross-platform QUIC protocol library. Built using Rust, TQUIC delivers high throughput, superior performance, and robust quality, supporting multiple congestion control algorithms such as BBRv3, BBRv1, COPA, and CUBIC to adapt to diverse network environments. Currently, TQUIC is widely deployed across Tencent's core services, including Tencent Video, Tencent Meeting, Tencent Advertising, WeChat, QQ, and gaming platforms.

In advertising bidding scenarios, integrating TQUIC increased real-time bidding rates by 30 percentage points, driving over 4% revenue growth. In live and VOD streaming scenarios, TQUIC optimizes first-play duration and reduces stuttering rates, enhancing user viewing experiences. Additionally, its multipath transmission capability ensures smooth service transitions across weak and cross-network environments.

Key advantages of TQUIC include:

- **Rapid Transmission**: As an industry-leading "toolbox" of congestion control algorithms, TQUIC supports multiple advanced algorithms, including BBRv3, BBRv1, COPA, and CUBIC, adapting to all transmission scenarios. In weak network conditions and certain critical scenarios, its transmission efficiency outperforms competitors by 2% to 30%, enabling data to travel across network links at lightning speed.
- **High Performance**: Refined through rigorous testing, TQUIC's single-machine processing performance surpasses comparable open-source products in most scenarios, with advantages reaching up to 20% in extreme conditions. This ensures efficient throughput for massive data volumes, laying a solid foundation for rapid business responsiveness.
- **High Quality**: Deeply rooted in the essence of the QUIC protocol, TQUIC encompasses over 10 core RFC standards or drafts spanning transmission, security, and application layers. With over 95% unit test coverage, 100% interoperability test pass rate against mainstream implementations, and formal specification testing, it ensures stable and reliable protocol operation.
- **Ease of Use**: Upholding a user-first philosophy, TQUIC offers multi-language interfaces including Rust/C/C++, with flexible and intuitive configuration. Its operational status is observable and monitorable. Future plans include expanding to popular languages like Kotlin/Swift, enabling developers across different tech stacks to master it effortlessly.

(a) TQUIC is currently deployed across multiple domains within Tencent, including:

- **Advertising Bidding**: In the high-stakes programmatic advertising arena, TQUIC boosted real-time bidding ratios by 30 percentage points and optimized single-bid ratios to 70%, directly driving over 4% revenue growth and injecting powerful momentum into advertising operations.
- **Audio–Video Entertainment**: In live streaming and video-on-demand scenarios, its superior congestion control significantly reduces video stuttering rates and loading times by over 20%. Key metrics like average full-length video views and effective viewing duration have markedly improved, delivering a smooth viewing experience. Services like Tencent Video and Tencent Meeting have leveraged this to achieve new highs in core user experience metrics.
- **Instant Messaging and Conferencing**: Addressing network switching challenges in weak network environments—such as mobile scenario transitions or

elevator entrances/exits—TQUIC ensures seamless, uninterrupted conferencing and instant messaging, enabling frictionless communication.

- **E-commerce Shopping**: Accelerates image loading by over 20%, helping e-commerce sites showcase products faster, boosting user decision-making efficiency, and reducing bounce rates.
- **Gaming Competitions**: Significantly enhances game responsiveness, extends player immersion time, and builds a more competitive network foundation for game developers, empowering exceptional gaming experiences.

7.3.4 Alibaba's Taobao Architecture Team Develops In-House XQUIC Service for Hundreds of Millions of Mobile Taobao Users

Figure 7.2 shows the evolution of Alibaba Taobao's XQUIC. In 2015, to optimize the slow handshake issue in standard TLS/1.2, Alibaba's Taobao team independently developed and launched Slight SSL, a lightweight proprietary encryption protocol. This protocol optimizes handshake and encryption by allowing session negotiation and data encryption to be combined into a single TCP segment, enabling 0-RTT when replay attack risks are absent.

Currently, HTTP2 + SlightSSL remains the primary carrier for Taobao Mobile's online traffic. Concurrently, past troubleshooting, service integration, and business requirements encountered complex or unmet challenges. Examples include: "Long-chain HTTPS fails completely under Wi-Fi, downgrading to short-chain HTTPS succeeds; switching to 4G restores long-chain functionality (SlightSSL private protocol blocked by Wi-Fi firewall)."

On the other hand, with the formal release of QUIC RFC9000 and HTTP3 RFC9114, evolving Taobao's network protocol to HTTP3/QUIC is not only essential for resolving the business pain points of the SlightSSL proprietary protocol but also crucial for enhancing network transmission performance and user experience. This evolution aligns with the prevailing trend in network protocol advancement.

Against this backdrop, Alibaba's Taobao Technology Team began developing the XQUIC implementation [9] in late 2018. Today, XQUIC's implementation of the IETF QUIC protocol has reached relative maturity and has undergone large-scale deployment within the Taobao ecosystem to validate its stability. Currently, XQUIC is applied for network acceleration in core scenarios within Taobao, including RPC requests for shopping guidance, short video downloads, and file uploads. The team continuously iterates on new features, conducts A/B testing, and optimizes Congestion Control algorithms through practical application.

A key distinction between XQUIC and other open-source solutions is its enhanced support for QUIC multipath, jointly developed by Taobao Mobile and the DAMO Academy XG Lab. Based on XQUIC, Alibaba pioneered the user-experience-driven multi-path transmission XLINK and conducted large-scale gray-scale validation in

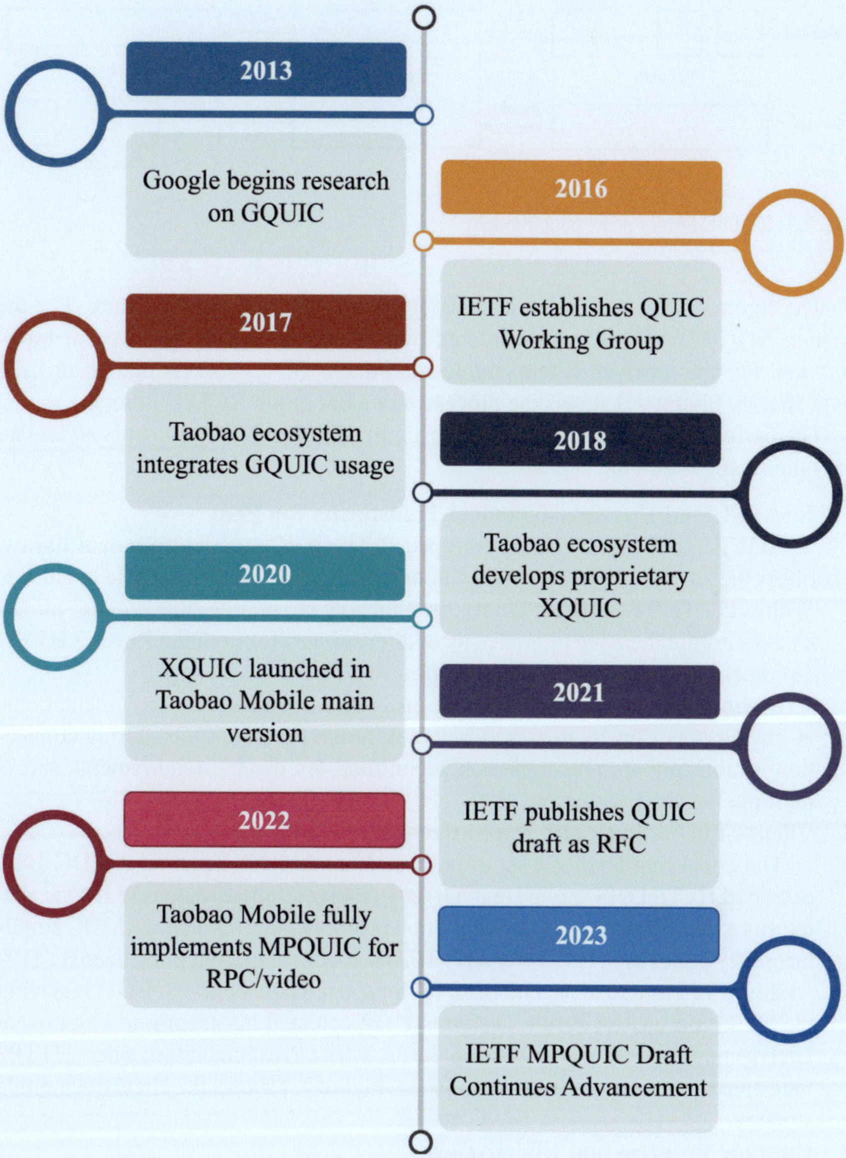

Fig. 7.2 Evolution diagram of Alibaba Taobao's XQUIC

Taobao's short video scenarios. This marks the industry's first multi-path QUIC transmission solution to complete extensive gray-scale validation, with related findings published at SIGCOMM 2021, a premier networking conference.

The XQUIC library processing model is as follows:

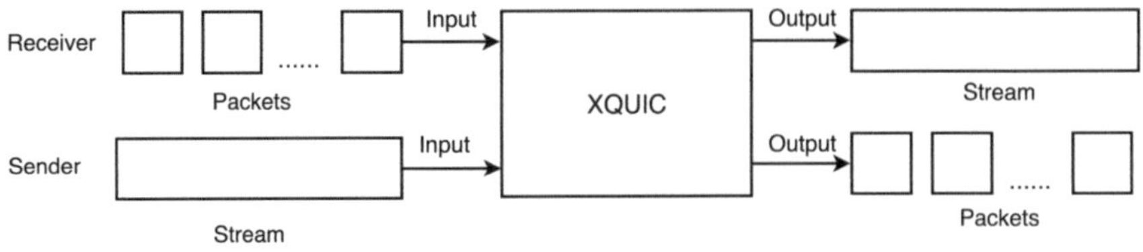

Fig. 7.3 XQUIC library processing model

The figure shows the simplified model of the XQUIC protocol stack. For the sender, XQUIC encapsulates an ordered byte stream into QUIC packets for transmission. For the receiver, it reassembles unordered QUIC packets into an ordered byte stream. Figure 7.3 shows the processing model of the XQUIC library.

The performance improvements achieved by HTTP3/QUIC protocols at Taobao encompass the following aspects:

1. **End-to-Cloud Upgrade Technical Transformation Plan**

   XQUIC, as Taobao's self-developed IETF QUIC standard protocol library, offers the advantages of complete autonomy, controllability, and rapid evolution. Within the TNET network library on Taobao's client-side, the XQUIC library enables comprehensive upgrades by adding support for both the Layer 7 HTTP/3 protocol and Layer 4 QUIC protocol.

   It simultaneously abstracts away differences in protocol implementations, al-lowing upper layers to simply select different protocol types during connection establishment. This approach accommodates diverse requirements across multiple business scenarios.

2. **Client-Side Fallback and Rapid Recovery**

   The client first fetches a set of policies from AMDC. Think of AMDC as an extended HTTP DNS service that not only resolves domain names to IPs but also returns extended attributes like supported protocols. At this stage, AMDC simultaneously issues both HTTP3 and HTTP2 protocols (the client prioritizes HTTP3, while HTTP2 is issued as a fallback for long-lived connections). Upon receiving the HTTP3 protocol, it first performs UDP connectivity testing to circumvent UDP limitations. Only after passing the network environment test, a new HTTP3 long-lived connection will be established. Figure 7.4 shows the client downgrade strategy.

3. **Upgrade Progress and Effectiveness**

   In 2018, Taobao Mobile completed the upgrade to HTTP/3 protocol coverage for IPv4 traffic across key business pathways. In 2019, following the completion of the Aserver main site's internal network QUIC over IPv6 link upgrade, the team migrated all relevant traffic—including shopping guides, transactions, short videos, and uploads—previously transmitted via TCP + IPv6 to the QUIC protocol. This marked the achievement of full-link coverage upgrades across multiple core business scenarios on Taobao Mobile. Data from platform-wide

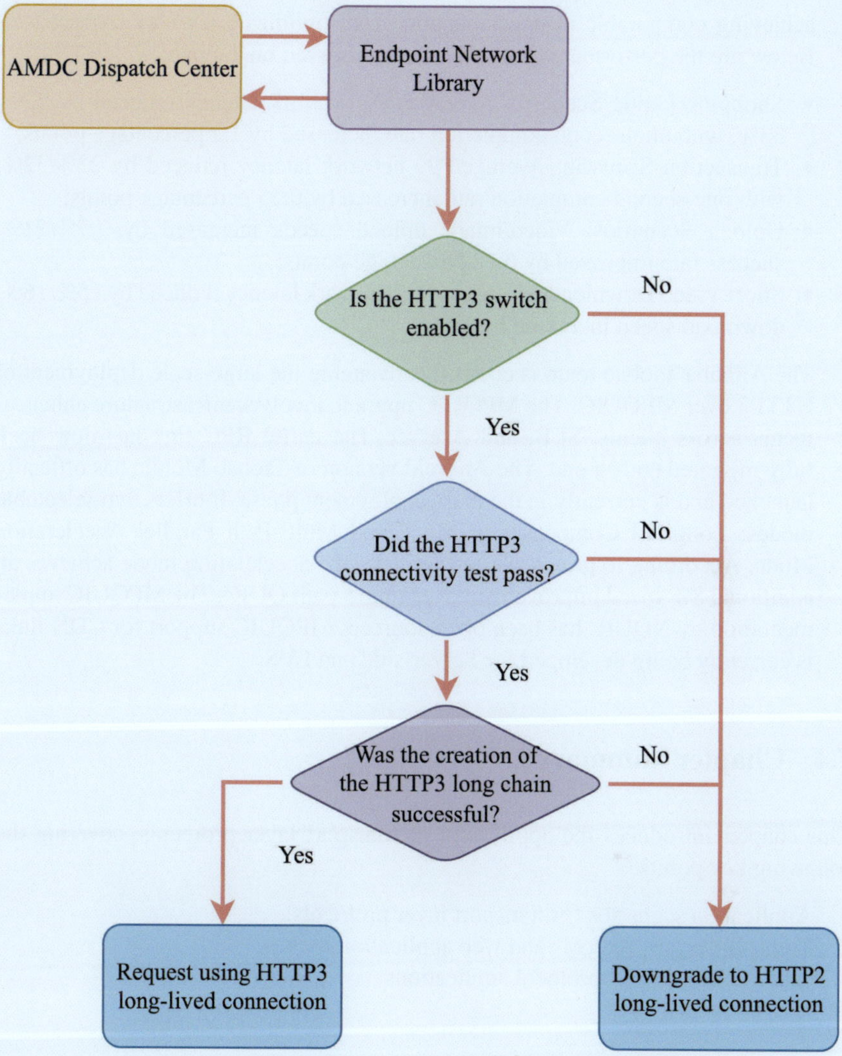

Fig. 7.4 Client downgrade strategy

metrics and business A/B testing indicates that both HTTP/3 and QUIC protocols deliver significant performance improvements across these diverse scenarios. They effectively enhance network transmission rates and average latency, resulting in better net-work performance (transmission rate/average latency). Additionally, they demonstrate superior performance in long-tail latency and request success rates under weak network conditions, ultimately providing users with a smoother online experience. Additionally, other Alibaba Group apps like Cainiao, and AliExpress have adopted our solution for HTTP3 upgrades, achieving comparable business benefits from optimized network experiences. Below are the performance improvements observed on Taobao:

- Shopping Guide Scenario: Average/P99 network latency reduced by 22%/33%, with one-second completion rate increased by 1.2 percentage points;
- Transaction Scenario: Average/P99 network latency reduced by 23%/32%, with one-second completion rate increased by 0.55 percentage points;
- Upload Scenarios: Video/image upload speeds increased by 7.7%/21%, success rate improved by 0.18 percentage points;
- Short Video Downloads: Average/P99 network latency reduced by 15%/16%, download speed increased by 18%;

The Alibaba Taobao team is currently advancing the large-scale deployment of HTTP3 over MPQUIC. The MPQUIC upgrade involves infrastructure enhancements across clients, SLB, and Aserver. The entire RPC link has now been fully migrated end-to-end. The Android version of Taobao Mobile has officially launched and is currently in the mass deployment phase. It offers two selectable modes: Long-tail Compensation Mode and Multi-Path Parallel Acceleration Mode. According to gray-scale testing data, the acceleration mode achieves an additional 8% speed improvement over single-path QUIC. The MPQUIC implementation by XQUIC has been open-sourced. MPQUIC support for CDN links is currently being developed for Server-side and LVS.

7.4 Chapter Summary

This chapter introduces the application of transport layer protocols, covering the following key points:

1. Application scenarios for transport layer protocols.
2. Transport layer protocols and web applications.
3. Enterprise transport protocol applications.

7.5 Experiment—Application Verification and Performance Analysis of Transmission Protocols

7.5.1 Experiment Objectives

1. Configure Chrome browser to enable HTTP/3 support and verify the QUIC-based HTTP/3 protocol.
2. Compare page loading performance between HTTP/2 (TCP-based) and HTTP/3 (QUIC-based).
3. Analyze HTTP/3 connection and stream information using browser developer tools.

7.5.2 Tools and Environment

1. Tools: Chrome browser (version 90 +), Wireshark.
2. HTTP/3-enabled websites: Cloudflare (https://cloudflare-quic.com) [10].

7.5.3 Experimental Steps

1. Configure Chrome browser to enable HTTP/3 support
   (1) Open Chrome browser, enter chrome://flags in the address bar and press Enter to access the experimental features configuration page (Fig. 7.5).
   (2) Enter HTTP/3 in the search box, locate the "Experimental QUIC protocol" and "HTTP/3" options, and set both to "Enabled." (Fig. 7.6).
   (3) Click the "Relaunch" button at the bottom of the page to restart the browser and apply the changes.
2. Verify HTTP/3 Protocol Connection
   (1) Open Chrome and visit the HTTP/3-enabled test site https://cloudflare-quic.com.
   (2) Open Developer Tools: Right-click the page → "Inspect" (or press F12/Ctrl + Shift + I).
   (3) Switch to the "Network" panel, refresh the page (Ctrl + R), and click any resource in the request list (e.g., index.html).
   (4) In the "Headers" panel on the right, check the "alt-svc" field. If it displays h3 or h3-29 (HTTP/3 protocol identifier), the resource loaded successfully using HTTP/3 (Fig. 7.7).
3. Comparing Page Load Performance Between HTTP/2 and HTTP/3
   (1) Testing HTTP/3 Performance:
      Keep HTTP/3 enabled in Chrome and visit https://cloudflare-quic.com.
      In the Developer Tools "Network" panel, click the "Refresh" button in the top-left corner and record key page loading metrics:
      Total load time (Finish time at the bottom of the panel).
      DOM parsing completion time (DOMContentLoaded event time).
      Observe resource loading concurrency (HTTP/3's QUIC stream multiplexing eliminates head-of-line blocking) (Fig. 7.8).
   (2) Testing HTTP/2 Performance:
      Disable HTTP/3 support: Re-enter chrome://flags, set "HTTP/3" to "Disabled," and restart the browser.
      Revisit https://cloudflare-quic.com, repeat step (1), and record the same metrics (Fig. 7.9).

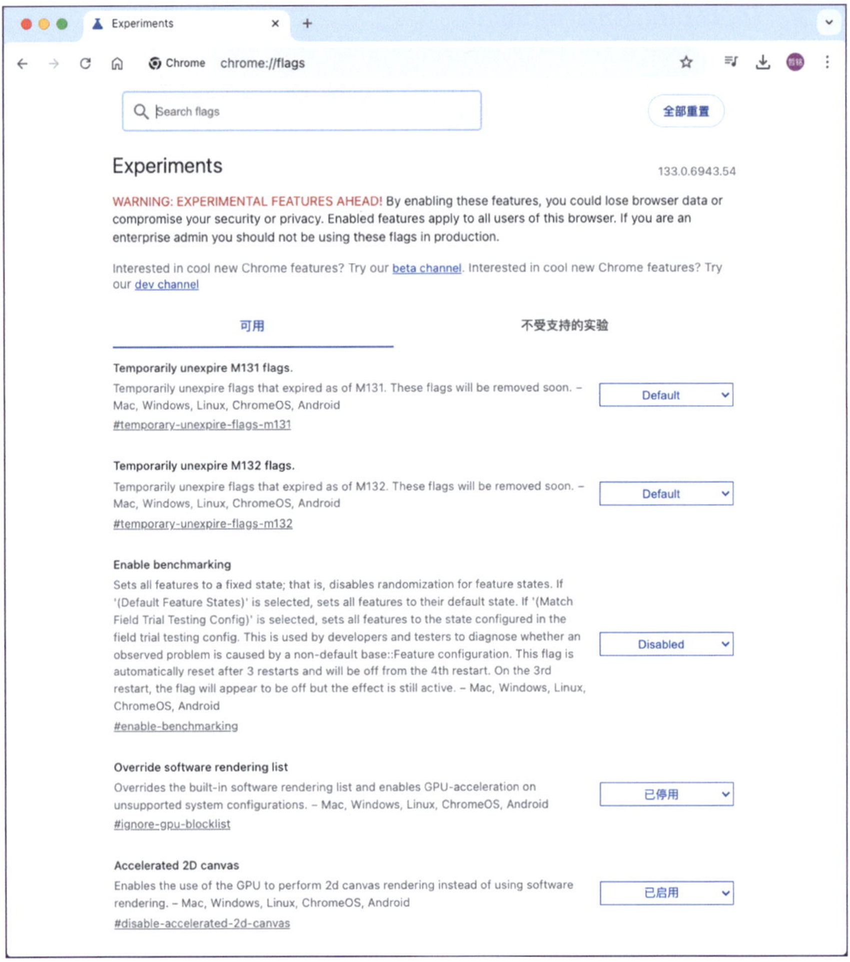

Fig. 7.5 Chrome browser configuration interface

(3) Compare HTTP/2 and HTTP/3 Performance:

Loading times demonstrate a significant performance improvement with HTTP/3 over HTTP/2, reducing loading time by nearly half.

7.5.4 Experiment Summary

This experiment provides a clear demonstration of HTTP/3's actual transmission process based on the QUIC protocol. It illustrates how stream multiplexing and 0-RTT handshakes enhance page loading performance, and how HTTP/3 optimizes network transmission efficiency by avoiding TCP head-of-line blocking issues compared to HTTP/2.

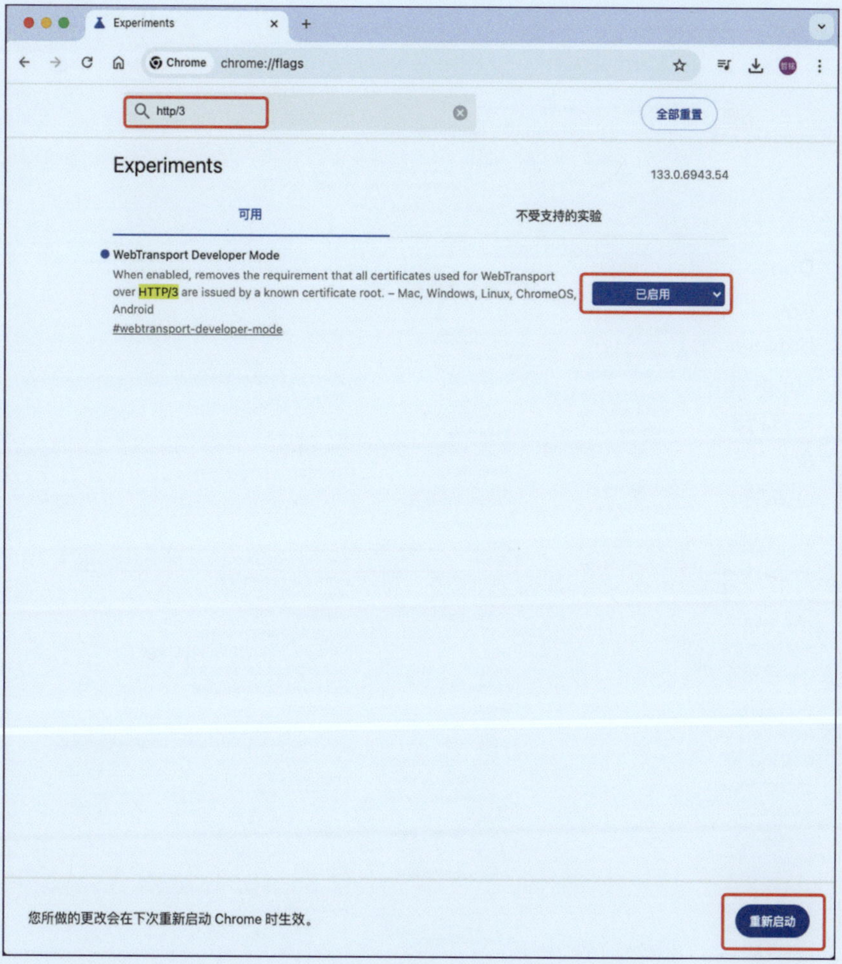

Fig. 7.6 Configuring HTTP/3 in chrome

7.6 Exercises

1. Briefly describe the application scenarios of transport layer protocols.
2. Briefly describe the application of the min-quic transport protocol.

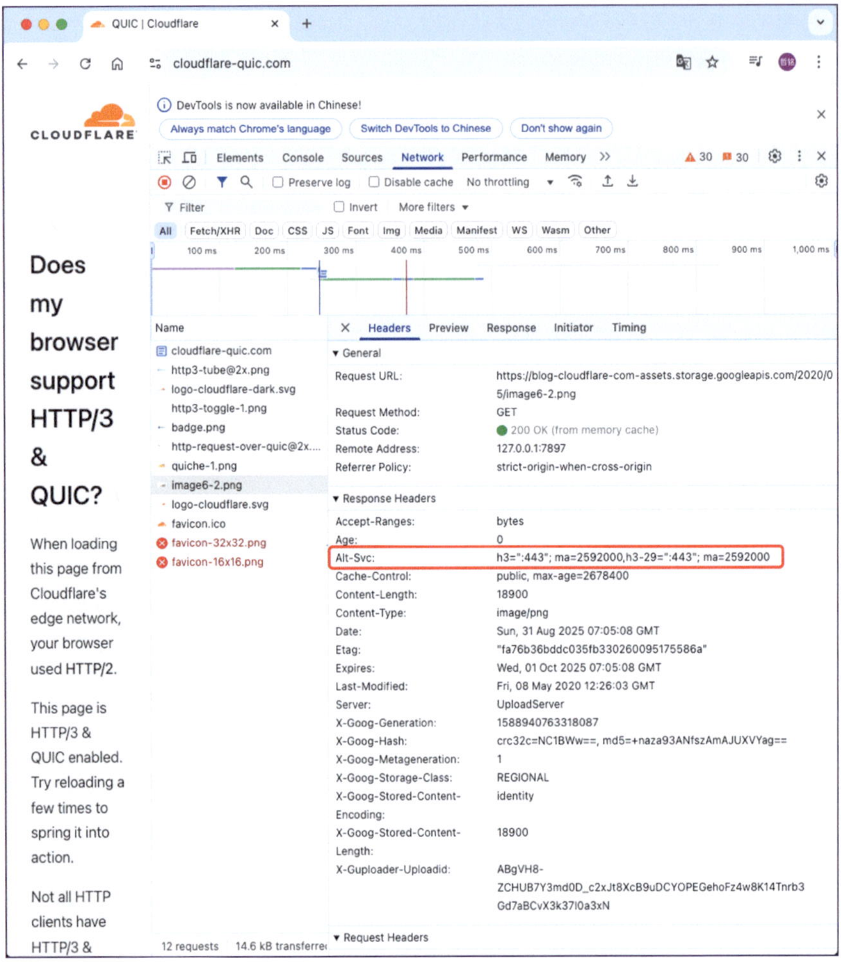

Fig. 7.7 Testing HTTP/3 connection

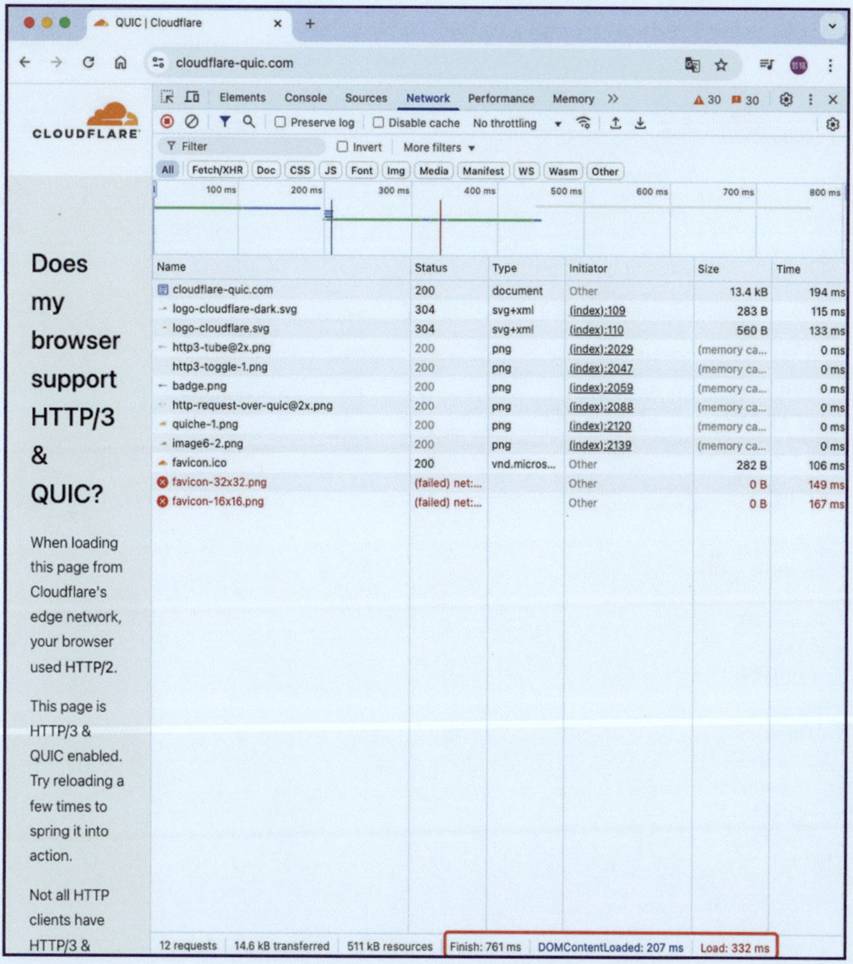

Fig. 7.8 HTTP/3 loading performance

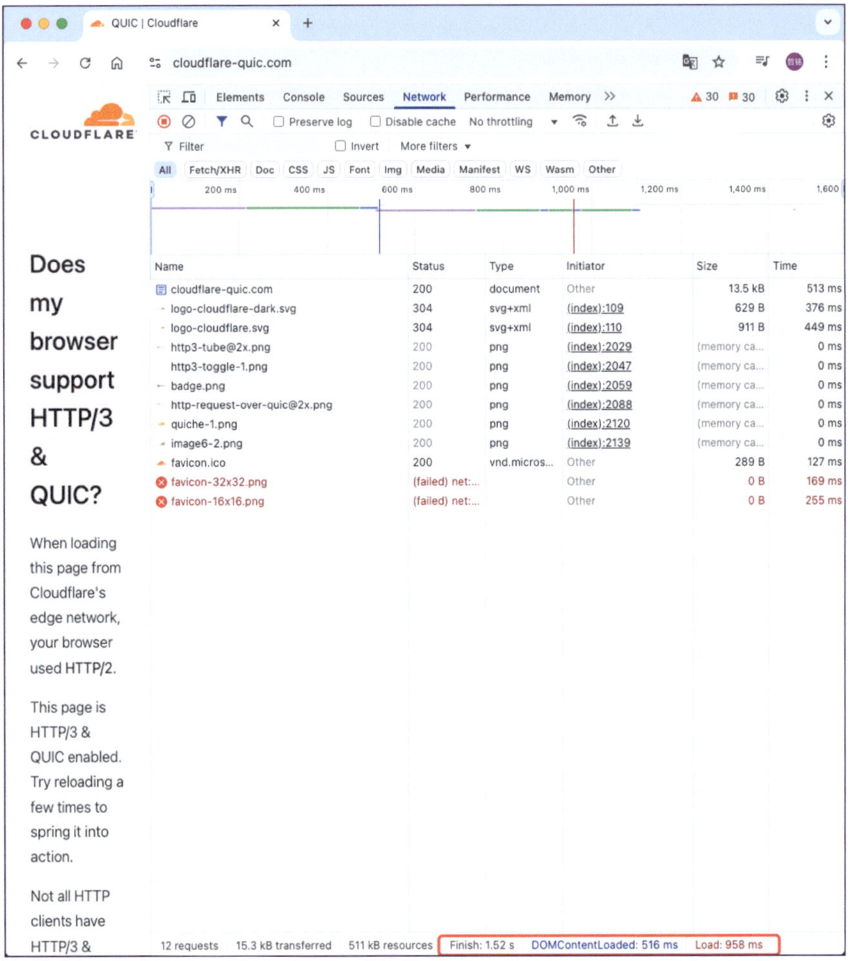

Fig. 7.9 HTTP/2 loading performance

References

1. Suznjevic M, Slivar I, Skorin-Kapov L. Analysis and QoE evaluation of cloud gaming service adaptation under different network conditions: the case of NVIDIA GeForce NOW. In: Proceedings of the 2016 eighth international conference on quality of multimedia experience (QoMEX). IEEE; 2016. p. 1–6.
2. Zhu Y, Eran H, Firestone D, et al. Congestion control for large-scale RDMA deployments. ACM SIGCOMM Comput Commun Rev. 2015;45(4):523–36.
3. Huang JW, Zhang LQ, Jiang ZY, et al. Heterogeneous parallel computing accelerated iterative subpixel digital image correlation. Sci China Technol Sci. 2018;61:74–85.
4. Li H, Bai H. Principle of architecture, protocol, and algorithms for CoG-MIN: a sustainably ecological and evolutionary solution for packet network system. Springer Nature; 2025 [cited 2025 Sept 14]. https://doi.org/10.1007/978-981-96-3596-2.

5. Xiao M, Bai H, Li H, et al. A secure and efficient transport protocol for multi-identifier network. In: 2023 9th international conference on computer and communications (ICCC). IEEE; 2023. p. 1653–1659.
6. Joras M, Chi Y. How Facebook is bringing QUIC to billions [EB/OL]; 21 Oct 2020 [cited 2025 Aug 17]. Meta Engineering. https://engineering.fb.com/2020/10/21/networking-traffic/how-facebook-is-bringing-quic-to-billions.
7. Volcano Engine. Full disclosure: Douyin Group's QUIC application practice at tens of millions of QPS [EB/OL]; 17 Aug 2023 [cited 2025 Aug 01]. https://developer.volcengine.com/articles/7268132377786843147.
8. Tencent Application Framework Team. TQUIC: a high-performance, lightweight, cross-platform QUIC protocol library [EB/OL]; 05 Dec 2023 [cited 2025 Aug 17]. https://tquic.net.
9. Alibaba Taobao Architecture Team. Alibaba Taobao's self-developed standardized protocol library XQUIC first public release [EB/OL]; 13 Aug 2020 [cited 2025 Aug 17]. https://www.infoq.cn/article/sy0kfj2pyjomb6sakqls.
10. Cloudflare, Inc. QUIC [EB/OL]; 2024 [cited 2025 Oct 5]. https://www.cloudflare.com/learning/performance/what-is-quic/.

Appendix

Solutions

Chapter 1: Overview of Transport Layer Protocols

1. Briefly Describe the Layered Model of Computer Networks

   Common network layered models include the OSI reference model and the TCP/IP model.

   OSI Reference Model: Divides network communication into seven layers, ascending from the bottom: Physical Layer, Data Link Layer, Network Layer, Transport Layer, Session Layer, Presentation Layer, and Application Layer. The Physical Layer is responsible for transmitting bit streams over physical media; The Data Link Layer assembles bit streams into frames and performs error detection and correction; the Network Layer handles routing and packet forwarding between different networks; the Transport Layer provides reliable end-to-end data transmission; the Session Layer establishes, maintains, and manages sessions; the Presentation Layer handles data formatting and encryption/decryption; the Application Layer delivers various network application services to users.

   TCP/IP Model: Divides network communication into five layers: Physical Layer, Data Link Layer, Internet Layer, Transport Layer, and Application Layer. The Physical Layer and Data Link Layer correspond to the Physical Layer and Data Link Layer of the OSI reference model and are responsible for transmitting data packets over physical media.; the Internet Layer corresponds to the Network Layer of the OSI reference model, responsible for routing and packet forwarding between different networks; the Transport Layer provides reliable end-to-end data transmission; the Application Layer corresponds to the Session Layer, Presentation Layer, and Application Layer of the OSI reference model, responsible for providing various network application services to users.

H. Li and Z. Bao, *Transport Layer for Computer Networks*,
https://doi.org/10.1007/978-981-95-7374-5

2. Briefly Describe the Definition of the Transport Layer

   The Transport Layer is a layer within the computer network layered model, positioned above the Network Layer and below the Application Layer. Its primary function is to provide reliable end-to-end data transmission services, ensuring data is correctly transmitted from the source host to the destination host. The transport layer establishes a logical connection between the source and destination hosts to achieve reliable data transmission. It also performs operations such as segmentation, reassembly, flow control, and congestion control to guarantee data correctness and integrity. Additionally, the transport layer provides a unified interface for the application layer, allowing it to focus on business logic implementation without concerning itself with underlying network details. It can also deliver different service qualities based on application layer requirements.
3. List at Least Three Key Technologies of the Transport Layer

   Reliable data transmission: Ensures data is transmitted accurately and in order from sender to receiver through acknowledgment mechanisms, sequence numbers and acknowledgment numbers, checksum mechanisms, and retransmission mechanisms.

   Flow Control: Primarily implemented via the window mechanism. The receiver notifies the sender of its window size based on its processing capacity, and the sender adjusts its transmission rate accordingly to prevent receiver overload.

   Congestion Control: In TCP/IP networks, prevents network congestion through slow start and congestion avoidance, fast retransmission and fast recovery, and congestion window adjustments. In Information-Centric Networks (ICN), congestion control is achieved through interest-based and packet-based mechanisms, supplemented by in-network caching, which helps reduce load and alleviate congestion.
4. Briefly Describe the Core Features of Multi-Identifier Networks

   CoG-MIN introduces a decentralized, blockchain-based co-governance model for hierarchical cyberspace management. Top-level identifiers are governed through consortium blockchain voting, ensuring global coordination, while low level identifiers are autonomously managed to preserve sovereignty and flexibility.

   Built with security as its core principle, CoG-MIN adopts a multi-level security framework that balances protection and manageability. This design fosters a secure, transparent, and democratic cyberspace environment.

   Through an identifier extension and rollback mechanism, CoG-MIN ensures sustainable evolution. By using identity as the core anchor, it supports seamless integration and scalability across diverse networks such as IoT, IoV, IIoT, and space-air-ground systems.

Chapter 2: Transmission Control Protocol

1. Briefly Describe the Fundamental Characteristics of the TCP Protocol
   TCP is a connection-oriented, reliable transport layer protocol. Its core features include providing a reliable delivery service, ensuring data arrives in order and error-free through sequence numbers, acknowledgments, and retransmission mechanisms; It employs a connection-oriented approach, requiring a three-way handshake to establish communication and a four-way handshake to release the connection upon termination. Additionally, it incorporates flow control and congestion control capabilities to adapt to network conditions, ensuring stable and efficient data transmission.
2. Briefly Describe the Difference Between Flow Control and Congestion Control in the TCP Protocol
   In TCP, flow control prevents the sender from transmitting data too rapidly, which could cause the receiver's buffer to overflow. It primarily limits the sender's transmission rate based on the window size indicated by the receiver, involving only interaction between the two communicating parties. In contrast, congestion control prevents network congestion caused by excessive data volume. It adjusts the transmission rate by detecting network congestion status, addressing the state of the entire network and serving as a global control mechanism.
3. List the Three Key Technologies of the TCP Protocol
   The three key technologies of the TCP protocol include the three-way handshake and four-way handshake. The former ensures orderly and reliable connection establishment and release processes. The retransmission mechanism upon congestion timeout guarantees reliability by setting a timeout timer and retransmitting data when no acknowledgment is received within the specified time. Congestion control algorithms, such as slow start and congestion avoidance, dynamically adjust the send window size to prevent network congestion and maintain transmission stability.

Chapter 3: User Datagram Protocol

In real-time scenarios such as video conferencing, online gaming, and live streaming, UDP's speed and efficiency make it irreplaceable. For applications demanding ultimate efficiency and low latency, the User Datagram Protocol (UDP) offers a minimalist alternative.

This chapter explores UDP as a lightweight, connectionless transport layer protocol, detailing its core characteristics and minimal header structure. This chapter delves into UDP's strengths and weaknesses (fast but unreliable) and how application-layer protocols like QUIC and RTP can optimize it. Finally, a hands-on experiment implementing UDP client–server communication and exercises comparing TCP and UDP helps students apply theoretical knowledge to real-world scenarios.

Chapter 3: User Datagram Protocol

1. Briefly Describe the Fundamental Characteristics of the UDP Protocol
   UDP is a connectionless transport layer protocol that does not provide reliable delivery services. It enables direct data transmission without establishing connections and does not guarantee ordered data arrival or include a retransmission mechanism. Its key features are high transmission speed and low overhead, making it suitable for scenarios demanding high real-time performance but less stringent reliability requirements, such as live video streaming and voice calls.
2. Briefly Describe the Differences Between TCP and UDP Protocols
   The primary distinction between TCP and UDP lies in their operational models. TCP is a connection-oriented, reliable protocol that establishes connections through a three-way handshake and releases them via a four-way handshake. It incorporates flow control, congestion control, and retransmission mechanisms to ensure ordered, error-free data transmission, though at the cost of higher overhead and slower speeds. Conversely, UDP is a connectionless, unreliable protocol that requires no connection setup and offers no reliability guarantees. It features low overhead and high speed, making it suitable for scenarios demanding high real-time performance.

Chapter 4: The QUIC Protocol

1. Briefly describe the fundamental characteristics of the QUIC protocol.
   QUIC is a novel transport layer protocol built on UDP, combining the reliability of TCP with the flexibility of UDP. It features low latency, enabling rapid connection establishment via 0-RTT or 1-RTT. It supports connection migration, maintaining continuity during network handoffs, while incorporating built-in encryption and authentication mechanisms for security. Additionally, it employs TCP-like flow control and congestion control mechanisms, balancing reliability with transmission efficiency.
2. List the advantages of the QUIC protocol over TCP
   Advantages of the QUIC protocol over TCP include: Faster connection establishment, enabling 0-RTT or 1-RTT handshakes, significantly reducing latency; Eliminates head-of-line blocking by implementing per-stream flow control to avoid global head-of-line blocking issues; Support for connection migration, maintaining uninterrupted connections during network transitions (e.g., switching from Wi-Fi to cellular); built-in TLS encryption eliminating additional handshakes for enhanced security; and more flexible congestion control that rapidly adapts to network changes, improving transmission performance.
3. List Three Key Technologies of the QUIC Protocol
   The three key technologies of the QUIC protocol are: the connection identifier mechanism, which enables connection migration through connection IDs independent of IP and ports; UDP-based multiplexing technology, where each

stream transmits independently, resolving TCP's head-of-line blocking issue; and an encrypted handshake integrating TLS 1.3, which combines connection establishment with encryption to reduce handshake latency while enhancing security and connection efficiency.

Chapter 5: Transport Layer Security Protocol

1. Briefly Describe the Primary Functions of the TLS Protocol

   The primary function of the TLS protocol is to provide security for network communications. By establishing an encrypted channel above the transport layer, it ensures the confidentiality, integrity, and authenticity of data during transmission. It prevents data from being eavesdropped on or tampered with, while also verifying the identities of communicating parties. TLS provides security support for application layer protocols such as HTTP, making it a crucial protocol for safeguarding network communications.
2. Briefly Describe the Main Technologies of the TLS Protocol

   The primary technologies of the TLS protocol include the handshake protocol, which negotiates encryption algorithms, exchanges keys, and verifies identities when establishing connections between communicating parties; the record protocol, responsible for segmenting, compressing, encrypting, and adding message authentication codes to application layer data to ensure secure and complete transmission; additionally, it involves various encryption algorithms (such as symmetric and asymmetric encryption), key exchange mechanisms, digital certificates, and identity authentication technologies, collectively building a secure communication environment.

Chapter 6: Frontier Exploration of Transport Layer Protocols

1. Briefly Describe the Changes in Demand Under Future Networks

   The evolving demands of future networks primarily stem from the diversification of internet applications and the upgrading of user needs. First, regarding communication paradigms: traditional networks centered on resource sharing between hosts, employing sender-driven push-based interactions. Future networks, however, prioritize content itself. User demands shift from "how to obtain resources" to "efficiently accessing content," driving communication semantics toward receiver-driven pull-based evolution. Simultaneously, compatibility with both push and pull modes becomes essential to accommodate complex scenarios.

   Second, network identification systems face expansion demands. Traditional IP addresses struggle to meet multi-dimensional identification needs like user and content identification. Future networks must support multi-identifier resolution and routing to enhance addressing efficiency and reliability, ensuring data transmission integrity and traceability.

2. Briefly Describe the Emerging Scenarios for Transport Layer Protocols

   Emerging scenarios for transport layer protocols primarily address specialized network performance requirements driven by diverse applications, including the following categories:

   Mobile network scenarios: With the proliferation of 5G and Wi-Fi 6, mobile devices' frequent handoffs and network instability demand protocols with rapid recovery and connection migration capabilities. Protocols like QUIC enhance transmission continuity in mobile environments through optimization mechanisms, while network coding technologies improve packet loss resilience in wireless settings.

   Data Center and Computing Networks: Data centers process massive volumes of data, demanding protocols that support high throughput, low latency, and high reliability. Technologies like RDMA and RoCE bypass kernel protocol stacks to reduce latency, while algorithms such as FASTFLOW optimize traffic burst issues during AI training.

   High-Performance Computing and Large Model Training Scenarios: Training trillion-parameter models involves coordinated communication among hundreds of thousands of GPUs, necessitating ultra-large-scale networking, ultra-high bandwidth, and ultra-low latency. RDMA and emerging protocols like UET and Falcon serve as core enablers, meeting high-concurrency data transmission demands.

Chapter 7: Applications of Transport Layer Protocols

1. Briefly Describe the Application Scenarios of Transport Layer Protocols

   The application scenarios of transport layer protocols are primarily determined by their design characteristics: TCP is connection-oriented, providing reliable transmission suitable for applications requiring high integrity and ordering, such as web browsing (HTTP/HTTPS), file transfer (FTP), and email (SMTP/POP3). It establishes connections through a three-way handshake and employs sliding window traffic control and congestion control mechanisms to ensure error-free data delivery. UDP is connectionless, emphasizing efficiency and low latency. It suits applications demanding high real-time performance and tolerating minor packet loss, such as video streaming, online gaming, voice calls (VoIP), and DNS queries. Its minimal header (8 bytes) and multicast support further optimize transmission efficiency. Additionally, specific scenarios like data centers enhance throughput through RDMA (e.g., RoCEv2), while cloud gaming and web transmission rely on the QUIC protocol combined with UDP to optimize latency and dynamically adapt to network fluctuations. Protocol selection requires balancing reliability, real-time requirements, and data scale demands.

2. Briefly Describe the Application of the Min-Quic Transport Protocol

   MIN-QUIC is a transport layer protocol that integrates QUIC protocol features into the MIN network. Its application focuses on enhancing transmission efficiency and flexibility in scenarios like the Web: It employs stream multiplexing to prevent head-of-line blocking, ensuring stable parallel transmission of multiple resources (e.g., images, scripts) within complex pages; Combined with MIN network's multi-identifier system, it enables more precise resource location and routing; Its pluggable congestion control strategy adapts to diverse network environments (e.g., home broadband, mobile networks), maintaining efficient transmission even under high latency or packet loss scenarios, thereby delivering superior user experiences for web applications.

MIX
Papier aus verantwortungsvollen Quellen
Paper from responsible sources
FSC® C105338

If you have any concerns about our products,
you can contact us on
ProductSafety@springernature.com

In case Publisher is established outside the EU,
the EU authorized representative is:
Springer Nature Customer Service Center GmbH
Europaplatz 3, 69115 Heidelberg, Germany

Printed by Libri Plureos GmbH
in Hamburg, Germany